EPIC
HIKES
of the
WORLD

Explore the planet's most thrilling treks and trails

CONTENTS

Easy   Harder   Epic

© Eventh | Getty, © Australian Scenics | Getty, © My Good Images | Shutterstock, © Andrew Montgomery | Lonely Planet

INTRODUCTION

Why do we hike? To exercise? To enjoy some pleasant scenery? To get from A to B? When we asked our global network of 200 travel writers to tell us about their most memorable hikes, it soon became abundantly clear that the reasons went much deeper than that. 'Life-changing' was a phrase that cropped up numerous times. For some it seems hiking is about the personal challenge – the sense of reward and confidence born of completing a long-distance trail from end to end, or reaching the summit of a mountain. For others it is about gaining an understanding – to follow historic or religious trails and learn (and feel) how our ancestors got about before motorised transportation. One common theme is the sense of connection you can achieve with a destination when you put one foot in front of the other, repeatedly, for hours, and days, on end. In his classic 1879 hiking memoir, *Travels with a Donkey in the Cévennes*, Robert Louis Stevenson explains, 'The great affair is to move; to feel the needs and hitches of our life more clearly; to come down off this feather-bed of civilisation, and find the globe granite underfoot and strewn with cutting flints.'

This book is intended to inspire hiking in all its myriad and flinty forms. We have selected 50 of the best and most inspiring routes suggested by our pool of travel writers, from athletic one-day summits to months of pacing through valleys and across ridgeways and international borders. These hikes cover almost every corner of the globe. The classics are well represented by the likes of the Pacific Crest Trail, Angels Landing and the Long Trail in the USA, the 'W' Trek in Patagonia, and several of the Great Walks in New Zealand. Wildlife and walking have always gone hand in hand and we have included hikes that involve encounters with giraffe and zebra (the Zambian walking safari), moose and grizzly bear (the Skyline Trail), and echidna and koala (the Gold Coast Hinterland hike). The intrepid will not be disappointed: we feature hikes in remote areas of India, Indonesia and the Caucasus, and walks across empty stretches of the Great Wall of China. We commune with pilgrims in Tibet and venture on expeditions deep into the South American jungle. And let's not forget the planet's great cities: urban areas can be rich and invigorating hiking destinations themselves, from the bridges of Sydney to the history and architecture along the Thames in London to the skyline trails of Hong Kong.

HOW TO USE THIS BOOK

The main stories in each regional chapter feature first-hand accounts of fantastic hikes within that continent. Each includes a factbox to help plan the trip – the best time of year to hike, how to get there, where to stay. But beyond that, these stories should spark other ideas. We've started that process with the 'more like this' section that follows each story, offering other ideas along a similar theme, not necessarily on the same continent. On the contents page, the hikes have been colour coded according to their difficulty, which takes into account not just how long, remote and challenging they are but their logistics and local conditions. The index collects different types of hike for a variety of interests.

It's important to note that many of the routes in this book are difficult and challenging. Whether you're a fleet-footed, seasoned hiker or a novice embarking on your very first trek, please ensure that you're adequately prepared and have taken appropriate safety precautions to help prevent against risks or dangers to yourself and others.

Clockwise from left: trekking
through snow in the Swiss Alps;
the lost city of Choquequirao;
regarding the view on the
Routeburn Track, New Zealand.
Previous page: hikers at the top of
Mt Kinabalu in Borneo

CAPE TOWN'S THREE PEAKS IN THREE DAYS

Instead of admiring Cape Town's mountains from the city, flip things around and scale the Mother City's peaks for a view of the skyline, hills and coast.

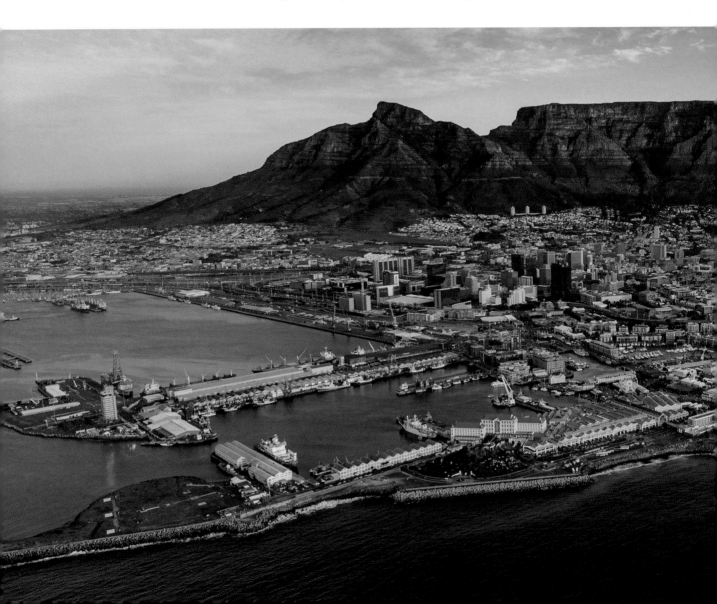

We stood, shivering, on Table Mountain's famously flat top. A sense of achievement was in the air, and not just because we'd managed to ascend the mountain on a day when the infamous 'Table Cloth' was blissfully absent. The layer of thick cloud is renowned for its tendency to roll in and obliterate the vistas of Cape Town below. But our view was unobscured and for the third time that weekend we surveyed the city panorama far beneath our feet.

Over the past three days we had tackled the trio of peaks that watch over Cape Town – Lion's Head, Devil's Peak and Table Mountain. These are not the most daunting peaks in the world to scale. All three added together still fall short of South Africa's highest mountain – and that in turn is half the height of Kilimanjaro. Yet climbing one, two or three of the peaks is a beautiful way to see one of the most beautiful cities in the world.

Hard-core hikers like to up the challenge by tackling all three peaks in one day, but for mere mortals, the hikes are

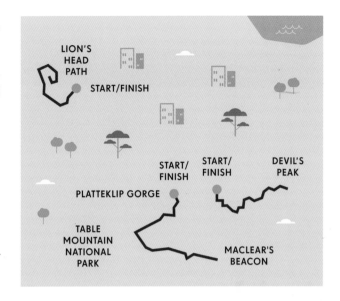

LION'S HEAD PATH

START/FINISH

PLATTEKLIP GORGE

START/FINISH

START/FINISH

DEVIL'S PEAK

TABLE MOUNTAIN NATIONAL PARK

MACLEAR'S BEACON

best completed over the course of a weekend, interspersed with shopping, beach trips or long lunches in Cape Town's side streets. And so, one Friday evening we joined the after-work crowd gathering on the road leading towards Lion's Head.

It doesn't matter what time of day you choose to ascend the 2195ft (669m) hill – you're always going to have plenty of company. Early risers head up for a sunrise over the city, a steady line of hikers climb throughout the day and on a full moon the diminutive peak is packed with wine-toting walkers here to watch the sun set and the moon rise.

It's only about an hour from the car park to the top, but just because it's short and slap bang in a city, that doesn't make the walk easy. There are vertiginous ledges, steep inclines and for those who crave a touch of adventure, a route that involves clinging on to ladders and chains manacled to the mountainside. If you're a little queasy with heights, you can bypass the ladders – just keep an eye out for the sign marking the detour.

As the hike circles Lion's Head, you get an ever-changing view of the city, the coast, the port, and once at the peak you can enjoy a vista that is considered by many to be superior to that from the top of Table Mountain, largely because the mountain itself is the central feature of the view. The downward scramble takes another hour and dusk is settling in when we head home to find a clean pair of socks for the next day's hike.

Although when seen from afar Devil's Peak seems to jut above Table Mountain, its jagged peak is in fact some 280ft (85m) shy of Table Mountain's highest point. Of course, the main lure of

"As the hike circles Lion's Head, you get an ever-changing view of the city, the coast, the port and Table Mountain"

all three of the peaks is the varied vistas over Cape Town, but there's also plenty to see on the mountainside itself, particularly for botanists and flower fans. The whole Table Mountain range is layered with fynbos – indigenous shrub-like vegetation unique to the region – and the overgrown vegetation provides a little shade on an otherwise exposed route.

It's not just sun you're likely to meet on Devil's Peak – the mountain, much like the city it resides in, is notoriously windy and as we emerge at the 3287ft (1000m) summit we're almost blasted back down to road level. It's instantly obvious why everyone quickly retreats to the eastern side of the peak to crack open the picnic. Once sheltered from the wind, we munch on slightly soggy sandwiches and try to pick out landmarks in Woodstock, the southern suburbs and as far away as the Cape Flats.

It's an out-and-back hike, and the loose gravel and sometimes steep incline make for a knee-jarring descent. By the time we're back at the car, my legs are wobbling in a way that makes me very happy that on the final hike there's an alternative way to get down the mountain.

There are many routes to the top of Table Mountain but we're joining the shortest and most popular route, Platteklip

DASSIES OF TABLE MOUNTAIN

Wildlife along the three peaks is largely limited to lizards, bugs and birds, but you are fairly likely to meet a dassie, particularly on top of Table Mountain. Looking a lot like a big fat rodent, the fluffy mammals are actually most closely related to the elephant. Also known by the name of rock hyrax, the cute creatures hop between rocks and provide photographers with an adorable alternative to all those cityscape shots.

From left: hiking the path up Lion's Head; a dassie watches on. Previous page: the magnificent cityscape of Cape Town

Gorge. It's a steep, 2-mile (3km) climb and admittedly isn't the prettiest of the Table Mountain routes, but that's not to say it's an unattractive hike. There's no disappointing way to reach the top of Table Mountain, particularly if the peak is free from clouds. I mean to count the uneven and occasionally enormous steps as we go, but after about 50 or so my mind wanders to more important things – photographing the slowly retreating city behind me, not tripping over loose rocks, keeping an eye out for dassies scurrying in the undergrowth.

We eventually emerge from the narrow gorge, but our climb is not quite done. You can't really call it a peak unless you reach the highest part, so we walk the extra half-hour to Maclear's Beacon. At 3563ft (1086m), it's only 62ft (19m) higher than the upper cableway station, but it's the principle of the thing that counts, so we save the celebratory high five for our arrival at the pyramidal pile of rocks marking Table Mountain's apex. By this point I wish I had followed the 'dress warm' advice that I always offer to others heading up Table Mountain, but I had failed to bring anything more than a very light sweater and the wind is whipping straight through it.

It's as good a time as any to join the queue for the cable car – the easiest and least knee-knocking way to descend. We might not have managed the Three Peaks in record time – the speediest to date is under five hours to scale the trio back-to-back – but at least the slow pace gives time to get back to sea level and enjoy the sights and bites of the city we've now viewed from every possible angle. **LC**

ORIENTATION

Start // The Lion's Head hike starts at the car park on Signal Hill Rd. The easiest route up Devil's Peak leaves from Tafelberg Rd, a little further on from the starting point for the Platteklip Gorge hike.

End // All three are out-and-back hikes, or you can opt to take the cable car back down the Table Mountain section.

Distance // Lion's Head 3 miles (5km); Devil's Peak 5.3 miles (8.5km); Maclear's Beacon via Platteklip Gorge 5 miles (8km); all distances are for a round trip.

Getting there // Cape Town airport is 11 miles (18km) from the city. The hikes are best reached by car or taxi – all are a short drive from the city centre.

What to take // The weather is extremely changeable so be sure to have a light rain jacket and warm layers plus sunscreen and a hat.

*Opposite: admiring the rocky
landscape of Cederberg from
beneath the Wolfberg Arch*

MORE LIKE THIS
SOUTH AFRICAN DAY HIKES

MALTESE CROSS, CEDERBERG

If you want to soak up the sandstone
scenery of the Cederberg on foot, but
are not quite up to an all-day scramble
up precipitous rock faces, the Maltese
Cross hike is perfect. Undulating but never
steep, the three-hour round-trip walk takes
in all that is best about the Cederberg
– scuttling lizards, big blue skies, hardy
endemic plants and weird rock formations.
The usual turn-around point is the Maltese
Cross, a curious monolith seemingly
sprouting from the rocks scattered around
it. If you're feeling energetic – and you
already have a permit – you could continue
up Sneeuberg, the range's highest peak at
6647ft (2026m).
Start/End // Sanddrif Holiday Resort
Distance // 4.3 miles (7km)
**More info // Permits must be obtained
in advance from Sanddrif**

SENTINEL PEAK, DRAKENSBERG

Also known as the 'chain ladder walk', this
is not a route for the vertigo sufferer. After
an initial steep climb, the path flattens
out for a while, but the real challenge
still awaits. Scaling the chain ladders up
the sheer face of the Mont-Aux-Sources
massif takes a bit of nerve, but there is
an (admittedly steep) alternative if you
just can't face the two ladders. Once at
the top, a fairly flat walk takes you above
the Tugela Falls, the second highest in the
world. Allow at least seven hours for the
round-trip hike.
**Start/End // Sentinel Car Park,
Free State**
Distance // 9 miles (14km)

SHELTER ROCK, MAGALIESBERG

Within easy access of Johannesburg,
the Magaliesberg is a playground for
outdoorsy Gauteng dwellers. Although
dwarfed by the Drakensberg, the
Magaliesberg has its own majesty thanks in
no small part to the quintessential African
panoramas viewed from mountaintops.
Leaving from an adventure camp that
also offers abseiling and rock climbing,
the hike transports you to the top of the
Magaliesberg range. There's plenty of
interest along the way, including glimpses
of antelopes in the distance, Boer War
relics, enough birdlife to have you whipping
out your field guide and of course Shelter
Rock itself, a very climbable hulk of ochre-
coloured sandstone.
Start/End // Shelter Rock Base Camp
Distance // 5 miles (8km)
**More info // Advance bookings are
required and there is a fee to access
the trail. Call +27 (0) 71 473 6298**

TOP OF THE WORLD: KILIMANJARO

Trek to the top of this mighty mountain in Tanzania for the greatest high you can get without crampons, and stand on the roof of Africa.

The wake-up call came a little before midnight – but I didn't need it. I'd barely slept a wink. Part of me was relieved the moment had finally arrived: I wanted to get this over with. Another part could think of nothing worse: I didn't want to get up because, beyond the safety of my sleeping bag, outside those tent flaps, the air was bitter-cold, perishing-thin and thick with impending doom.

Finally, steeling myself, I unzipped my warm cocoon and stepped out into my fears. Having climbed three-quarters of the way up Mt Kilimanjaro, it was time to make the final throat-scraping, limb-aching, head-mushing push for the top.

Four days earlier I'd set off as part of a group of 10 hopeful trekkers, accompanied by no less than 34 crew. This obscenely sized entourage of porters, cooks and guides was tasked with getting us to the top of Africa.

Kilimanjaro isn't like other mountains. At 19,341ft (5895m), it's the continent's highest peak by far. It's the world's biggest free-standing summit, rising isolated and enormous from the Tanzanian plains. But it's the mountain's combination of huge heft yet relative accessibility that makes it unique. No technical climbing skills are required, so Kilimanjaro tantalises with possibility: mere mortals might reach the summit. 'Might' being the operative word...

It's estimated that around 35% of the 30,000-or-so trekkers who take to Kili's slopes each year fail to reach Uhuru ('Freedom') Peak, the mountain's very highest point. 'Many people are defeated from the start,' head guide Samuel said as we set off *pole pole* (slowly, slowly) along the Machame route, the most popular and scenic of the mountain's five main trails. 'They see Kilimanjaro and think, "I can't do that".'

Many others, however, are defeated by the dizzying heights. Altitude sickness commonly kicks in above 11,500ft (3500m), and a high proportion of climbers feel some effects, from breathlessness, headaches and nausea to vomiting, confusion and, well, death. Kili is a 'manageable challenge' but not one to be taken lightly.

Our start was fairly tough, not because of the altitude – the trailhead was at around 5577ft (1700m) – but the morale-dampening downpour. It seemed churlish to moan, though. I toiled with only a daypack, while the porters dashing past in their cheap shoes lugged everything from paraffin canisters to folding tables and chairs.

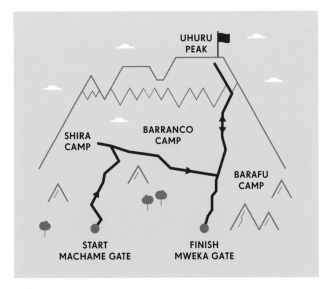

After around six hours of walking through a rainforest that lived up to its name – rain dripped off the tree ferns and turned the path to chocolate milkshake – we reached our first camp, now at 10,500ft (3200m). Everything was soggy except our spirits: nothing brings a new band of brothers together like the sharing of both a common goal and bodily functions (flatulence is a curious by-product of altitude acclimatisation). We huddled and giggled in the dining tent, eating popcorn and pasta, listening to our crew's soft Swahili songs float up to meet the drizzle.

The following days fell into a pattern. Mornings involved 20 minutes of psyching myself up to leave my sleeping bag, a quick 'bath' (a once over with a wet wipe), packing and repacking, a big breakfast. We soon trekked out of the forest zone, advancing into the moon-like upper slopes, oxygen becoming rarer with every stride. We walked amid phallic lobelia, tough everlastings, crumbled boulders and putrid long-drop loos. We rose higher, gaining views down on to the clouds and up to Kili's ever-nearing crest. By the time we reached 15,000ft (4600m) Barafu Camp, our final base before our attempt on the top, I felt stinky, sunburnt and bunged up, but overjoyed.

Then came our final briefing. 'Tonight is not a good night,' Samuel told us frankly. The summit climb is a steep, relentless schlep of almost a vertical mile. It's about digging in; giving everything to cross the finish line. We would all likely find ourselves in dark places. 'But self-confidence,' he concluded, 'all you need is self-confidence.' In bed by 6.30pm, I lay wide awake, trying to believe in me.

"After what seemed like an age, I looked at my watch. I'd only been going for an hour. There were still five or six to go"

THE FALLING SNOWS OF KILIMANJARO

In 1849 Swiss-German missionary Johannes Rebmann became the first European to see Kilimanjaro. When he sent back reports of snow on the equator, scholars sneered; the president of the Royal Geographical Society declared it 'a great degree incredulous'. But he was right. And Kilimanjaro, which sits just 3° south of the earth's middle, is still topped by glaciers – just. Between 1912 and 1989, the ice cover decreased by 75%. Some scientists predict that it could be gone by 2030.

Clockwise from top: above the clouds at Shira Camp; another peak looms; elephants on the plains; if nature calls at 15,000ft (4600m) Barafu Camp. Previous page: destination Kilimanjaro

Thankfully, it was a beautiful night; freezing cold but windless, dry and star-spangled. At around midnight we joined the procession of head-torches curling up the mountain, falling into a steady robotic trudge. All was quiet save for the guides, who showed off by belting out pop songs. I wished I had the breath to sing; I wished I could escape the throbbing monotony inside my own head. With nothing to focus on but the heels in front and the darkness everywhere else, time was stretching out. And as the minutes dragged, so the ground steepened, the cold bit harder, the nausea yanked and the air thinned. After what seemed like an age, I looked at my watch. I'd only been going for an hour. There were still five or six to go.

It was at this point I gave myself a stern talking to. I either surrendered to the mountain – gave in, got beat. Or I surrendered to the challenge – stopped fighting and fretting, and simply got on with it; one foot in front of the other. Thus I shuffled on, moving slowly upwards. Eventually the minutes ticked by; the hours. The sky seeped from inky black to hazy purple to dawning pink. And then, finally, there it was, up ahead: the sign confirming our arrival on the roof of Africa.

The sun burst through the pillowy cloud below. I felt its creeping warmth. I felt relief. And I felt the beginnings of euphoria tugging at the sleeve of my fatigue. I wasn't quite ready for it – I needed to get down this mountain first. But I had an inkling of just how good this moment was going to feel. **SB**

ORIENTATION

Start // Machame Gate
End // Mweka Gate
Distance // Approximately 37 miles (60km)
Duration // Six to seven days
Getting there // Kilimanjaro International Airport is between the towns of Moshi and Arusha. The Machame trailhead is a one-hour drive from Moshi, two from Arusha. Climbing independently is not allowed – trekkers must have a guide or join an organised trip.
What to wear // Expect to be hot, cold and wet. Thermals, fleeces, T-shirts, a down jacket, waterproofs and hats (sun and woolly) are essential.
When to go // January to March and June to October, namely the drier seasons.
What to take // A head-torch, good sleeping bag and water purification tablets. Ask your doctor about Diamox, a drug that combats the effects of altitude sickness.

*Opposite, from top: a gelada enjoys the
high life at Simien Mountains National
Park; Morocco's Mt Toubkal, the
tallest mountain in North Africa*

MORE LIKE THIS
AFRICAN HIGH PEAKS

MT KENYA, KENYA

Another great hulk of Rift Valley volcanicity,
Mt Kenya is Africa's second highest peak. It
soars up to an impressive 17,057ft (5199m)
but is often ignored by peak-baggers with
their eyes on the bigger prize – climbing
Kenya doesn't have quite the same cachet
as conquering Kilimanjaro. That's a shame
because Kenya is a fine climb: less crowded
than Kili, richer in wildlife, arguably more
scenic. Mt Kenya's two highest summits –
the sharp shards of Batian (17,057ft/5199m)
and Nelion (17,021ft/5188m) – are for
technical climbers only. Trekkers aim
for 16,355ft (4985m) Point Lenana,
conquerable in three days, though four is
better for acclimatisation. The classic hike
is via the Sirimon route, which ascends
through wildlife-rich national parkland.
Look out for elephants, zebra and other
ungulates on the lower slopes, while the
more alien upper reaches are home to
shrieking rock hyraxes and various strange
senecio and lobelia plants.
**Start/End // Sirimon Gate
(Sirimon route)**
Distance // 33 miles (53km)

MT TOUBKAL, MOROCCO

Apex of the Atlas Range, 13,671ft (4167m)
Mt Toubkal is also the highest peak in
North Africa. You can get up and down it
in two days if summiting is all that matters,
but making a longer circuit not only helps
with acclimatisation, it also offers a greater
insight into local Berber culture. From
the Imlil valley make a clockwise loop via
walnut groves and cherry orchards, high
passes and boulder fields, mud-brick
houses and neat green terraces, wandering
shepherds and wind-wizened juniper
trees. The final ascent from the Neltner
refuge is a stiff but steady clamber up
scree, rewarded by views across a starkly
spectacular landscape that the hardy
Berber have made their own.
Start/End // Imlil
Distance // 45 miles (72km)

RAS DASHEN, ETHIOPIA

The Simien Mountains National Park, a
dramatic spread of 13,000ft+ (4000m)
peaks dimpling northern Ethiopia, has been
designated a World Heritage Site. And it
is quite a sight: the basalt layers here have
been eroded into striking escarpments,
broad valleys, plunging precipices and
spiky pinnacles, most notably 15,0157ft
(4620m) Ras Dashen, the country's highest
point. The range is also home to rare and
endemic gelada baboons, walia ibex,
Simien foxes and Egyptian vultures, as well
as ancient shepherd paths that provide
plenty of exploring options. A classic route
is to start in Sankaber (near the market
town of Debark) to trek via the Geech
Abyss and wildlife-abundant Chenek. The
climb up Ras Dashen itself leads through
giant lobelia forests and goat pasture, with
an easy scramble to the summit for views
over the Unesco-listed landscapes and to
Eritrea beyond.
Start/End // Sankaber
Distance // Various

ANIMAL MAGIC: ZAMBIAN WALKING SAFARI

Delve into the raw African bush on a walking safari for electrifying encounters with elephants, lions and buffalo – and facetime with countless smaller species.

What does hyena smell like?

My Zambian guide, Abraham Banda, was in no doubt. Passing a clump of tall grass, he sniffed the still air then crouched beside the reedy stems. 'Can you smell the scent?' I knelt, and tried to look as if, well, obviously that unfamiliar aroma couldn't be anything but... What, exactly? 'Hyena. The males mark their territory by secreting that distinctive odour on to the leaves.'

Sniffing a whiff of scavenger pheromones – now, that's something you can't experience sitting in the cab of a jeep. It was just one of countless moments of connection with the African bush experienced only on a walking safari, where there's nothing separating you from the natural world – no windows blocking vision, no engine noise drowning out growls or birdsong, no exhaust fumes masking scents.

I was enjoying Abraham's impromptu lesson in aromatics on stage one of a three-day hiking safari in South Luangwa National Park. Zambia's flagship wildlife destination is also the home of the walking safari, devised by near-legendary ecotourism pioneer and conservationist Norman Carr more than 50 years ago. Its mosaic of grasslands, lagoons and riverine woodland is a haven for creatures great and small, including four of the Big Five (rhino were sadly poached out across Zambia by 1998, though they've since been reintroduced). But what makes it a treat for wildlife watchers is the chance to roam its vastness on foot alongside some of Africa's finest guides.

The dawn chill was evaporating as we set out from Luwi Camp on the first leg of our stroll between a quartet of bushcamps, roughly tracing the Luwi River to its confluence with the larger Luangwa. I say 'roughly' – we weren't following a set trail, but instead relying on the expertise and experience of Abraham and our armed ranger, Johns. The emphasis was very much on quality, not quantity; distances are modest, measured in animal encounters, not miles or metres.

Within our first couple of hundred steps I was absorbing titbits of Abraham's bush lore. The trunk of a young tree was bent double, half-snapped from the attentions of an itchy elephant; while along the path another bush showed signs of spoor – dried mud scraped on its side, marking a buffalo's transit. Past that hyena-marked grass we found the scavengers' droppings, flecked white with

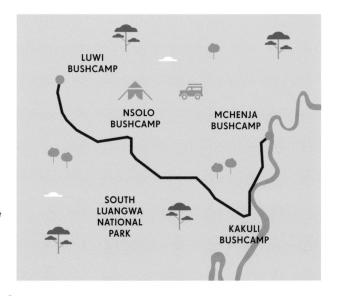

LUWI BUSHCAMP

NSOLO BUSHCAMP

MCHENJA BUSHCAMP

SOUTH LUANGWA NATIONAL PARK

KAKULI BUSHCAMP

© Ian Cumming | Getty

bone. Add a visit to a hippo midden, a teetering pile of dung at the water-horses' al-fresco toilet, and the morning was a veritable poop patrol, topped off when Abraham broke open a football-sized elephant dropping to extract a marula nut. 'They're very sweet – good for jam,' said Abraham, 'and a lot easier to open once an elephant's had a go at digesting them.'

We paused frequently: to laugh at warthogs, always comical, squealing and scattering before us; to examine the empty husks of lizard eggs, their incubation mound dotted with millipede tracks; to watch a snake eagle tearing at a monitor lizard in a branch above us. The gentle rustle of our footsteps was occasionally drowned by the whir as flocks of queleas and Lilian's lovebirds took flight from a seed-laden patch of dust. And at this delightfully stop-start pace, by late morning we reached the dried-out bed of a tributary of the Luangwa River.

We sat out the dry, breathless African noon in the shade of a buffalo-thorn; bird calls had receded, the vivid carmine bee-eaters nowhere to be seen. The sandy riverbed was a virtual walk of fame where the stars of the park had pressed their prints – the dinner-plate pads of elephants, the cloven hoofs of giraffes and the tiny paw prints of elephant shrews framed within lion pugmarks – but the animals themselves were elsewhere.

Then to our left, I spotted a movement: a young lion padded around a bend in the riverbed and headed straight for us. As it advanced, another juvenile appeared behind, and then two more: 300 yards away, 200, 100... they flowed towards us with liquid grace, and Johns tightened his grip on the rifle, as Abraham weighed up the approaching predators.

> *"A young lion padded around a bend in the riverbed and headed straight for us. Another juvenile appeared behind"*

OLD BULL BUFFALO

Born in what's now Mozambique in 1912, Norman Carr worked as an elephant control officer in Northern Rhodesia (today's Zambia), but in the 1940s virtually invented eco-tourism. In 1950 a local chief granted him permission to establish a reserve on the Luangwa River, and during the 1960s 'Kakuli' ('Old Bull Buffalo'), as he was nicknamed, developed walking safaris. A vocal proponent of conservation, Carr – ever adamant that local people should benefit from tourism – established one of Africa's finest guide-training programmes.

Seconds later, the increasing tension was broken as two of the lions decided it was time for fighting practice. A halo of dust rose around the young animals as they collapsed on to the riverbed, rolling, nipping and growling softly while their companions stood haughtily watching, clearly considering themselves above such childish shenanigans. Then some movement from our group betrayed our presence; the lions froze and sniffed the air before leaping on to the far bank and evaporating back into the brush.

That day's hike was punctuated by such big encounters and small incidents, each providing a better appreciation of the park's varied habitats. Mopane and acacia stands lined the river across which echoed the gutsy guffaws of male hippos. In scrubby grassland we passed herds of buffalo, jumpy impala, waterbuck and puku. Elephants materialised anywhere, at any time, herds rumbling across the plains, browsing branches and gathering at the river's edge.

And there were plenty more aromas to enjoy. As we approached the Nsolo Camp late that afternoon the fragrances of African lavender and sage faded and the scent of baking potatoes wafted towards us. Dinner?

'That's not the camp kitchen,' smiled Abraham. 'It's the smell of the potato bush.' As we ambled into camp after seven captivating hours, serenaded by the calls of turtle doves urging us to 'Drink harder! Drink harder!', my brain was whirling with the addition of yet another nugget of wilderness wisdom. So it continued, day by day, and step by step. A Zambian walking safari packs in more magic moments per mile than any other hike. **PB**

Clockwise from top: in South Luangwa you'll find elephant, zebra and southern carmine bee-eater. Previous pages: eye-to-eye with a giraffe; lions at rest

ORIENTATION

Start/End // Various bushcamps, mostly in the Mfuwe sector of South Luangwa National Park

Distance // Not more than about 7.5 miles (12km) each day

Getting there // Safari companies pick up guests from Mfuwe Airport, a one-hour flight from Lusaka (Zambia's capital) or Lilongwe (Malawi).

Tours // Various companies offer walking safaris between their camps in the park. The best-known and longest-established include Norman Carr Safaris (https://timeandtideafrica.com/norman-carr-safaris), Robin Pope Safaris (www.robinpopesafaris.net) and the Bushcamp Company (www.bushcampcompany.com).

When to go // June to October, during the cooler dry season – animals and birds seek out water, ensuring excellent wildlife watching.

*Opposite from top: a gorilla in the
midst of Bwindi Impenetrable Forest,
Uganda; wildebeest migrating through
the Masai Mara*

MORE LIKE THIS
AFRICAN WALKING SAFARIS

GORILLA TRACKING, BWINDI, UGANDA

The total population of mountain gorillas
is tiny: fewer than 900 are believed to
survive in the Virunga Mountains straddling
DR Congo, Rwanda and Uganda, and in
the latter's Bwindi Impenetrable Forest.
Whacking up through the lush, dense
vegetation of Bwindi to locate one of the
habituated family groups is not for softies:
it's steep, it's muddy, it's overgrown, and
it can be wet, cold, hot, or all three in
one day. Until recently, limited numbers
of permits costing US$600 per person
allowed visitors to spend up to one hour
with a family (if you can find them). But
you can now join rangers habituating new
groups, and enjoy gorilla company for
several hours.
**Start/End // Depends on the family
being tracked, but treks usually depart
from park headquarters**
Distance // Various
**More info // Habituation experience
permits cost US$1500 per person.
www.visituganda.com**

MASAI MARA CONSERVANCIES, KENYA

Kenya's most famous game-viewing area,
the Masai Mara National Reserve, hosts
the great migration of some 1.5 million
wildebeest, zebra and Thomson's gazelle
each August to October, but also a
permanent array of large herbivores and
the predators that stalk them. But whereas
the reserve itself can get woefully crowded
with jeeps ringing lion kills, surrounding
private conservancy areas offer equally
fine wildlife watching, with the boon that
walking safaris – forbidden in the reserve
proper – are permitted. Join an expert
Maasai guide and spotter to roam the bush
savannah of Mara Naboisho Conservancy
and witness the secondary wildebeest
migration through the Loita Hills, watching
for elephant, giraffe and lion.
**Start/End // Conservancies set up for
walking safaris include Naibosho, Mara
North, Olare Motorogi, Ol Kinyei and
Siana Group Ranch**
Distance // Various
More info // www.expertafrica.com

NYALALAND TRAIL, KRUGER NATIONAL PARK, SOUTH AFRICA

Kruger is known as a terrific destination for
self-drive camping safaris, but to really get
under the skin of the park and its diverse
wildlife, join one of the official three-night
Wilderness Trails guided tours. Based in
a small, rustic camp on the Madzaringwe
River, overshadowed by the looming
Soutpansberg Mountains, you'll be among
just eight guests led out on consecutive
days for hikes among baobab trees to spot
both the biggest game – including lion,
leopard, rhino, buffalo and elephant – and
local specialities such as spiral-horned
nyala and Sharpe's grysbok, or prized
birders' favourites Verreaux's eagle and
Pel's fishing owl.
Start/End // Punda Maria Rest Camp
**Distance // Up to about 12 miles (20km)
each day**
More info // www.sanparks.org

A WINTER DESCENT OF THE GRAND CANYON

An off-season Grand Canyon geology class offers fresh perspectives on the USA's most iconic national park, from snow on the canyon rim to improvised riverbank saunas.

For geologists, there's no place on earth like the Grand Canyon. Nearly two billion years of the planet's history are encapsulated in the canyon's mile-high jumble of fossil-laden rock layers, allowing scientists to take a mesmerising walk back through time.

Alas, science was never really my thing. Even the simplest paragraph in a made-for-dummies textbook went in one ear and out the other. Still, universities have their expectations, and mine wanted me to complete three science classes before graduation. So when I saw 'Geology of the Grand Canyon' listed among the autumn course options during my sophomore year at Stanford, it was like manna from heaven.

Taught by two long-haired graduate students, this course's big appeal was that its weekly classroom sessions would be complemented by a semester-ending Thanksgiving trek under the full moon into the depths of America's greatest natural wonder. I signed up on the spot. Two months later, on a chilly late-autumn evening, I found myself driving through the night from the San Francisco Bay Area to the canyon's South Rim, serenaded by the Grateful Dead in a car full of like-minded renegades.

We arrived just as dawn was sending red shoots through the steely November sky, illuminating a couple of inches of snow on the canyon rim and the endless folds of the chasm beyond. Starting from the New Hance trailhead, we were to chart a precipitous 7-mile (11km) course down to the Colorado River via the Red Canyon ravine, returning via the more gradual Tonto and Grandview Trails. Our instructors had chosen this route – one of dozens that descend into the canyon – because of its varied geological interest and its relative efficiency in reaching the

bottom. The pitfalls of this approach soon became apparent: this entire first day would be down, down, relentlessly down from rim to river. (For several weeks afterwards, the toll on my knees was palpable; as even climbing a simple staircase back home became excruciatingly painful.)

Once you get below the rim, the world changes. Sheltered from the harsher conditions of the high-altitude Colorado Plateau, the trail soon exited the snow and we entered a world of layered desert landscapes, where the intricacies of Kaibab limestone, Coconino sandstone and Bright Angel shale we had seen traced on the classroom blackboard suddenly emerged into vivid real-world

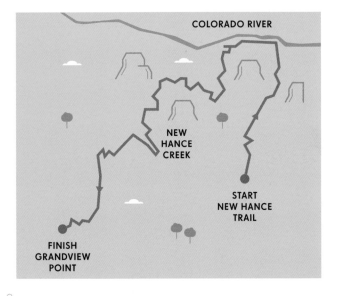

© Matt Munro | Lonely Planet

focus. The canyon, so huge and limitless from above, took on greater intimacy as we stair-stepped down into it, winding between piñon- and juniper-dotted rocky outcroppings and losing sight of the Colorado River. Here, the manifold colours of the canyon walls – reds, whites, greenish-greys, creams, oranges and ochres – became charged with more tangible meaning as we came face to face with them, a layer at a time.

After hours of dogged descent, we finally reached the river at Hance Rapids, setting up camp above a sandy beach at the foot of a jagged red-rock pinnacle. Down here, the early winter sun managed to nudge the thermometer to around 15°C (60°F) and some of us were tempted to take a dip. But with the river temperature below 4°C (40°F), even a quick swim bordered on the suicidal; I paddled about two arms' lengths into the water before reconsidering and racing to shore, my innards converted instantly to ice cubes. Later, as sunset yielded to a full moon, casting eerie illumination over the river and surrounding desert, our instructors constructed an impromptu sweat lodge from the coyote willows lining the river bank, and we took turns getting overheated and refrozen on repeat journeys between the sauna and the river.

Our day on the bottom was filled with teachable moments, as the canyon itself became an impromptu classroom. Along with exploring the beaches, climbing the pinnacle above camp and rustling up a pale imitation of a Thanksgiving dinner, we passed the time discussing geologic esoterica like Vishnu Schist and the Great Unconformity, while recuperating for the long climb ahead.

> *"The canyon, so huge and limitless from above, took on greater intimacy as we stair-stepped down into it"*

ROUTE MANOEUVRES

Ready to plan your own hike into the canyon? There are nearly two dozen routes to choose from, each with its own appeal. For first-timers an obvious choice is the well-maintained and relatively shady Bright Angel Trail, equipped with two ranger stations and frequent potable water sources. For something more off-the-beaten-track, head to the canyon's less accessible North Rim. Wherever you hike you'll need a permit, which should be reserved four months in advance at www.nps.gov.

Clockwise from top: cloud fills the Grand Canyon as seen from Yaki Point; an elk enjoying the view; the South Rim's Bright Angel Trail. Previous page: standing on the edge of one of America's epic sites

© RooM the Agency | Alamy

The next two days would be spent relentlessly slogging back uphill from 2608ft (795m) to 7400ft (2255m). (Exiting the canyon in a single day is generally out of the question, except for the supernaturally fit or the borderline insane.) Our plan was to make an intermediate overnight stop at the 4900ft (1493m) Horseshoe Mesa, a hulking semicircular rock outcropping where prospector Pete Berry struck a rich vein of copper in 1890 and founded his legendary Last Chance Mine.

Signs of the region's mining history appeared everywhere as we passed through the imposing cliffs of Redwall limestone at the base of the mesa. Openings in the hillside hinted at the 19th-century mine shafts just below, while rocks flecked with dazzling blue and green crystals of azurite and malachite littered the trail's edges, reminders of the eternal appeal of glitter to the human eye. Our last night in the canyon was spent in moonlit exploration, wandering past the foundations of abandoned mine buildings to the mesa's far northern reaches, where the now-distant Colorado River could be seen dimly sparkling in hallucinogenic half-light, 2300ft (701m) below.

Another day, another climb. Our final exit route to the canyon rim retraced the steps of the mules that were employed to haul copper off Horseshoe Mesa up to Pete Berry's Grandview Hotel. The hotel is long gone, but the route remains. Feeling a bit like overburdened mules ourselves, we headed back up through the familiar Coconino, emerging again at the snow-covered rim where our trip had started four days before – exhausted, elated and ready to do it all again. And maybe, just maybe, having learned a little something about all those beautiful rocks. **GC**

ORIENTATION

Start // New Hance trailhead
End // Grandview Point
Distance // 21 miles (33km) round trip
Getting there // The nearest domestic airport is Flagstaff Pulliam Airport (FLG), 84 miles (135km) away; international flights come into Phoenix, 228 miles (366km) away.
When to go // April, May and October.
Where to stay // The National Park Service operates lodges on both the South and North Rim. For lower-cost accommodation, camp or look further afield.
What to take // An animal-proof food container, water-purifying supplies and plenty of water.
What to wear // Dress in layers for the large temperature variations between the rim and river.
More info // www.nps.gov/grca/index.htm
Things to know // Reserve your trail permit months in advance, or be prepared to wait several days for the limited supply of 'first come, first served' permits issued on site.

*Opposite: winter snow settles on the
spectacular hoodoos of Bryce Canyon
National Park*

MORE LIKE THIS
OFF-SEASON CLASSICS

INCA TRAIL, PERU

The Inca Trail to Machu Picchu is a
perennial rite of passage for every would-
be South American explorer. The iconic
four-day trek is deservedly the stuff of
legend – crossing two 13,000ft (3962m)
passes, traversing ancient Incan steps
and tunnels, and visiting other magnificent
ruins en route to breathtaking views of
Machu Picchu at dawn through the Gate
of the Sun. Peruvian government efforts to
safeguard the trail have resulted in new
restrictions limiting access to 500 people
per day, which means that permits for the
dry-weather months of May to October
typically book up months in advance. If
you're willing to put up with slightly less
dependable weather, consider a trip in
the off-season, when trails are quieter and
competition for reservations less daunting.
**Start // Km 82 along Río Urubamba
railway from Cuzco
End // Machu Picchu
Distance // 27 miles (43km)
More info // www.incatrailperu.com**

MT TEIDE, TENERIFE, CANARY ISLANDS

At 12,198ft (3718m), Spain's highest
mountain is an enjoyable and surprisingly
rigorous summer challenge, but outside
high season, when the Parque Nacional
del Teide's four million or so annual visitors
trickle down to manageable numbers, it
comes into its own – particularly in early
spring, when the lower slopes start to
bloom in flowers and, if you're lucky, the
summit area still has a hat of snow. The
ascent to the volcano's peak is the real
challenge, especially if you opt for the very
tough six-hour hike, but if weather or lung-
power make this impossible, the cable car
will still give you the views, and the park's
73 sq miles (190 sq km) plenty of other
enjoyable hikes. The Unesco site protects
nearly 1000 Guanche archaeological
sites and contains examples of 80% of
the world's different forms of volcanic
formations, as well as 14 plants found
nowhere else on earth.
**Start // Montaña Blanca
End // Peak of El Teide
Distance // 10 miles (16km)
More info // www.telefericoteide.com**

FAIRYLAND LOOP, BRYCE CANYON NATIONAL PARK, UTAH, USA

For another off-season take on the rare
beauty of the American Southwest, head
for Bryce Canyon National Park in winter.
Nothing enhances the fairy-tale quality of
Bryce's multi-hued, whimsically sculpted
hoodoos (rock spires) like a dusting of
newly fallen snow. The red rock, evergreen
trees and frosty whiteness combine to
create a classic Christmas card colour
scheme during the winter months, while
the trails themselves are nearly deserted
– in stark contrast to summertime, when
the annual influx of visitors from the USA
and abroad, coupled with helicopter
sightseeing flights, can make the place
feel like a theme park. The Fairyland Loop
takes in some of the park's most gorgeous
scenery, including Sunrise Point, Fairyland
Canyon, China Wall and the otherworldly
Tower Bridge. Verify trail conditions with
rangers before setting out; foot traction
devices are advised in icy weather.
**Start/End // Fairyland Point, Bryce
Canyon National Park
Distance // 8 miles (13km)
More info // www.nps.gov/brca**

TREKKING THE 'W' IN CHILE

Expect the unexpected in this climatically challenging but rewarding backcountry trek past glaciers, lakes, plains and peaks, including the magnificent blue towers of Torres del Paine.

I f there's one thing you learn hiking in the mountains of Torres del Paine, it's that there isn't one kind of wind; there are many, and none is quite like another.

There are cool breezes and gentle zephyrs. There are soft drafts and sudden gusts. There are whirlwinds that sneak up out of nowhere, whipping dust from the trail and snatching maps from your hands. There are keening squalls that scream down from the mountains, knifing through jackets and chilling fingers to the bone. And then, there's the general, all-purpose kind of wind, the one for which Patagonia is notorious – a persistent, obstinate wind that never disappears, even on the calmest of days, and which, without any warning, can accelerate from mild to murderous. It's my first day on the W, and I reckon I've already experienced all of them, and a few more besides.

Stretching for 44 miles (71km) across the southern half of Torres del Paine National Park, the W is Patagonia's most celebrated hiking route. Its name comes from the fact that it forms the rough

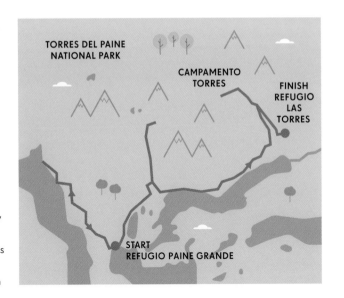

outline of a letter W, looping from Laguna Amarga in the east to Lago Grey in the west. It's a five-day route that affords access to some of South America's wildest mountain scenery – razor-edge mountains, wind-scoured valleys, tawny pampas and icy glaciers. It deserves its reputation; few places feel quite as raw, or wild.

Most hikers tackle the trail from east to west, but I'm walking in the opposite direction, as I want to end my journey by watching sunrise over the Torres del Paine, the rock towers after which the park is named. Unfortunately, Patagonia's capricious weather means there's no guarantee they'll be visible by the time I get there – but there's little point worrying about that now.

I spend my first day tracking the left line of the W, following the shores of Lago Grey, a glacial lagoon formed by meltwater from the Grey Glacier, itself an offshoot of the Southern Patagonian Ice Field. I look out over one of the glacier's tongues as it melts into the lake, calving into icebergs or fracturing into columns that collapse with a boom and splash. Like most of the world's glaciers, the Southern Patagonian Ice Field is melting fast due to climate change; on average, thinning by 6ft (1.8m) per year.

I spend the night at a rustic *refugio*, or mountain hut, near the lakeshore, before pushing eastwards towards the middle of the W. It's a long, tiring trek: through swaths of land scarred by bush fires, along the blue sweep of Lago Pehoé and Lago Scottsberg, over the wild creek of Rio Frances and under Los Cuernos (The Horns), a chain of summits along the valley's eastern edge. I pitch my tent among twisted lenga trees as darkness falls and the wind whines around the mountaintops.

> "I pass a sign on a ranger's hut: 'Do not ask about the weather today,' it reads. 'This is Patagonia. We do not know.'"

Day three covers the middle line of the W: the Valle Francés or French Valley, supposedly one of the most scenic parts of the trek. Unfortunately, the weather has noticeably worsened. Dense black cloud squats over the mountains, and the wind has become a gale, hurtling down from the mountains and scouring scree from the trail. Occasionally the cloud splits and peaks briefly materialise from the murk – Fortaleza (the Fortress), La Espada (the Sword), La Hoja (The Blade). But by the time I reach the glacial cirque at the valley's head, I'm in a whiteout, and the bitter wind and rain force me to beat a frustrated retreat.

The weather feels equally grim on day four as I follow Lago Nordenskjöld east towards the towers. I pass families of guanacos, the wild cousin of the llama, huddling together for shelter against the biting wind. Spindly trees shiver and rattle against the steel-grey sky, and the wind sends ripples and eddies through the yellow pampas. All I can do is plod on, head down, bent into the wind; the W has become a test of endurance as much as fitness. I pass a sign nailed on a ranger's hut: 'Do not ask about the weather today' it reads. 'This is Patagonia. We do not know.' I boost my spirits with a snack of wild calafate berries; a legend says that anyone eating the sweet fruit is sure to return

ANIMAL MAGIC

Torres del Paine National Park is one of the last strongholds for the wild puma in South America. A relation of the cougar and mountain lion, pumas can reach 8ft (2.4m) from nose to tail tip, run at 40mph (64kph) and leap up to 18ft (5.4m) in the air. They're solitary predators, with a territory covering as much as 80 sq miles (129 sq km), and survive mainly on a diet of small mammals and their favourite prey, guanacos, although occasionally their fondness for sheep also brings them into conflict with Patagonia's gauchos.

to Patagonia, but right now, I feel like I'd rather be anywhere than here. By the time I pitch camp that night at Campamento Torres, I should be able to see the towers from my tent, but there's no sign of them. The mountains are locked behind a wall of cloud. As I fall asleep, listening to the gale buffet and batter against the walls of my tent, I feel gloomy. It looks like the Patagonian weather might get the better of me after all.

However, the next morning, miraculously, the wind has completely dropped. There's not the faintest breath of a breeze. The mountains are quiet and still, and the night sky is clear, illuminated by the star-spangled arc of the Milky Way. Elated, I pull on my boots and half-walk, half-run along the trail. By the time I reach the base of the towers, daylight is breaking over the mountains. I round a corner, and there they are: the mighty Torres themselves, high, craggy and tall, soaring skywards like a cluster of Saturn rockets.

I watch sunlight spill over the valley. Slowly, the towers blush, then glow, then glare, and soon enough they're blazing, bright as pokers pulled from a furnace. Gradually, they turn yellow, then grey, then smoke-blue, like shards of metal cooling, and I finally understand their name: in the local Tehuelche dialect, Torres del Paine translates as the Blue Towers. And then, of course, this being Patagonia, the weather makes its presence felt: the breeze picks up, the cloud rolls in, and the towers vanish into haze.

As I trudge back through the Valle del Silencio – the Valley of Silence – I reflect on how fitting its name is. Like me, every single hiker I pass seems to be utterly lost for words. **OB**

Clockwise from left: that top-of-the-world feeling at Lago Grey; a puma keeps watch; trekking ever upwards. Previous page: another dramatic Torres del Paine panorama

ORIENTATION

Start // Refugio del Paine
End // Refugio Las Torres
Distance // 44 miles (71km)
Getting there // Torres del Paine National Park is 70 miles (112km) northwest of Puerto Natales. Shuttle buses and private transfers can easily be arranged.
When to go // October to April.
Where to stay // Hotel Lago Grey (www.lagogrey.cl), Hotel Explora (www.explora.com).
More info // www.swoop-patagonia.com has guided hikes.

Opposite from top: king cormorants
gather in the remote Beagle Channel;
drinking in the awesome vista of the
Fitz Roy mountains

MORE LIKE THIS
PATAGONIAN EPICS

LAGUNA DE LOS TRES, LOS GLACIARES

Hikers visiting Torres del Paine often add on an expedition to the national park of Los Glaciares, which offers equally stunning scenery, not to mention a wealth of day hikes and multi-day treks. This 14-mile (22km) hike is one of the classics, carrying you deep into the mountains of the Fitz Roy range. The name – the Lagoon of Three – refers to the trio of mountains that lie in wait at the end of the trail: Cerro Fitz Roy, Aguja Poincenot and Torre, rising like rocky guardians around the lakeshore. It's a long but rewarding day hike, with the added bonus that you get to sleep in a proper bed and get a good meal at the end of the day: the town of El Chaltén has plenty of accommodation options for hikers.
Start/End // El Chaltén
Distance // 14 miles (22km)
More info // www.losglaciares.com

HUEMUL CIRCUIT

This little-known backcountry route in Los Glaciares National Park is much, much quieter than many of Patagonia's trails, but it's for a reason. This is a challenging and technical trek that occasionally teeters over into scrambling and rock climbing; at certain points, you'll also have to ford rivers, which can be a nerve-wracking proposition when they're in spate. The reward? Hiking in the kind of solitude that's almost impossible to find in the better-known parts of Patagonia – not to mention an unforgettable view across the Southern Patagonian Ice Field.
Start/End // El Chaltén
Distance // 37 miles (60km)
More info // www.losglaciares.com

DIENTES DE NAVARINO

If you really want remote, then this hike is the one to choose. It starts with a flight by prop plane from Punta Arenas to the southernmost town on earth, Puerto Williams, located on the Chilean island of Isla Navarino, before heading off into areas of the Patagonian Andes where few people, let alone hikers, ever tread. At 55°S, this is a hike that very nearly takes you off the bottom of the map as you go through the chain of spiky mountains that rise up from the middle of the island. At the hike's summit, you'll get stunning views over the Beagle Channel and, on a very clear day, all the way to the distant tip of Cape Horn.
Start/End // Puerto Williams
Distance // 23 miles (37km)
More info // www.swoop-patagonia.com

BOSTON'S FREEDOM TRAIL

Stroll through America's revolutionary past on a historical hike visiting early settlers' cemeteries, patriots' meeting places and key sites in the struggle for independence.

At first glance, Boston Common doesn't seem so remarkable. Sure, there's a bandstand, and a pond, and on the balmy September morning of my visit the trees teased with glimpses of their flaming fall finery. But it's much like any other city park, populated by ordinary folk strolling, lolling, or browsing a newspaper on a bench.

Except it's not. This 50-acre (20-hectare) emerald swath is the oldest public park in the USA, established in 1634 by Puritan settlers. It's witnessed the hangings of heretics and 'witches'; it's been trampled by redcoats; it's hosted Judy Garland, Martin Luther King Jr, Pope John Paul II and Mikhail Gorbachev. And it's the starting point for possibly America's most intriguing urban hike: the Freedom Trail. This 2.5-mile (4km) route snakes between key historic sites, most relating to the 18th-century American struggle for independence. It's also simply a fine walk – a great way to introduce yourself to the buzzing heart of Boston, bars and markets as well as churches and museums.

The first stop beckoned brightly just steps from the start point at Boston Common Visitor Center: the gilded dome of the Massachusetts State House. Twenty years after his famous nocturnal ride to Lexington, Paul Revere joined John Hancock in presiding at the laying of the building's cornerstone, and went on to copper-plate its dome.

But though such monumental landmarks are impressive, more fascinating are the sites that speak of the day-to-day lives (and deaths) of early Bostonians. Following the line of red bricks embedded in the pavement, I ambled down Park St to its namesake church and the adjacent Granary Burying Ground, where I paid homage to pivotal patriots John Hancock, Samuel Adams

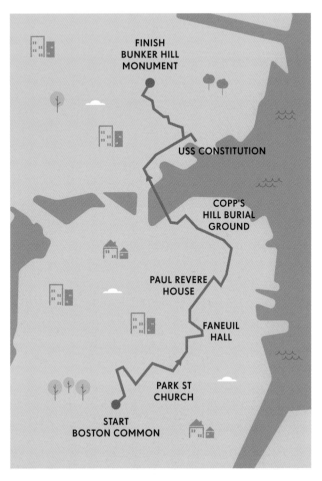

FINISH
BUNKER HILL
MONUMENT

USS CONSTITUTION

COPP'S
HILL BURIAL
GROUND

PAUL REVERE
HOUSE

FANEUIL
HALL

PARK ST
CHURCH

START
BOSTON COMMON

and – there he was again – Paul Revere. Those patriots are the big draws, but I found the earliest gravestones, some decorated with winged skulls, more evocative still.

Past King's Chapel I wandered, saluting Benjamin Franklin en route down School St. His statue peers down from a pedestal near the site of the Boston Latin School, the country's first public school, founded in 1635. Such education bore fruit among the 19th-century writers who congregated at the nearby Old Corner Bookstore, built around 1812 and now a Mexican restaurant. Here, poets and novelists including Longfellow, Hawthorne, Emerson and Beecher Stowe gathered; among the fried food and chillies, I hoped (but failed) to detect a whiff of literary genius still.

They say talk is cheap. Not so in pre-independence Boston: some of the most costly and influential was exchanged across Washington St at the Old South Meeting House. Unlike at the former bookstore, this red-brick church built in 1729 exudes an atmosphere of past activism. Here, in the late 1760s, mutinous mutterings against repressive British rule and taxation swelled to a roar, climaxing in the Boston Tea Party of 1773 in which hundreds of colonialists rushed from the meeting house to toss heavily taxed tea into the harbour.

Heading north up Washington St, I found myself engulfed by skyscrapers, beneath which cluster three of the most notable venues of independence action. The 1713 Old State House is

> "The 1713 Old State House stands as proud as it did when the Declaration of Independence was read from its balcony"

hemmed in by high-rises but stands as proud as it did nearly 250 years ago, when the Declaration of Independence was read from its balcony in July 1776. That triumph was in marked contrast to the bloody clash that had erupted just outside it six years earlier. On 5 March 1770, a mob of aggressive Bostonians surrounded British soldiers, who fired into the crowd, killing five in what became known as the Boston Massacre. And steps away, Faneuil Hall hosted 1764 protests against the British sugar tax, meetings led by John Hancock discussing the tea taxation question, and a century later rallies against slavery addressed by the likes of Frederick Douglass.

History makes me hungry. Fortunately, the central colonnade of Faneuil Marketplace behind the Hall is lined with tempting stalls peddling all manner of delectables; a hefty lobster roll later and I was fuelled for the second half of the trail.

Not that there's any shortage of eating opportunities en route. Along Union St, the western edge of Blackstone Block – Boston's oldest commercial district – the Union Oyster House has been

BLACK HERITAGE TRAIL

Another fascinating route winds through the streets of Beacon Hill. The Black Heritage Trail (maah.org/trail.htm) links sites connected with the African-American community who settled here and in the North End. It includes the 1806 African Meeting House (the USA's oldest surviving black church) and Abiel Smith School, founded in 1835 and now home of the Museum of African American History.

From left: anchored in Boston Harbor, the 18th-century USS Constitution; the historic Old State House. Previous page: cobblestoned Acorn St in the Beacon Hill district

dishing up seafood treats since 1826, in a shop built more than a century earlier. And on Hanover St, the main artery of the North End – Boston's Little Italy – I watched pizza aficionados lining up on the pavement for the city's finest slices and arancini; I joined the (just as lengthy) line across the road in Mike's Pastry to choose from 18 flavours of cannoli, baked here for over 70 years.

With blood-sugar levels soaring, I delved into Paul Revere's simple shingle-clad house, built in 1680 and bought by the famed silversmith and patriot 90 years later. Today it's a true time machine, a treasure trove of period furnishings (even Revere's wallpaper), giving a palpable sense of Boston life centuries ago.

Turning northwest on to his namesake mall, I was confronted with the spire of the Old North Church. I pictured its spindly tower in 1723, when it was first raised on a promontory at that time surrounded by the waters of the Charles River. And again on that night half a century later, when Revere's two lanterns hung from the steeple alerted his patriot comrades in Charlestown of the British plans. I envisioned its view of the bloody battle at Bunker Hill across the river two months after Revere's ride, and of 'Old Ironside' – USS *Constitution* – being constructed in Hartt's shipyard nearby two decades later.

There, on the water's edge, I ended my journey of the imagination, having covered just 2½ miles (4km), but over two-and-a-half centuries of drama. **PB**

ORIENTATION

Start // Boston Common
End // Bunker Hill
Distance // 2.5 miles (4km)
Getting there // Park Street T (subway) station, at the junction of the Red and Green Lines, is close to the start of the trail at Boston Common Visitor Center (www.bostonusa.com/about-gbcvb/contact-us), which sells Freedom Trail guidebooks and maps. Buses 92 and 93 return downtown from near Bunker Hill. Boston's Logan International Airport is connected with the city centre by Blue Line T, Silver Line bus and water shuttle. For public transport information visit www.mbta.com.
Tours // Walk into History tours led by guides in period costume run frequently year-round (http://thefreedomtrail.org/book-tour).

Opposite: San Antonio's San Fernando Cathedral, the oldest standing church building in Texas

MORE LIKE THIS
US URBAN HISTORICS

THE CONSTITUTIONAL, PHILADELPHIA, PENNSYLVANIA

US capital for a decade before DC took up its duties in 1800, Philly is understandably proud of its role in the foundation of the nation. This self-guided tour snakes past more than 30 sites connected with the struggle for independence and the first years of the fledgling country. You'll visit the Pennsylvania State House – now Independence Hall – where Thomas Jefferson's pivotal document was adopted on 4 July 1776. You'll admire the Liberty Bell, now famously cracked but which may have rung to announce the first reading of the Declaration. And you'll see a wealth of firsts: the sites of the first US Capitol and Supreme Court, the First Bank of the United States, and the Betsy Ross House where that matron was reputedly commissioned to create the first American flag in 1877.
Start // National Constitution Center
End // African American Museum
Distance // 3.3 miles (5.3km)
More info // www.theconstitutional. com/tours

SAN ANTONIO RIVER WALK, TEXAS

Remember the Alamo? That fateful clash in 1836, at a former Spanish Catholic mission that had become a stronghold for Texan soldiers, is seared into the memories of all American schoolchildren. The remains of the battle-scarred monument now lie in downtown San Antonio, forming the centrepiece of a walk through the city's most historic districts. An exemplar of urban riparian regeneration, the River Walk incorporates walking, cycling and boating trails tracing the San Antonio River from Brackenridge Park south through Downtown to Mission Espada. For a day of heritage hiking, begin at the Alamo, roam the two-centuries-old arts village La Villita, pause in the Plaza de las Islas and San Fernando Cathedral, founded by Canary Islanders in the 1730s, then stride south past old-time saloons to a cluster of Spanish missions.
Start // Brackenridge Park
End // Mission Espada
Distance // 15 miles (24km)
More info // visitsanantonio.com

BARBARY COAST TRAIL, SAN FRANCISCO, CALIFORNIA

At the start of the 1840s, the city now called San Francisco was neither a city, nor called San Francisco (it was then Yerba Buena), nor in the United States. Yet just a decade later, within two years of the California gold-rush frenzy sparked in 1848, the population had boomed to more than 25,000. Follow the Barbary Coast Trail, waymarked with dozens of bronze medallions and arrows embedded in the pavement, to explore sites tracing the city's history from the gold rush to the earthquake of 1906, including the Old Mint of 1874, the Pony Express Headquarters, the Wells Fargo Museum, the ships of the Maritime Historic Park, and reminders of waves of immigration from China, including the USA's first Asian temple.
Start // Old Mint
End // Ghirardelli Sq
Distance // 3.8 miles (6km)
More info // www.barbarycoasttrail.org

ROCKIES ROAD: THE SKYLINE TRAIL

One of Canada's backcountry classics, the Skyline is an unforgettable adventure straight through the heart of the Rocky Mountains.

A red sky is rising over the Rockies as the shuttle bus pulls out of Jasper and rattles into the backcountry. The bus is rammed with hikers, chatting and double-checking their packs for supplies. Outside, pine forest blurs past the windows, and above the treeline, I catch glimpses of saw-tooth peaks, crests tinted pink by the morning sun. Everyone's excited about the hike, but there's a crackle of trepidation too: an adventure's guaranteed, but no one's sure quite what the mountains have in store.

Running for 27 miles (44km) between Maligne Lake and Maligne Canyon, the Skyline is considered the crème de la crème of Canadian hiking. It's aptly named: over half the trail runs way above the treeline, a high-level, big-sky route offering some of the grandest views in the Rockies. Unfortunately, its altitude means it's exposed to the weather, and its wildness means wildlife encounters are a constant possibility. Reflexively, I check my belt for my canister of bear spray as I step off the bus, bid farewell to the driver and take my first step on to the Skyline.

Most hikers cover the route in two or three days, staying at backcountry campgrounds dotted along the trail. I've been hiking in the Rockies for a few months, so I feel confident about tackling it in two – although looking up at the craggy peaks ahead, I wonder if I might have overestimated my abilities.

The first stretch, at least, is a gentle one. From the trailhead, the path winds through stands of tall pine and fir. After a few miles, the silvery pools of Lorraine Lake and Mona Lake appear, and I stop to pitch a stone across the still water before pressing on to Little Shovel Pass, where I'm treated to a postcard view over Maligne Lake and the Queen Elizabeth Ranges. I break for lunch, watching

a family of hoary marmots play on the rocks, whistling and hooting softly to each other, their ears twitching and fur rippling in the breeze.

Further up the mountain lies the sprawling meadow known as the Snowbowl. It's late August now, and the meadow is laced with snowmelt pools, interspersed amongst a carpet of wildflowers and tundra. It feels thrillingly wild and empty, and I stop for a while to watch a hawk circling high above the mountaintops, scanning the valley below for unseen prey.

By the time I reach my overnight spot at Curator Campground, it's early evening, and the sky's the colour of candy floss. It's not

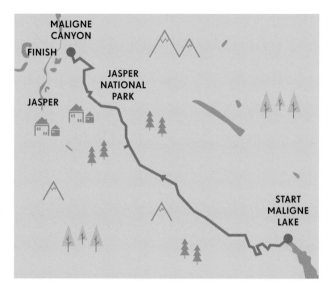

far from the famous Shovel Pass, named by plucky adventurer Mary Schaffer, who got stuck here in deep snow in 1911; she and her guide Jack Otto had to dig their way through using shovels fashioned from tree trunks. I find a patch of grass and pitch my tent, boiling some tea as I stretch out my sleeping bag and give my aching legs a rest. Soon enough, I get chatting to some other hikers, and we share hiking tales over a supper of camp-cooked chilli, followed by biscuits, chunks of dark chocolate and mugs of hot tea. Afternoon drifts into evening, evening into night; stars prick the darkening sky, and a chill descends over the valley. I head off to bed by the light of my head-torch, but not before I've strung up my food bag; I haven't caught sight of any bears yet, but I know they're out there, and tonight, I'm camping out in their backyard.

I wake with the lark, muscles aching. Mist hangs on the meadow as I fry up a quick breakfast, then get an early start on the trail. Grey cloud squats on the mountains, and the wind is getting up, rattling through the trees and whipping up dust devils along the rocky trail. It gets fiercer as I climb to the trail's highest point, the Notch, a rocky pass perched at 8235ft (2510m). The wind is howling over the mountain now, keening and whooshing across the rock face in great buffeting gusts. Grimly, I remember a ranger

"Looking up at the craggy peaks ahead, I wonder if I might have overestimated my abilities"

MARMOT OR PIKA?

Once prized for their pelts, fuzzy mountain-dwelling marmots are a member of the squirrel family. They live in burrows in close-knit family groups; like meerkats, the family keeps watch for predators, and you're bound to hear their distinctive hooting, whistling cries if you get too close. Pikas are much smaller, with round bodies and big ears that make them look rather like oversized mice – but they're actually more closely related to rabbits.

Clockwise from top: a marmot; Jasper mountain stream; the Skyline Trail. Previous page: Maligne Lake

telling me that the Notch was the most dangerous section of the Skyline; the high-wire point, he called it. Several hikers have been struck by lightning here during storms. Still, I can't help pausing to shoot the view – a widescreen panorama over the Athabasca valley, with the ghostly silhouette of Mt Robson looming on the horizon.

Then, as I trudge along the ridgeline of Amber Mountain, the wind suddenly drops, as though someone's flicked the off switch. Stillness returns to the mountain, and buttery sunshine bathes the trail as it switchbacks down to Tekarra Lake. Pikas appear from their burrows, chirruping as they dart over the rocks. Above me, a line of bighorn sheep pick their way along a narrow precipice. Gradually, barren rock gives way to tundra, then to scrubby forest, and as I pass beneath the shadow of Excelsior Mountain, I know I've finally stepped off the high-wire on to safer ground.

From here, I'm on the home stretch, which is an old fire-road that leads down into Maligne Canyon, but there's time for a stop at the lookout on Signal Mountain for one last panorama. Ragged peaks zig-zag along the horizon, crusted with glaciers fed by the great Columbia Icefield, and the blue thread of the Athabasca River snakes along the valley floor. But I don't have very long to enjoy the view; ink-black clouds are massing overhead, and as I trudge down the fire-road, a boom of thunder cracks over the valley like cannon fire.

By the time I make it to the trailhead and the shelter of the shuttle bus, rain is hammering against the windshield, and I'm soaked to the skin. But I don't mind. A cold beer is waiting for me in Jasper Town, and I feel like I've earned it. **OB**

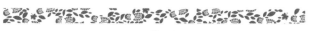

ORIENTATION

Start // Maligne Lake
End // Maligne Canyon
Distance // 27 miles (44km)
Getting there // Edmonton is the nearest international airport, some 225 miles (362km) east of Jasper. The Maligne Lake shuttle runs to the trailhead from Jasper Town.
When to go // Late July to late September.
Where to stay // There are campgrounds at Evelyn Creek, Little Shovel, Snowbowl, Curator, Tekarra and Signal. Bookings are mandatory in summer, as is a valid Backcountry Pass.
What to take // Bear spray, plasters, wet-weather gear.
More info // Jasper Park Information Centre (www.jasper. travel), Parks Canada (pc.gc.ca/en/pn-np/ab/jasper).
Things to know // All the Skyline's campgrounds are equipped with barrel toilets and bear poles for food storage. Campfires are sometimes allowed when the fire risk is low, but gas stoves are cleaner and more efficient.

Opposite, clockwise from top: Hopewell Rocks in the Bay of Fundy, New Brunswick; black bears are frequently spotted in BC; negotiating a footbridge through the West Coast Trail

MORE LIKE THIS
GREAT CANADIAN HIKES

WEST COAST TRAIL, VANCOUVER ISLAND

Constructed in 1907 as a means of rescuing sailors shipwrecked along the Vancouver Island's rocky, reef-lined coast, this 47-mile (75km) trail has become one of Canada's most popular hiking trails. Part of the Pacific Rim National Park, it provides a fabulous introduction to the island's natural environment, traversing old-growth forest, wild beaches, muddy bogs and tumbling waterfalls. Ladders, boardwalks and stone staircases all form part of the route, and there are several sections where you can choose to veer up into the highlands or stick close to the pebbly, sea-washed shore. Much of the time, you're walking on ancient paths first trodden by First Nations people some 4000 years ago, and the land here remains sacred to native tribes – so this is definitely a trail to tread with reverence. Most people take five or six days to complete it.
Start // **Pachena Bay**
End // **Gordon River**
Distance // **47 miles (75km)**
More info // **www.westcoasttrail.com**

THE FUNDY FOOTPATH, NEW BRUNSWICK

Well off the beaten track on Canada's under-appreciated east coast, this seaside trail explores the wild, unspoilt stretch of coastline between Labrador and Florida, one of the last untouched areas of true coastal wilderness left in North America. Running for 25 miles (41km) around the Bay of Fundy, it's a wonderful wild hike that gives access to dramatic cliffs, tumbling cascades, pristine rivers and countless hidden sandy beaches where you're unlikely to spot another soul. Unsurprisingly, the cliffs here are a haven for all kinds of seabirds, and if you're really lucky, you might even spy a pod of dolphins or right whales playing in one of the numerous isolated coves. But it's the tides here that provide the real challenge: they're some of the highest on earth, and several sections of the trail are cut off by rising water. Along with a good map, a tide timetable is a must-have accessory.
Start // **Big Salmon River**
End // **Fundy National Park**
Distance // **25 miles (41km)**
More info // **www.fundyhikingtrails.com**

THE GREAT DIVIDE TRAIL, BRITISH COLUMBIA/ALBERTA

This is it: the big kahuna, the granddaddy, the trail to end all trails. Sprawling for a truly epic 745 miles (1200km) along the borders of British Columbia and Alberta, this long-distance route traces the course of the so-called Great Divide – the continental ridge that separates North America's west and east. To the west of the trail, all rainfall runs into the Pacific Ocean; to the east, it trickles down to the Atlantic or the Gulf of Mexico. The trail zig-zags across the divide numerous times, traversing areas of wilderness that have only recently been opened up to hikers. This is the big-sky Canada you've been dreaming of, complete with all the wild critters you'd expect to encounter – including moose, wolves, black bears, grizzlies and, unfortunately, hordes of biting insects in summer. The reward? Canada's most challenging hike, bar none.
Start // **Waterton**
End // **Mt Robson**
Distance // **745 miles (1200km)**
More info // **www.greatdividetrail.com**

CONCEPCIÓN VOLCANO HIKE

Wake before dawn in Nicaragua to summit the sheer slopes of this active volcano, climbing through field and forest all the way to the steam-shrouded crater.

It is dawn, and I'm nervous. 'Just how active is "active"?' I ask the guide. 'Don't worry, we always check the seismic forecast before we leave,' he assures me.

There are certain things you want to know before summiting a 5282ft (1610m) live volcano. I'm on the island of Ometepe in the middle of vast Lake Nicaragua. The island is shaped like a figure of eight lying in the water, each side a volcano. On the southeast side there's Maderas, its slopes covered in cloud forest. Its last known eruption was in the Pleistocene epoch. Concepción, the one I'm hiking up today, last erupted a bit more recently. Like, 2010 recently. It was no big deal, though, the hotel owner tells me. Just a big ash cloud.

Oh, OK then.

Seen from the distance, Concepción looks like a child's drawing of a volcano: a perfectly symmetrical cone with a flat top haloed by clouds. Many consider reaching its summit to be the most difficult hike in all of Nicaragua, no small thing in a nation with several major mountain ranges and 40-odd volcanoes. This isn't my first Nicaraguan volcano hike, but it will definitely be the longest. We're aiming to get up and back within eight hours, though it can take 10 or more.

Rising in the bluish predawn, we begin our summit assault in the tiny hamlet of La Concepción. We walk through fields of coffee and banana plantations, nodding greetings at several early-rising farmers. But the easy stroll gets challenging very quickly, as the trail takes a steep turn up the slope and into the forest. This is dry tropical forest, dense with vines and ferns. It's still early, and the first weak rays of sunlight barely penetrate the canopy. Howler monkeys screech overhead, an eerie sound that reminds me of

the spooky stories I heard from the proprietor of the hotel where we stayed the night before, stories of a man-devil named Chico Largo who roams the nature reserve south of Concepción, turning men into cows and worse. We climb and climb, sometimes walking up stairs hacked by machete out of the earth. They're slippery beneath our feet, still wet with morning dew. I trip on a root and nearly land face first in the mud.

Finally we come to El Floral, a lookout point at about 3280ft (1000m). In the morning light we can see down across the treetops to the patchwork fields below and all the way across the navy waters of Lake Nicaragua to the mainland. On some days you

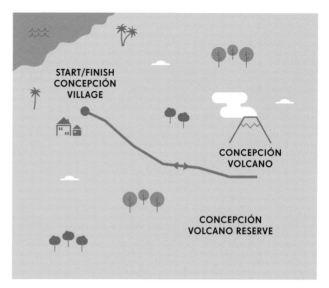

© Riderfoot | Shutterstock

can actually see the Pacific Ocean, our guide tells us, but today is a little hazy. We crouch and eat our sandwiches of avocado and salty farmer's cheese, then share a ripe, sweet local mango. Fortified, we push on.

From here on, the path becomes very exposed, rocky and unnervingly steep. The forest has dropped away and we find ourselves climbing through alpine meadows of low, spiky shrubs. Soon, the shrubs are replaced with grass, which becomes shorter and shorter before petering away entirely. We're now walking on volcanic scree, the slope strewn with boulders the size of beach balls. Our feet slip on the loose grit, and at times I find myself on all fours, like a very awkward mountain goat. It's also chilly, with a raw wind whipping up the dust. I'm glad I brought a windbreaker. We ascend like this for what feels like ages, no longer bothering to speak because of exhaustion and the noise of the wind. The smells – sulphur, and something even more harsh – grow stronger.

Slowly, then all at once, we are enveloped in cloud. But it's not ordinary cloud. This is cloud mixed with volcanic steam emanating from deep inside the mountain, acrid and yellow. Visibility turns to nearly nothing. Our guide is only a few feet ahead of us, but

"We're at the edge of the crater. This must be what it's like to visit Mars"

at times I can only see his shoes or his swinging arms. The smell is overwhelming, rotten eggs and sharp metal odours. You can understand why ancient peoples from many cultures described this as the stench of hell.

Then our guide turns and stops. We're at the edge of the crater, he tells us. It's so cloudy we wouldn't have known. We snap a few pictures of ourselves, though we won't be able to see much. I become aware of a warm wind, which I realise is heat coming from the nearby fumaroles, those rents in the earth leading deep inside the volcano. This must be what it's like to visit Mars.

Not everyone who summits Concepción has this steam and cloud and sulphur experience. Some days the volcano is quieter and wind patterns mean there's little or no cloud on top. On those days you can see for hundreds of miles across lake and land and ocean. But I'm glad to experience this, this strange grey hellscape.

Now all we need to do is get back down. As every mountain climber knows, descent is often the most dangerous part of the climb. This is especially true when the descent is down hundreds of yards of volcanic boulders and grit with the wind blowing in your eyes. But we catch a lucky break as we reach the relatively safety of the high meadows. The clouds dissipate, opening up a view over the patchwork of farmland spreading out below. We still can't quite see the ocean, but the shining waters of Lake Nicaragua look pretty darn glorious.

Exhausted, bug-bitten and muddy, we stumble back to our hotel. Time for a shower, a huge plate of *gallo pinto* (beans and rice), and a dreamless sleep in the shadow of the volcano. **EM**

OMETEPE'S DIVERSITY

Inhabited since 2000 BC, Ometepe Island's earliest peoples left behind thousands of petroglyphs, pottery shards and stone idols. Today, its residents farm coffee, plantains and cacao in the rich volcanic soil. The forests are home to howler monkeys, armadillos, sloths and 80 types of migratory birds. One variety of tree and a type of salamander occur nowhere else but Ometepe.

Opposite, clockwise from top: cloud shrouds Concepción volcano; white-throated magpie jays on Ometepe Island; a female howler monkey. Previous page: the full volcanic vista

ORIENTATION

Start/End // Concepción village
Distance // 9 miles (14km)
Getting there // Nicaragua's main airport is in Managua. From here, reach Ometepe by ferry from the lakeside town of San Jorge. Moyogalpa is the main town on Ometepe, so most hikers stay here the night before their climb.
When to go // The December-to-March dry season is best for clear summit views, while September to November can be so rainy it's dangerous to go past the lookout point.
What to take // Plenty of water, snacks and sunscreen, and a windbreaker for the summit.
Things to know // Two trails up the volcano start from villages near Moyogalpa, and another from La Sabana, east of the volcano. Start as early as 4am as the afternoon often brings bad weather. Guides are mandatory.

Opposite: steam escapes from thermal springs in Yellowstone National Park

MORE LIKE THIS
VOLCANO HIKES

VESUVIUS' CRATER, ITALY

Although the climb up Vesuvius is the busiest, most commercialised hike in Italy, the magnitude of what you witness makes up for the aggregation of panting, sweating, flip-flop-wearing humanity. Most of these won't have realised that they are required to leave their vehicles at the Quota 1000 car park, 922ft (281m) below Vesuvius' modern summit, necessitating a 282ft (86m) steep and stony scramble to the rim of the gaping crater. From the car park, the trail rises in a southwesterly direction, switching back after a couple of hundred metres then climbing steadily at an average gradient of 14 percent towards the crater. Remember that Vesuvius will erupt again sooner or later, so you climb it at your own risk. Be aware, too, of vipers – and illegal taxi drivers...

Start/End // Quota 1000 car park
Distance // 1.9 miles (3km)

ASCENT OF VOLCÁN LANÍN, ARGENTINA

Towering over the northern Lakes District, Volcán Lanín rises from a base plain of around 3609ft (1100m) to a height of 12,388ft (3776m). Its thick cap of heavily crevassed glacial ice makes it look almost impossible to climb, but up its eastern side is a strenuous, though straightforward, ascent. In fact, Lanín is probably the highest summit in Patagonia safely attainable without ropes. An ice axe and crampons are mandatory, however, as are suitable mountain clothing and kit. The summit is normally tackled between November and February and an early start is imperative, since after midday the snow often becomes soft and slushy, making the going tiring. The volcano's steep slopes are no place for tents, so trekkers must stay at one of three unstaffed *refugios*, roughly halfway up the mountain. We suggest the rustic, tin-roofed Refugio CAJA at 8727ft (2660m) for the end of both your first day's ascent and the following night on the way back down.

Start/End // Guarderia Tromen
Distance // 15 miles (25km)

MT WASHBURN AND SEVENMILE HOLE, YELLOWSTONE NATIONAL PARK, USA

This long day or overnight shuttle hike climbs 1400ft (425m) from Dunraven Pass to the summit of 10,243ft (3122m) Mt Washburn, all that remains of a volcano explosion some 600,000 years ago that formed the vast Yellowstone Caldera. From the small car park at Dunraven Pass, a wide trail grants a comfortable but steady sidling ascent through forests of subalpine fir. Broad switchbacks and a narrow ridge lead to Mt Washburn's lookout tower, which affords majestic views across the Yellowstone basin. The trail then drops southeast towards undulating wildflower meadows and campsite 4E1, about 90 minutes from the top. You'll continue southwest through boggy grassland and the boiling mud pools at Washburn Hot Springs. From the southern rim of the Grand Canyon of the Yellowstone, which plunges some 1312ft-deep (400m), the views become ever more spectacular en route to the Glacial Boulder Trailhead. Bear in mind that this is grizzly country, and bears are populous here in late summer and early autumn.

Start // Dunraven Pass
End // Canyon
Distance // 16.6 miles (26.7k)

BORDER PATROL ON THE PACIFIC CREST TRAIL

Bursting with US mountain panoramas and challenging backcountry terrain, this cross-country corridor is perfect for anything from a weekend escape to an epic five-month adventure.

I t is late April, and dawn is breaking over the southern Californian desert as the dust kicked up by my friend's car settles. I watch as she disappears into the distance, then turn around and approach a large wooden marker standing a few feet from the US/Mexico border fence. It reads 'Pacific Crest National Scenic Trail; Southern Terminus; Mexico to Canada 2650 Miles'. A dirt footpath meanders away from the site. I snap a picture, hoist my backpack on to my shoulders, mutter something reassuring and take my first few steps along the Pacific Crest Trail (PCT) towards Canada.

The PCT truly is epic, traversing the country's wilderness virtually unbroken between Mexico and Canada. It cuts the states of California, Oregon and Washington in half by following the spines of the Sierra Nevada and Cascade mountain ranges, passing through 25 national forests, seven national parks and climbing over 90 vertical miles along the way. And I'm attempting a hike of its 2650 miles (4265km) in a single season, a feat commonly referred to as a 'thru-hike' and usually met with some combination of confusion, awe and bewilderment when announced to the general public.

Timing is key: a late-April start will get me through the desert before it becomes too hot and dry, let me reach the Sierra Nevada mountains just as the snow from the previous winter has melted, and then give me three quick months to make it through Oregon and Washington to Canada before winter.

The first section of the PCT is known as 'the Desert', though that betrays the astonishing diversity of landscapes it passes through. From the barren hills near Mojave to the dense pine forests surrounding Big Bear Lake, this section is all about variety. The desert is also a refreshing social experience, with dozens of

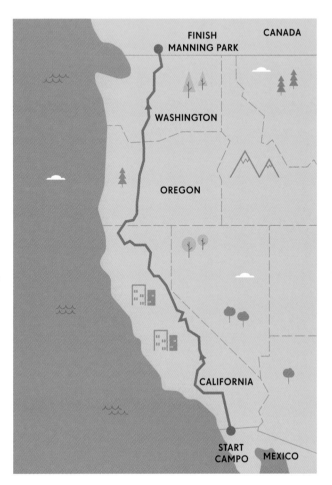

hopeful hikers starting northbound from the border each day in April (more than 90% of hikers walk northbound). Many lifelong friendships are forged in these first 700 miles (1126km).

The popularity of the PCT has skyrocketed over the past decade, largely due to the movie adaptation of Cheryl Strayed's best-selling 2012 novel *Wild: From Lost to Found on the Pacific Crest Trail*. In two decades numbers have grown from a couple of hundred intrepid hikers annually to more than 3000 in 2016, which can be a mixed blessing; it makes it easy to find a group to hike with, but those seeking solitude may want to consider a southbound hike starting at the Canadian border instead.

A month after leaving the southern terminus I arrive at the outpost of Kennedy Meadows, which marks the end of the desert. By now I've got my 'trail legs'. I can walk 25 miles day after day with a full pack without a problem, my feet have callused up and resemble a hobbit's leathery soles, and my constant caloric deficit means I'll devour anything I can get my hands on. The High Sierra awaits. Stretching nearly the entire length of California, the Sierras are a section of outstanding natural beauty and spirit-testing isolation. Containing 10 snow-veiled passes above 10,000ft (3048m), countless river crossings and minimal resupply or evacuation routes, it's a landscape that demands respect and in

"Stretching nearly the entire length of California, the Sierras provide a section of outstanding natural beauty"

return delivers some of the most dramatic hiking anywhere on the planet. Translucent mountain lakes, sheer granite cliffs and raging rivers teeming with fish are just some of the remarkable vistas the trail traverses for 600 miles (965km) between Kennedy Meadows and Lassen Volcanic National Park in northern California.

North of Lassen the landscape undergoes a geological shift as the granite peaks of the Sierras fade into the distance and give way to the volcanoes of the Cascade Range. Dotting the landscape like breadcrumbs from northern California all the way through Washington, these behemoths dominate my views for the next 1000 miles (1609km). The frequent ascents/descents of the Sierras are replaced by the mellow rolling hills and forests of Oregon as the PCT crosses ancient lava fields and passes close to each of the Cascade volcanoes. A highlight of Oregon is hiker-friendly Timberline Lodge on the flanks of Mt Hood, famous for a breakfast buffet that puts even the most voracious hiker's appetite to the test.

KIND HEARTS AND CORONAS

A cooler in the middle of the desert stocked with beer, soda, and chocolate? It's not a mirage, it's 'trail magic'! Along its entire length, the PCT has a vibrant local community of 'trail angels' who selflessly give their time and resources to help hikers on their journeys. Whether it's a cold drink or a ride into town, their generosity is unparalleled and can turn a bad day into something magical.

From left: Rainbow Falls in California's Mammoth Lakes; tackling the trail through Oregon; marking the route. Previous page: California's Lassen Volcanic National Park is one of seven on the Pacific Crest Trail

With Oregon behind me, I descend towards the Columbia River and savour the crossing into Washington, the final state of my journey. Here Oregon's forgiving terrain comes to an abrupt end and almost instantly I'm climbing up and down the deep glacial valleys of the northern Cascades. Three weeks after crossing the Columbia I've reached Stehekin, the final town on the trail and possibly the most charming. Sitting on the northernmost coast of a large mountain lake, it can only be reached by foot, boat or seaplane, an isolation that give it a uniquely laidback feel. The people are friendly, and relaxing days of soaking in the magnitude of my journey come easy.

After leaving Stehekin, I savour the three-day hike to the Canadian border and use the time to reflect on how lucky I've been to spend my summer experiencing all the ups and downs of the PCT – both physically and mentally. As a Canadian, part of what kept me going was a sense of walking home, though after months on the PCT the concept of 'home' had become a bit abstract. I eventually arrive at the northern terminus on a late afternoon in mid-August and am greeted by a monument that is near-identical to the one I left behind at the Mexican border. It reads 'Canada to Mexico 2650 Miles'. This time I'll go home instead, wherever that is. **AB**

ORIENTATION

Start // Southern Terminus: Campo, CA, USA
End // Northern Terminus: Manning Park, BC, Canada
Distance // 2650 miles (4265km)
Getting there // San Diego is the closest airport to the southern terminus, Vancouver to the northern.
When to go (earliest recommended start dates) // Northbound, 15 April; southbound, 1 July
What to take // Overnight backpacking gear; sleeping bag rated to at least -10°C (14°F); ice axe and crampons if in the Sierras or Washington before July; extra sun protection and water in the desert.
Maps and apps // Maps from www.pctmap.net and apps *Halfmile's PCT* and *Guthook's Pacific Crest Trail Guide*.
More info // Pacific Crest Trail Association: www.pcta.org
Things to know // Download a report providing near real-time status of water sources in the desert at pctwater.com.

Opposite from top: re-enacting a bygone age at George Washington's home at Mt Vernon; Florida's lush Big Cypress National Preserve

MORE LIKE THIS
US SCENIC TRAILS

ICE AGE NATIONAL SCENIC TRAIL, WISCONSIN

Take a hike 15,000 years back in time, to when mammoths last wandered the earth. During the last ice age and North America's most recent glacial period (known as the Wisconsin glaciation), a frosty crust lay over vast swaths of the USA, leaving impressive marks on the land, from rippling hills to gouged-out river valleys and dramatic ridges. Wisconsin's Ice Age National Scenic Trail, which skirts the edges of North America's last continental glacier, is like walking through a 3-D geography lesson, with added birdsong, fresh air and a sense of freedom. Only around half of the proposed 1200-mile (1930km) trail is currently complete, but it's still possible to walk day-long or multi-day segments, or even the whole trail: the finished off-road sections range from 2 miles (3km) to 40 miles (65km) and are linked by temporary routes along quiet country roads.
Start/End // Interstate State Park/ Potawatomi State Park
Distance // 1200 miles (1930km)

FLORIDA NATIONAL SCENIC TRAIL, FLORIDA

Explore the alternative Sunshine State – that is, its estimable wild side, far from fairytale castles or talking mice... The Florida National Scenic Trail trail (which is around three-quarters complete) begins in the Panhandle, on the crunchy-white, turquoise-lapped beaches of the Gulf Islands National Seashore near Pensacola. From here it wiggles east and south, via salt marshes, crystal-clear springs, lakes, prairies, old-growth forests and historic urban areas. It finishes in Big Cypress National Preserve, bordering the Everglades, amid a lush swampland of bright bromeliads and giant ferns. This semi-tropical state is incredibly bio-diverse, and most of the trail is also a wildlife corridor, protecting both common and rare species. Possible sightings include black bear, deer, otters, alligators, gopher tortoises and sea turtles, plus a plethora of birds – the crested caracara and red-cockaded woodpecker are particularly sought-after species.
Start/End // Big Cypress National Preserve/Fort Pickens, Gulf Islands National Seashore
Distance // 1300 miles (2090km)

POTOMAC HERITAGE NATIONAL SCENIC TRAIL, VIRGINIA, MARYLAND, PENNSYLVANIA AND DISTRICT OF COLUMBIA

Linking the Potomac and upper Youghiogheny river basins, this scenic trail isn't one continuous walking route but a network of heritage, cultural and get-out-in-nature pathways across the region. Thus, thru-hiking isn't the point here. Better to pick a part that sounds intriguing. For instance, those short on time could try Virginia's history-laced Mt Vernon Trail, which runs for 17 miles (27km) along the Potomac from Theodore Roosevelt Island to George Washington's home at Mt Vernon, via memorials, a 19th-century lighthouse, the old trading town of Alexandria and marshes prolific with birds. Multi-dayers might like the 150-mile (241km) Great Allegheny Passage or GAP, a hiker-biker route throughout parts of the Appalachian Mountains, linking Cumberland (Maryland) and downtown Pittsburgh using defunct corridors of the USA's old railroads; this includes traversing cast-iron truss bridges, lofty viaducts and the 1968ft (600m) tunnel under Big Savage Mountain.
Start/End // Various, between Pittsburgh and the mouth of the Potomac River
Distance // 708 miles (1140km)

HELI-HIKING IN THE BUGABOO MOUNTAINS

To elevate your hiking to a totally epic level, fly by helicopter to remote trailheads among Western Canada's mountains, glaciers and blue-green lakes.

The helicopter's rotors whirl and roar above us, a dozen hikers squatting together, our heads low to the dirt. It's the first day of our heli-hiking trip in British Columbia's Bugaboo Mountains, and we're learning to do the 'heli huddle'. To stay out of the helicopter's landing path, we crouch and cluster on cue, attempting to shield ourselves from the swirling propeller's knock-you-over winds.

Heli-hiking is the warm-weather equivalent of heli-skiing, where a helicopter whisks you into the mountains in search of pristine terrain. But instead of seeking to make first tracks in untouched powder, you're looking for remote hiking routes that are difficult or impossible to reach unless you fly in.

Canadian Mountain Holidays (CMH), a tour company that pioneered heli-skiing back in the 1960s, now runs summer hiking adventures as well. Forty of us are headed for three days of hiking, based at the CMH Bugaboo Lodge on the edge of Bugaboo Provincial Park, a vast wilderness covering 33,700 acres (13,600 hectares) named for the Bugaboo Spire, one of several glacier-carved granite spikes that jut towards the sky.

For our first flight, a 10-minute hop from the helipad outside Kootenay National Park, the red-and-white Bell 212 helicopter shuttles us in small groups, flying low over the green hills. We land in a gravel field in front of the wood-and-stone lodge building.

I can't help but say 'wow' as I walk into the lodge and look through the windows framing the view: the snow-topped Bugaboo Spire, more than 10,500ft (3200m) tall, with a carpet of evergreens beneath it and several peaks nearby.

In the equipment room, we meet several of the guides who'll be accompanying us out on the trails. They chat with us while we

try on boots, rain jackets and daypacks (you can bring your own or borrow from the CMH supply), to assess our hiking experience and comfort with different types of terrain. They weigh us – for helicopter load balancing – and by the time we go into the dining room for lunch, they have sorted us into groups of eight to 10 like-minded hikers.

After we eat, each group climbs into the helicopter in turn, for our first adventures on the trail. Even though it's the middle of July, the height of Canada's summer, the skies are overcast, and when the helicopter deposits us above a jade-coloured lake, we layer fleece sweaters under our jackets. Our guide, Paul, who tells us

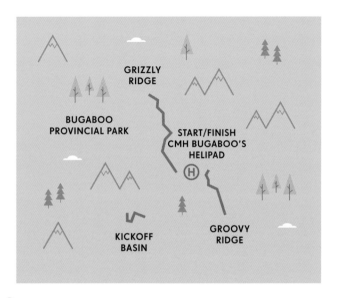

he's been guiding for more than two decades, is very visible in his bright red parka. We follow him along a shale-covered trail that descends into a valley and climbs gently up towards the snow-capped mountains.

As we hike higher on the ridge and across a field of snow, the clouds drop like a curtain around us, until it feels as if we could reach up and hold the heavy grey mist. The wind comes up, too, and we pause to pull on hats and gloves. We walk a little further, before Paul turns his face to the wind and scans the sky. He tells us it's time to get off this ridge before the weather worsens. He radios for the helicopter, and after we snap a few quick photos with our feet in the summer snow, we hike down to a more sheltered spot, where the craft can land. When we pull up into the clouds, fat raindrops begin splattering the windshield.

We're back at the lodge in time for 'tea goodies', when everyone gathers in the lounge (or hot tub) for cocktails and snacks, swapping stories about their day's adventures. Dinner is served family-style, and we dig into Caesar salads, baked salmon and lemon tarts.

The next morning, the sun peeks through the clouds during my pre-breakfast stroll outside the lodge. White and yellow wildflowers surround a nearby pond, a perfect foreground for photos of the pointed peaks. One group sets off early, boarding the helicopter to tackle a via ferrata or 'iron way', a climbing route assisted with a system of iron rings, cables, ladders and bridges fixed into the

"The helicopter whisks you into the mountains, looking for remote hiking routes difficult to reach unless you fly in"

TACKLING THE BUGABOOS

The spiky peaks known as the Bugaboos are in the Purcell mountain range, near the provincial border between British Columbia and Alberta, west of the Canadian Rockies. Since the early 1900s, these spires have drawn mountaineers who attempt to summit their rocky faces. Austrian-born Conrad Kain became a Bugaboos legend after he climbed both the Bugaboo Spire and the nearby North Howser tower in 1916. A remote mountain hut today bears Kain's name.

Clockwise from top: a precipitous via ferrata in the Bugaboo; scaling sheer rock walls; the helicopter prepares to ferry a new group of heli-hikers. Previous page: backcountry skiers on Bugaboo Glacier

rock. I opt for 'regular' hiking, and the helicopter zips our group to a ridge, where we set out for a lagoon at the base of the Vowell Glacier. In less than an hour, we reach the blue-green pool below the glacier-topped mountains. Right on schedule, the clouds lift, and the sun glimmers off the water.

The helicopter returns and flies us to Tamarack Glen, where evergreens frame snowy granite hills. We have a picnic lunch overlooking another jade lake. Next, we fly around to the opposite side of the spires, landing on a rock outcropping with an expansive vista across a green valley and an up-close view of the spires. We hike through a meadow, across several small rushing streams and over rock slabs to an alpine lake.

Paul yanks off his boots and wades in to the lake. 'It feels great', he insists. I cautiously dip my toes into the icy water, and after the initial shock – yikes, it's absolutely freezing! – it does rather perk up my flagging feet.

We trek over another crest, and Paul radios the helicopter. As it hovers above our hikers' huddle, I'm stunned to see that the pilot can land on a flat rock not much larger than a queen-size bed.

The chopper flies us over to one more trail, where we hike amid evergreens and across several snowfields. The terrain is gentler here, but that's OK with us. We've been out all day between the turquoise lakes, mountaintop glaciers and the spiky Bugaboo Spires. And with our helicopter to shuttle us from trail to trail among these remote Canadian mountains, we haven't seen another soul. **CH**

ORIENTATION

Start/End // Canadian Mountain Holidays (CMH) Bugaboos trips start in Banff or Lake Louise, Alberta, or in Golden, British Columbia.

Distance // Varies

Getting there // Calgary (Alberta) is the closest international airport. CMH staff can help arrange transportation to the trip starting point. They'll take you by coach to the helipad.

When to go // July, August, early September.

Where to stay // The comfortable 32-room CMH Bugaboo Lodge has an outdoor hot tub, indoor climbing wall and spectacular mountain views.

What to take // Prepare for variable mountain weather, from summer sunshine to whipping winds, rain, even snow. Layers are your friends. CMH stocks hiking boots, rain jackets, daypacks and hiking poles for guests to borrow if you're travelling light or don't have the gear you need.

MORE LIKE THIS
HELI-HIKING AROUND THE WORLD

CANADA

Several heli-hiking operators offer trips in British Columbia, Canada's westernmost province. In addition to the Bugaboos trip, Canadian Mountain Holidays (CMH) runs heli-hiking adventures in two other BC destinations. Multiday trips based at its 26-room Bobbie Burns Lodge, north of Bugaboos Provincial Park, give guests the option to trek near the Conrad Glacier or tackle North America's longest via ferrata. The newest CMH trip, from the 28-room Cariboo Lodge, takes hikers into the more remote Cariboo Mountains, west of Jasper National Park. If you don't want to commit to a multiday heli-hiking trip, try out the sport in Whistler, a two-hour drive from Vancouver. Though this mountain community is best known for its skiing and snowboarding, it's a year-round destination for outdoor adventures, including Blackcomb Helicopters' half- and full-day heli-hiking excursions. For more heli-hiking options, contact Glacier Helicopters or Heli Canada Adventures, both based in the town of Revelstoke, in eastern BC's Selkirk and Monashee Mountains.
More info // www.canadian mountainholidays.com; blackcombhelicopters.com: www.glacierhelicopters.ca; helicanada.com

CHILE

While the Chilean Andes have become a centre for winter heli-skiing, heli-hiking in this South American adventure destination is still in its infancy. But if the idea of heli-hiking in the world's longest mountain range makes your heart beat faster, here are a couple of operators in Chile who organise helicopter-based hiking experiences. Lodge Andino el Ingenio, a small adventure lodge 40 miles (65km) southeast of Santiago, offers guests an optional day of heli-hiking. A 15-minute flight takes you into the Piuquenes Valley, where you'll hike up for views of turquoise lagoons and the towering Andes. Located in the Andes, 95 miles (150km) southeast of Chile's capital, between Río Los Cipreses National Reserve and the Argentine border, Noi Puma Lodge enables its guests to heli-hike into the nearby mountains. These day treks reward with vistas across valleys, glaciers and snow-topped volcanoes.
More info // www.lodgeandino.com; www.noihotels.com

NEW ZEALAND

In New Zealand, heli-hikers head for the South Island, particularly the region around the Aoraki/Mt Cook and Westland Tai Poutini National Parks in the Southern Alps, where a helicopter can fly you in to trek on massive glaciers and snowfields. Both Southern Alps Guiding and the Helicopter Line run heli-hiking trips to the country's longest glacier, the Tasman Glacier in Aoraki/Mt Cook, which extends more than 15 miles (24km). These half-day excursions combine a helicopter flight with trekking on the glacier. The Helicopter Line also takes heli-hikers out to the Franz Josef Glacier, a 7.5-mile (12km) span of ice. On these half-day trips, you'll fly over the glacier and then take a guided hike through dramatic glacial ice formations.
More info // www.mtcook.com: www.helicopter.co.nz

CHOQUEQUIRAO: THE CROWD-FREE INCA TRAIL

Some 500 people hike the Inca Trail to Machu Picchu daily, yet a smaller path nearby leads to an even larger 'lost city' of Peru that remains remarkably untouched.

Rambling along the bumpy road from Cuzco out to Cachora, it becomes abundantly clear that I've left the feverish Machu Picchu crowds behind and am now entering the less polished corners of the Peruvian Andes. These are the fabled hills of the Inca, though they're not the ones most visitors fly across oceans to see.

There's only one reason travellers go out of their way to visit the rural village of Cachora, and it's to see a set of ruins that lie just out of sight at the far end of the Apurímac Valley: Choquequirao. Said to be up to three times the size of the more widely known Machu Picchu, these ruins astoundingly see only about two dozen visitors each day.

I've always wondered what it must have been like to visit Angkor Wat, Chichén Itzá or Machu Picchu before the roads and tour buses arrived. Then I found out about Choquequirao, a citadel so far up in the Andes of Peru that archaeologists have only freed about 30% of it from the jungle.

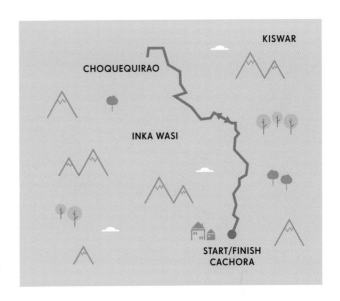

Before American explorer Hiram Bingham ever laid eyes on Machu Picchu, he was whacking his way through the Apurímac Valley, surveying the remarkable carcass of its so-called sister city. Scared off by the prospect of a gruelling, four-day round-trip journey, however, few tourists have bothered to visit over the years. I set off on my own journey to the ruins with a muleteer in tow. There are 28 miles (45km) ahead of me before I'll see Cachora again, so it's a relief knowing I won't have to carry my pack, food and camping gear the entire way.

Cachora lies in a bowl of terraced farmland, so my first objective is to climb out. I spend the remainder of the first day descending 4920ft (1500m) into the Apurímac Valley, walking ever closer to the orange-brown waters of its namesake river. I camp at Playa Rosalina, along the Apurímac River's windy edge, and wake up early the following morning to cross over to the sun-baked side of the valley. It's here that I'll begin my ascent to the base of the ruins high up in the clouds at 10,000ft (3050m).

It's a vertical desert of thorny cacti and dusty switchbacks for the first hours of morning light, but the landscape becomes exceedingly greener the higher I climb. By the time I reach the remote village of Marampata that afternoon, I've entered a high-altitude jungle.

About a hundred people have etched out a meagre existence in Marampata, some two days away from the closest road and far removed from modern comforts. Marampata is the gatekeeper to Choquequirao and home to the humble headquarters of the archaeological park that protects it. This hilltop settlement also

"Some historians believe this hidden outpost was the last refuge of the Inca"

has a basic campground and a store to purchase whatever provisions may have been hoofed up to these Andean heights in recent days by pack mules.

I overnight in Marampata and am awake on day three in time to arrive at the ruins for sunrise. I've prepared a traditional cup of coca tea (from the leaf used to make cocaine) to stave off altitude sickness. It serves the additional purpose of jolting me awake with euphoria by the time the archaeological site's tumbling terraces come into view.

Sprawled across three hilltops and 12 sectors, Choquequirao is less immediately photogenic than Machu Picchu. But this towering citadel, occasionally buried within the clouds, offers a level of solitude unimaginable at most ancient marvels. It also has innumerable tentacles for would-be archaeologists to explore. Abandoned in the mid-16th century, it was 'rediscovered' several times over the intervening three centuries before preservation efforts began in earnest in 1992. Modern archaeologists believe it was geo-cosmically placed in line with its ceremonial sister, Machu Picchu, with a temple and administrative buildings situated around a central square and living quarters clustered further afield.

A high level of sophistication is evident in the gabled ceremonial halls, stone 'refrigerators' and elaborate irrigation

© Yuri Zvezdny | Shutterstock

channels hewn into rock. Climb up to the main plaza and you get astounding views of the frosted 16,000ft (5000m) peaks of the Willkapampa range, as well as soaring condors below. Take the stairs down from the main plaza and you reach one of the most iconic sectors: a set of terraces decorated in a mosaic of white llamas. A longer and windier path leads to the Casa de Cascada cluster, where stone buildings perch on the edge of a cliff overlooking a ribbon waterfall.

The name Choquequirao means 'cradle of gold' in the local Quechua language. Some historians believe this hidden outpost was the last refuge of the Inca as the empire crumbled and royalty fled Cuzco during the 40-year uprising against Spanish conquistadors. But perhaps it was the administrative hub and ceremonial centre linking Cuzco with the Amazon. Or maybe the royal estate of Túpac Yupanqui, the 10th ruler of the Inca Empire. The answers, for now, remain buried deep in the jungle.

Some visitors to Choquequirao will continue onward, and upward, to Machu Picchu on an epic nine-day journey in the footsteps of the Inca. My plan, however, is to head back to Cachora, retracing my own footsteps down the Apurímac Valley to climb, yet again, up the flanks of its far side.

When I reach Playa Rosalina for the second time I'm told of on-again, off-again plans to build a US$50-million cable car to these ruins that would make them accessible in just 15 minutes. Choquequirao will undoubtedly remain one of the great mysteries of the Inca Empire, but this lesser-known 'lost city' appears, at long last, to be finally opening up to the wider world. **MJ**

'DISCOVERING' THE LOST CITY

Choquequirao is so remote, so high up in the Andes, that Spanish conquistadors never found it, though that doesn't mean it was ever truly lost. The first Westerner to visit was Spanish explorer Juan Arias Díaz in 1710, and it was a mapping and surveying trip to Choquequirao in 1909 that inspired Yale professor Hiram Bingham to return to Peru in 1911 for the investigation that led him to rediscover Machu Picchu.

From left: on the trail to Choquequirao; depiction of a llama at the site; the ancient city is thought to be sister to Machu Picchu. Previous page: Choquequirao on its lofty perch in the Andes

ORIENTATION

Start/End // Cachora, Peru
Distance // 28 miles (45km)
Duration // Four days/three nights
Getting there // From Cuzco airport catch a bus 3½ hours west to Cachora. Many guided treks include private transport to and from Cuzco, though operators in Cachora arrange tents, guides and/or mules at about half the cost. The trailhead is accessible by vehicle from Cachora town.
Going solo // While most visit on a guided tour, it's possible to do it alone as the path is clearly marked and there are small camps and shops along the way to purchase water or snacks. However, the trek is extremely steep with little shade, so hiring a muleteer to cart gear is wise.
When to go // May to October is the dry season.

*Opposite: the circa millennium-old
Unesco-listed ruins of Pueblo Bonito,
New Mexico*

MORE LIKE THIS
LOST CITIES OF THE AMERICAS

LA CIUDAD PERDIDA TREK, COLOMBIA

Ciudad Perdida is a lost city hidden deep in the Sierra Nevada de Santa Marta mountains of northern Colombia. Built and occupied by Tayrona Indians between the 8th and 14th centuries, this ancient town was abandoned during the Spanish conquest and only rediscovered in the 1970s by local tomb raiders. It's believed to be one of the largest pre-Columbian settlements in the Americas, though much of the site remains buried beneath the jungle at an altitude of between 3115ft (950m) and 4265ft (1300m) – the modern indigenous inhabitants of the area won't allow further excavations. To reach its 169 mountain-carved terraces and 1200 stone steps you'll need to book a guided tour from Santa Marta in advance, because visiting this site alone is prohibited. The four- or five-day return journey traverses a steamy jungle and includes a number of river crossings and steep climbs. Your reward at the end: a private citadel in the sky.
Start/End // The small village of El Mamey, accessible from Santa Marta
Distance // 27 miles (44km)

THE PUEBLO ALTO LOOP, USA

New Mexico's remote Chaco Canyon is home to the most extensive collection of pueblos in the American Southwest. Built between the 9th and 13th centuries, they were among the largest buildings in North America until well into the 19th century. They're now preserved under the desert sun in one of Unesco's most sorely underappreciated World Heritage Sites. The Pueblo Alto Loop through Chaco Culture National Historical Park offers the perfect introduction to the Chaco world. Climb steps hewn into rock out of the canyon to the mesa above to take in panoramic views of Pueblo Bonito and other Chacoan buildings visible from the canyon rim. Then visit the trail's namesake Pueblo Alto, an 89-room 'great house' that was probably used for ceremonial rituals. Complete the circuit by tramping through the rust-red dirt and descending back into the canyon below where more great houses await.
Start/End // Pueblo del Arroyo Trailhead, accessible from Albuquerque
Distance // 5 miles (8km)

EL MIRADOR HIKE, GUATEMALA

The world's largest pyramids are not in the deserts of Egypt, but rather in the jungles of Mesoamerica at places such as El Mirador, a pre-Columbian complex discovered in 1926 in northern Guatemala. This Mayan centre is among the largest ever found by archaeologists and flourished from about the 6th century BC to the 1st century AD with upwards of 250,000 inhabitants. To reach it, you'll need to trek five days (return) along a mule trail into the dense Guatemalan jungle past the many Mayan satellite centres of the Mirador Basin. A guide is essential, while most hikers also use a mule to transport food, water and supplies. Expect to trek more than 20 miles (30km) in a day and sleep in basic campgrounds near the minor ruins. The view atop 236ft (72m) La Danta, the largest of the three main pyramids at El Mirador, makes it worth all the sweat, as it's pure green as far as the eye can see.
Start/End // The village of Carmelita, accessible from Flores
Distance // 75 miles (120 km)

THE LONG (AND WINDING) TRAIL

Running the length of Vermont's Green Mountains and with 185 miles (300km) of side trails, America's oldest long-distance walking trail showcases the diverse beauty of northern New England.

Before the Appalachian Trail, the Pacific Crest Trail and all the other epic hiking routes of North America, there was the Long Trail. America's oldest long-distance footpath was born in 1910, when two dozen outdoors enthusiasts formed Vermont's Green Mountain Club. What started in 1912 as a 30-mile (48km) spur between Mt Mansfield and Camel's Hump – Vermont's two most beloved peaks – had expanded by 1930 to run the entire length of the state, from Massachusetts to Québec.

In a place best known for its pastoral beauty, the Long Trail offers total immersion in a wilder sort of nature. Running north-south along the Green Mountains' spine, it undulates through dense maple, beech and birch forest, down into ferny gulches and rocky creek beds and up to the state's highest summits.

The classic Long Trail odyssey is a 272-mile (438km) marathon from Vermont's southern border near Williamstown, Massachusetts to the village of North Troy on the doorstep of French Canada. Depending on your pace, you can hike it in two to four weeks, staying at any of the 70-plus overnight shelters along the trail. These range from no-frills tenting platforms and open-sided lean-tos to more elaborate options like the restored, polychrome-shingled Bolton Lodge, dating to 1928 and reminiscent of an Irish cottage. Spaced every 5 miles (8km) or so along the path, the Long Trail's shelters are first-come, first-served. Most are free of charge, with a few bringing in summer caretakers and charging a nominal US$5.

Like many New Englanders, I've adopted a piecemeal approach to the trail, tackling it one section at a time on shorter excursions. The Long Trail regularly intersects with state highways and passes near villages, meaning there's a convenient network of trailheads throughout Vermont where you can embark on a day hike or

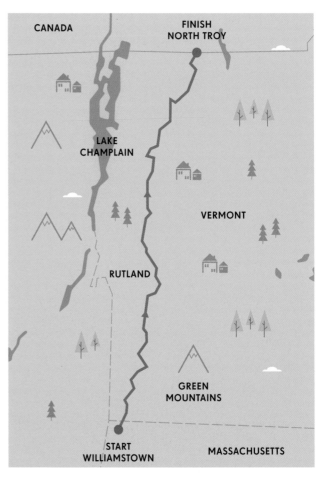

CANADA

FINISH
NORTH TROY

LAKE
CHAMPLAIN

VERMONT

RUTLAND

GREEN
MOUNTAINS

START
WILLIAMSTOWN

MASSACHUSETTS

© Aurora Photos | AWL

a weekend adventure, getting a taste of the trail's allure without committing to a multi-week ramble. (Some may consider this cheating, but the Green Mountain Club still awards its coveted 'End-to-End' patch to anyone who has hiked the trail in its entirety, whether over the course of two weeks or a lifetime.)

Over the years, I've ticked off sections on a regular basis, choosing good-weather weekends to explore the mountains near my twin homes of Brattleboro and Middlebury. As a native East Coaster, I find that these gentle green mountains speak to something in my spirit. So much of Vermont's beauty lies in its forests, and there are days when I like nothing better than plunging deep into the trees, hiking down from unpaved Mt Tabor Rd near Danby into the Big Branch Wilderness. Anyone who has ever spent a crisp autumn day looking up through white-barked birches and brilliant red and golden maple leaves to a cloudless blue sky understands the incandescent beauty of these woods.

However, I also spent 20 years living among the wide-open spaces of the American West, and I still pine for far-ranging vistas, for the places where the Long Trail emerges above the tree line.

One of my favourite moments involved joining a group for a climb of Camel's Hump – the only major summit in the Green Mountains that hasn't been developed for skiing, and, with its abrupt, exposed cliff face, the most distinctive peak in the state. We set off from the Montclair Glen Lodge at the mountain's base, trudging in places through knee-deep snow and clambering between icy boulders to reach the summit near dusk, an awe-inspiring experience in the grey winter light. After dark, we retraced

> "After dark we formed a single-file row of headlamp-clad silhouettes against the mountain's ghostly white flanks"

HUMP DRAWN ON QUARTERS

One of Vermont's unmissable icons, the distinctive profile of Camel's Hump (4083ft, 1244m) has long stirred people's imaginations. The native Abenaki called it 'saddle mountain,' and French explorer Samuel de Champlain dubbed it 'le lion couchant' (the sleeping lion). Back in the early 2000s, when the United States treasury minted commemorative quarters for every state in the union, artists competing to design Vermont's coin were given just one requirement: the Camel's Hump had to appear somewhere in the picture!

Clockwise from top: just your regular Vermont inhabitant: a young moose; a tent platform in the Green Mountain forest; the Brandon Gap in autumn. Previous page: hiking the distinctive Camel's Hump

© MH Anderson Photography | Shutterstock

the trail back down the mountain, a single-file row of headlamp-clad silhouettes against the mountain's ghostly white flanks.

Another spot of pure magic is the summit of Mt Mansfield, whose long exposed ridgeline has been anthropomorphised to bear names like 'The Nose', 'the Chin' and 'the Forehead'. Hiking this ridge atop Vermont's tallest mountain is the ultimate Long Trail experience, with stunning sustained views west to Lake Champlain, east to New Hampshire, south past Camel's Hump and north to Montreal. Along the way you enter a rare universe of alpine tundra, dominated by plants that normally occur 1500 miles (2414km) north in sub-Arctic Canada. To hook up with this section of Long Trail on a day hike, nothing beats the strenuous 3-mile (5km) ascent of the Sunset Ridge Trail from Underhill State Park, one of the prettiest walking routes in the state.

Other high-altitude experiences along the Long Trail are less demanding. Few offer more satisfaction than the 0.8-mile (1.3km) climb from Brandon Gap to the Great Cliff of Mt Horrid, where awe-inspiring vistas unfold over beaver and moose country at the base of the cliffs and vast waves of mountains beyond.

But perhaps my favourite Long Trail memory is accompanying my one-year-old daughter, Chloe, on her first big climb from Lincoln Gap to Mt Abraham, one of the state's rare 4000-footers, and watching her break out into an ear-to-ear grin as she supported herself against the back of a tolerant dog on the summit, with the great green expanse of Vermont's Champlain Valley spread out behind her. Thirteen years later we regularly hike sections of the trail together, and I've begun to envision walking the whole thing end-to-end with her one day, as it was meant to be done. **GC**

ORIENTATION

Start // Williamstown, Massachusetts
End // North Troy, Vermont
Distance // 272 miles (439km)
Getting there // Albany International Airport (ALB) is a one-hour drive from the southern trailhead near Williamstown, MA. Burlington International Airport (BTV) is 90 minutes by car from the northern trailhead.
When to go // June to October.
Where to stay // Supplementing the Long Trail's 72 rustic shelters, the full-service Inn at Long Trail (www.innatlongtrail. com) makes a good halfway splurge.
What to take // A tent (shelters fill up in summer), camp stove (open fires are discouraged), water-purifying tablets.
What to wear // Dress in layers, including hat and gloves.
More info // www.greenmountainclub.org/the-long-trail
Things to know // High-altitude sections around Mt Mansfield and Camel's Hump typically close during Vermont's 'mud season' (late March to late May), when trailside vegetation is especially vulnerable to trampling.

*Opposite: the John Muir Trail weaves
its way through the Sierra Nevada*

MORE LIKE THIS
LONG-DISTANCE USA

APPALACHIAN TRAIL

For outdoorsy Americans living east of the Mississippi River, the Appalachian Trail is the Holy Grail of long-distance hiking. This venerable footpath charts an uninterrupted 2200-mile (3540km) course along the slopes and ridgelines of the Appalachian Mountains, crossing through 14 states on its way from the lush deciduous forests of the Deep South to the piney wilds of northern New England. Along the way it crosses through the eastern USA's most iconic mountain ranges, including the Great Smokies, the Blue Ridge Mountains, the Poconos, the Catskills, the Berkshires, the Taconics, the Greens and the Whites. Conceived of in 1921 and completed in 1937, it was recognised as the USA's first National Scenic Trail in 1968.
Start // **Springer Mountain, Georgia**
End // **Mt Katahdin, Maine**
Distance // **2200 miles (3540km)**
More info // **www.appalachiantrail.org**

CONTINENTAL DIVIDE TRAIL

Still a work in progress, the 3100-mile (4989km) Continental Divide Trail celebrates the grandeur of the American West, running the length of the USA's high-altitude ridgelines through New Mexico, Colorado, Wyoming, Idaho and Montana. Rivers to the west of the trail flow into the Pacific Ocean, while rivers to the east flow into the Atlantic Ocean or Hudson Bay. Currently a mix of dedicated walking trails, unpaved roads and paved highways, the route offers hikers magnificent perspectives on snow-capped peaks, deserts and rangeland as it travels from the Mexican border up through Rocky Mountain, Yellowstone and Glacier national parks. The CDT was designated a National Scenic Trail in 1978, but has far fewer hikers than its sister routes, the Appalachian and the Pacific Crest trails.
Start // **Crazy Cook Monument, New Mexico**
End // **Glacier National Park, Montana**
Distance // **3100 miles (4989km)**
More info // **www.continentaldivide trail.org**

JOHN MUIR TRAIL

John Muir is something of a god to American conservationists. The father of Yosemite National Park and the founder of the Sierra Club, Muir spent his whole life exploring and advocating for the preservation of California's mountain wilderness. It's only fitting, then, that the state's premier long-distance walking trail bears his name. Completed in 1938, the 215-mile (346km) John Muir Trail showcases California's most spectacular high-altitude scenery, travelling from Yosemite Valley southeast to 14,505ft (4421m) Mt Whitney, the state's tallest peak. Along the way, it passes through three national parks (Yosemite, King's Canyon and Sequoia) and traverses the heart of the Sierra Nevada mountain range, affording close-up perspectives on legendary natural landmarks such as Nevada Falls, Half Dome, Tuolumne Meadows, Devils Postpile and the Ansel Adams Wilderness.
Start // **Happy Isles, Yosemite Valley**
End // **Mt Whitney**
Distance // **215 miles (346km)**
More info // **www.johnmuirtrail.org**

ANGELS LANDING

Zion National Park's rock star is this spirit-soaring US day hike that zig-zags up to a precipice so heart-poundingly sheer it seems only angels could reach it.

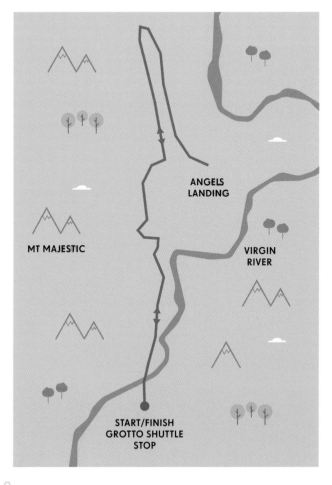

ngels Landing is a fitting name for the 1490ft (454m) fist of rock so vertiginous that hiking along its knife-edge ridge feels more like a high-wire act. 'Surely not' is what springs to mind when you catch a panicked glimpse of the last insane stretch of the trail. Then, wiping your anxious brow and double-checking your laces are tightly done up, you decide 'to hell with it', and push up and on even though it seems like utter madness. Angels might be able to wing down to the eyrie-like incline but, let's face it, they'd be missing out on one of finest and most fearsome day hikes in the USA. Angels Landing is Zion National Park's top-of-the-beanstalk hike – sure, there are higher treks, but nowhere are the 360-degree views more mind blowing. Despite just being a 5-mile (8km) round hike, it's also the kind of stuff that makes even experienced hikers quiver in their boots.

I hiked it on a sweltering August day, with white heat pounding relentlessly down on the buckled Navajo sandstone cliffs, rippled with reds, golds and milky whites. Way up there on America's greatest national park list, Zion was founded as Utah's first national park in 1919. The 229-sq-mile (593-sq-km) park is now a gigantic rock playground for hikers, climbers, cyclists and campers. And staying true to its original conservation ethos, Zion's free shuttle buses whisk visitors between trailheads to ensure the park is largely traffic-free.

The beginning of the trek is deceptively easy. Starting on level ground at the Grotto trailhead, it crosses a footbridge over the north fork of the Virgin River, hooking up with the 30-mile (48km) West Rim Trail for a while. So far so simple. But soon the steady climb begins on an exposed path where the sun beats down, with temperatures hitting 35°C (95°F) and barely any shade. The sweat

ANGELS LANDING

MT MAJESTIC

VIRGIN RIVER

START/FINISH GROTTO SHUTTLE STOP

is running off in rivulets. But if the heat is unforgiving, the views are spectacular, with rust-red mesas and buttes towering above a stippling of cottonwood trees, junipers and pinyon pines below that seem almost thirst-quenchingly green in the arid surrounds.

The glimmering river is now just a distant ribbon of silver as the trail wends ever upwards, hugging cliff faces to emerge at a narrow gap between Angels Landing and Cathedral Mountain. I breathe a sigh of relief as a waft of blissfully chilled air – as if someone suddenly opened the deep-freeze door – greets me in what is nicknamed 'Refrigerator Canyon'. The blast of refreshing wind in the ravine, where bigtooth maple and white fir trees grow, is a delicious reprieve from the blistering sun.

Angels Landing eases you in gently, but the gradient soon steepens, giving a taste of what's to come. The challenge presents itself in the form 'Walter's Wiggles'. Zig-zagging steeply up the cliff face, the 21 tight switchbacks are named after Walter Ruesch, Zion's very first ranger, who had the dubious honour of helping to construct the switchbacks back in 1926. While the name has an endearing ring to it, this is where the trail cranks up a notch in terms of difficulty, and I find myself cursing the fact I hadn't begun the hike earlier in the cool of morning. I have to hand it to Walter, though – the trail is an impressive feat of engineering that still makes hikers elicit little gasps of wonder today.

The 'Wiggles' squiggle up to a saddle called Scout Lookout, where the view suddenly cracks open to reveal the entire Zion Canyon splayed out before you. Here chipmunks scamper among the straggling trees that have managed to take root in the rock.

> *"I'm acutely aware that one misplaced footstep will send me spiralling down into the valley like a sycamore seed"*

THE MAKING OF ZION

The spectacularly buckled and contorted landscape that is now squashed into the 229-sq-mile (593-sq-km) confines of Zion National Park has been formed over millennia by the Virgin River that flows through Zion to the desert below. Zion began life as a massive desert some 250 million years ago, with winds dragging one dune on top of another to create the impressive rock strata visible today, which includes narrow slot canyons, slickrock peaks and Navajo sandstone cliffs.

Clockwise from top: 'Walter's Wiggles' zig-zag up Angels Landing; it is home to many chipmunks; Zion Canyon. Previous page: the trail's precarious final stages

© Kevin Crowley | J Kev

Many hikers give up at this point, gulping as they clap eyes on the half-mile final hurdle and reassess their nerve and footwear (note: flip-flops are a no-no). Indeed, if vertigo kicks in at this point, there are few better places to enjoy a highly panoramic picnic.

I love heights but even I hesitate at the sight of the Hog's Back, with its breathtakingly steep incline, uneven steps and sheer drop-offs. Only one thing for it: bite the bullet. And so, along with a few other brave (or foolhardy) hikers, I inch my way up along the cable-secured trail, hacked into the solid rock, barely daring to peer into the void. The trail is slippery, polished smooth with many years of leather, and I'm acutely aware that one misplaced footstep will send me spiralling down into the valley like a sycamore seed. It's a curious paradox: death is so close but I've rarely felt so alive. It's so narrow that there are passing places to let other hikers go by – patience here is every bit as important as pluck.

Then, with a final exhilarated step and pounding heart I reach the summit. Relief washes over me and I survey the scene in all its glory. Here, 5791ft (1765m) above sea level, I am at eye level with Zion's natural landmarks: the Great White Throne, Observation Point, the puckered summit of Cathedral Mountain. Below, the Virgin River rages on. A storm is bubbling up on the horizon and late-afternoon shadows are throwing the rocks into relief. I know it's time to return soon but for a moment I savour Angels Landing. To get here you have to confront the fury of the devil himself, but the view you receive as a reward is nothing short of heavenly. **KC**

ORIENTATION

Start/End // Grotto shuttle stop
Distance // 5 miles (8 km)
Duration // Allow roughly five hours for the round trip
Getting there // The nearest major airport is Las Vegas, 175 miles (280km) over the state border. Park at the Zion Canyon visitor centre. From April to October, a free shuttle takes you to the trailhead.
When to go // Hiking here in summer is a sweaty affair, so it's better to come in spring or autumn. If you do hike in the hot months, get an early start.
What to take // A light daypack with snacks and plenty of water should suffice. Sturdy boots, a sun hat and sunscreen are also recommended.
More info // For the trail lowdown and maps, visit the park website: www.zionnational-park.com.

*Opposite: the 3460ft (1055m) Mt
Liathach rises sharply behind the
Scottish hamlet of Torridon*

MORE LIKE THIS
TOP OF THE ROCK HIKES

DEVIL'S PATH, USA

Spare a thought for the bewildered
early Dutch settlers who took one look
at the rugged, densely wooded Catskill
Mountains in southeastern New York
State and exclaimed that only the devil
could live there... Indeed, Devil's Path is
a fitting name for this beast of a 25-mile
(40km) hike, which runs along the spine
of the Catskills and deep into boreal
forest, ticking off five peaks: Indian Head
Mountain, Twin Mountain, Sugarloaf
Mountain, Plateau Mountain and West Kill
Mountain. So far so normal, but this isn't
dubbed 'the toughest hike in the East' for
no reason; the steep rock chutes, scrambles
and gruelling, relentless uphill trajectory
make this feel more like a climb than a
hike at times. Hardcore hikers tackle it in a
long day hike – but with no time to linger
– while others more sensibly factor in a
night at Mink's Hollow. It's not all about the
ascent: the technical descents can be real
thigh-burners, too.
Start // Prediger Rd (east)
End // Spruceton Rd
Distance // 40km (25 miles)

WAYNA PICCHU, PERU

Imagine Machu Picchu and the surrounding
ragged peaks cloaked in cloud forest, then
go one step beyond by following in intrepid
footsteps and climbing Wayna Picchu,
nicknamed the 'hike of death'. Seen from
a distance, you'd never believe it possible,
so sheer is this 8924ft (2720m) thumb of
rock sticking out above Machu Picchu.
Yet the industrious Incas hacked a trail
into it, which clambers 1180ft (360m) up
to the precipice. It's *steep*, with dizzyingly
sheer drops and ledges, vertigo-inducing
steps and only a few handrails for you
to grip with sweaty palms. But the brave
are rewarded with phenomenal bird's-eye
views of the ruined Inca city spread out
spectacularly before them. Allow around an
hour each way.
Start/End // Machu Picchu
Distance // 1.2 miles (1.9km)
**More info // Numbers on the trail are
restricted daily to 200 at 7am, 200 at
10am. Hikers must sign in and out**

LIATHACH, SCOTLAND

As any burly Scot will tell you, there are
Munros and then there are *Munros*.
Out on its lonesome in the Northwest
Highlands above Torridon, Liathach
('the grey one') most definitely belongs
to the second category. This is a starkly
beautiful, boulder-strewn landscape of
mountains that pucker up like wizard hats
and Lewisian gneiss rock that has been
around since dinosaurs roamed the earth.
On rare clear days, the ultimate day hike
takes you up to its knife-edge ridge, an
eight- to 10-hour monster of a Munro
bag. Hearts begin to pound at the gnarly
3460ft (1055m) ridge – both because of
the stiff climb and its near-vertical cliffs,
spires and buttresses. Summon the pluck to
teeter up to the summit, where the views of
Beinn Eighe, the Am Fasarinen pinnacles,
glittering Loch Torridon and the Hebrides
are out of this world. The tightly zig-zagging
descent provides a real workout and can be
boggy and slippery.
**Start/End // Small car park east of Glen
Cottage, Torridon**
Distance // 7 miles (11.5km) return

THE LOST COAST TRAIL

Tucked between dense redwood forests and forbidding cliffs, California's most dramatic untamed coastline offers hikers an unforgettable walk on the wild side.

In a state that is famous for the beauty of its shoreline, the Lost Coast is one of the most spectacular stretches of California, as rugged as either Big Sur or Malibu, yet still largely unknown even to natives of the state. From the minute I saw this mysterious patch of undeveloped coast on the map, I knew that I wanted to go there.

Long the domain of intrepid loggers, this coast was always a forbidding place, and even now, just reaching the trailhead remains a challenge. The dirt road turn-off from California State Highway 1 resembles an overgrown driveway, but look closely and you'll see a sign for Mendocino County Rd 435 buried in the bushes. Six miles further north along this steep and rutted access route lies Usal Beach, a black-sand beach in a wide valley between cliffs, and the southern terminus of the Lost Coast Trail.

My long-dreamed-of exploration of this remote coastal wilderness began on a sunny May morning. With an outdated USGS topographic map providing the only clues as to what might lie in store, I hit the trail with two old friends and headed north into the unknown. The route climbed quickly, zig-zagging along a scenic ridgeline to the summit of Timber Point, then descending through tangled evergreen forest, finally re-emerging into golden straw-coloured bluffs high above the ocean – a meditative spot for a midday break.

More afternoon rambling through deep forest and steep coastal gulches brought us to our first overnight camping spot, in a semicircular cluster of redwoods set about 200ft (61m) back from the Pacific. As twilight set in, we made the short pilgrimage down to Little Jackass Beach, a scant triangle of sand tucked below the ominously named Mistake Point, and lingered till

nightfall under the spell of sea arches and tortured-looking rock outcroppings at the foot of ashen cliffs. The sense of solitude here, at the trail's midway point, was profound; nothing but the steady roar of surf, the lonesome hooting of a distant owl, and the wind-blown rustle of alder leaves.

Inland, a side trip led off to the oldest stand of redwoods remaining on this stretch of coast – Sally Bell Grove, saved from the saw teeth of the Georgia-Pacific lumber company in 1986 and preserved as a small pocket of almost never-visited parkland. In stark contrast to the touristy Avenue of the Giants just over the mountains, it remains virtually inaccessible, without so much as

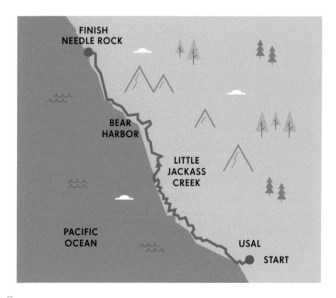

a trail marker to indicate its presence, a silent but comforting reminder of the world before we arrived.

Day two began with the trail's most gruelling climb, from sea level to 1064ft (324m) in less than a mile, followed by a steep downhill and another ascent. Our reward? The Lost Coast's most spectacular viewpoint at Anderson Cliff, reached by an unmarked side trail around the 3-mile (5km) mark. Perched 650ft (198m) above the ocean, this sheer-faced promontory affords astonishing bird's-eye perspectives stretching 20 miles (32km) north to Shelter Cove, with a half-moon shaped beach chomping into the otherwise uninterrupted wall of razor-sharp escarpments.

Back on the main trail we soon found ourselves descending to the same beach we had seen from above, a vast expanse of black sand on the threshold of the old Wheeler logging camp, where operations were abandoned in 1959. After so much time within earshot of the surf, yet hundreds of feet above it, it was pure exhilaration to plunge into the waves, despite the frigid water temperature. We broke for lunch, then climbed over a 4-mile (6.5km) ridge to our next campsite.

At Bear Harbor, the landscape abruptly emerged from the rugged cliffs and densely forested hills of the southern Lost Coast into the blissfully open coastal bluffs of Sinkyone Wilderness State Park. Our camp sat in a grassy clearing beside a creek, a few paces inland from a wild, pebbly beach. Nearby, open meadows and a venerable eucalyptus grove hinted at the Lost Coast's more settled history; in the 19th century, an influx of settlers established orchards, farms and ranches here, and a railroad was built to extract tan oak bark from the inland forests.

> *"When we awoke, the grasses beside our tent bore the imprints of the elks' massive bodies"*

THE END OF THE ROAD

Look at the map of California and you'll see one highway or another hugging the coastline most of the way from Mexico to Oregon. Then suddenly, up near Cape Mendocino, a 70-mile (112km) stretch of roadless coastal wilderness unfolds. Between the teeny northern Californian communities of Rockport and Petrolia, this so-called 'Lost Coast' escaped development thanks to its topography, so relentlessly rugged that California's highway engineers headed for the hills, rerouting Highway 1 inland to avoid the coastal cliffs.

Clockwise from top: the cliffs of the Lost Coast; backpackers make their way along the path; elks are commonplace. Previous page: trekking the lesser-trodden Lost Coast Trail

Few tangible remnants of this past remain, yet a different kind of domesticity has set in. Our home for the night was one of Sinkyone State Park's 15 'environmental campsites', a simple affair by US camping standards, but luxurious compared with the bare-bones sites we'd encountered further south. It had a picnic table, fire ring and outhouse, and we felt like royalty.

As the sun began to set over the low headland leading down to the beach, we detected other signs of life – silhouetted along the ridgeline was a small herd of Roosevelt elk. Originally native to this area, they were reintroduced in recent decades and have thrived in this pastoral habitat – the females grazing in the company of their calves in spring, and the males putting on tremendous foot-stomping, antler-clashing displays in the autumn rutting months. Throughout the night, the elk wandered through our campsite at will, grazing and snorting. When we awoke the next morning, the grasses beside our tent bore the imprints of their massive bodies.

The route back to civilisation was short and sweet. A 3-mile (5km) dirt road wove north from Bear Harbor along the bluffs, opening up more expansive vistas of grassy slopes and crashing sea. Within a couple of hours, we had reached park headquarters at Needle Rock, the simple wood cabin where we had parked our second vehicle. To the north of the cabin, another 2 miles (3.2km) of trail led to the park's remaining environmental campsites. And beyond that lay the King Range Conservation Area, a continuation of this same wild coastline, which is accessible only via a 24-mile (38km) beach walk. Another dream to be fulfilled another time. **GC**

ORIENTATION

Start // Usal
End // Needle Rock
Distance // 20 miles (32km) one way
Getting there // The California Redwood Coast-Humboldt County Airport (also called Arcata-Eureka Airport) is a 2½-hour drive from either trailhead.
When to go // April to October
Where to stay // Minimalist campsites at Usal, Anderson Gulch, Little Jackass Creek, Bear Harbor and Needle Rock.
What to take // Adequate water and purifying supplies; rope for hanging food; calamine lotion for poison oak.
What to wear // Coastal California gets cool at night, even in summer; dress in layers and bring a warm hat.
More info // lostcoasttrails.wordpress.com
Things to know // Hike the trail out-and-back, or bring two vehicles, parking one at each trailhead. Driving time between Usal and Needle Rock is about two hours, with extensive unpaved stretches. Beware the shiny, trifoliate leaves of poison oak, an abundant itch-inducing plant.

Opposite: beneath green and vivid cliffs, Kalalau Beach occupies an idyllic setting

MORE LIKE THIS
WILD COASTLINES

KALALAU TRAIL, KAUA'I, HAWAII

One of the world's great coastal walks, this exquisitely beautiful trail along Kaua'i's Na Pali Coast epitomises the rare beauty of the Hawaiian Islands. The path threads its way between patches of lush tropical jungle, mountains streaked with waterfalls, and idyllic coves backed by deeply fluted, colourful *pali* (cliffs). The juxtaposition of limpid turquoise seas against the brilliant greens and oranges of the shoreline create a dazzling scenic effect, but walkers should not be lulled into complacency by the trail's beauty or relatively short length. This is a rugged, physically challenging hike with substantial elevation gain and loss, best undertaken by people in excellent physical condition. Campsites at Hanakoa (6 miles/9km) and Kalalau (11 miles/18km) allow you to break the journey; get permits at https://camping.ehawaii.gov/camping.
Start/End // Ke'e Beach
Distance // 22 miles (35km) round trip
More info // www.kalalautrail.com

EAST COAST TRAIL, NEWFOUNDLAND, CANADA

Ask the average tourist where they'd like to take their next beach vacation, and Newfoundland isn't likely to be at the top of the list. But for anyone who appreciates wild coastal landscapes, the East Coast Trail is a rare treasure. Encompassing more than 186 miles (300km) of walking routes between Cape St Francis and Cappahayden, the trail showcases the geographic and biological wonders of Canada's North Atlantic, from fjords, sea stacks and icebergs to whales and caribou. Along the way, walkers experience a mix of pristine wilderness, historic fishing villages and archaeological sites.
Start // Cape St Francis, Newfoundland
End // Cappahayden, Newfoundland
Distance // 164 miles (265km)
More info // www.eastcoasttrail.com

SUPERIOR HIKING TRAIL, MINNESOTA, USA

Not all coastal hikes follow the ocean. As any North American geography student can tell you, Lake Superior is one of the world's largest bodies of fresh water, so it's only fitting that it has its own trail, a 310-mile (499km) monster that roughly parallels the lake's Minnesota shoreline from the Wisconsin border to Canada. Skirting clifftops and ridgelines above the lake for most of its length, the trail crosses through seven state parks and offers nearly 100 fee-free campsites for hikers. Much of the route is heavily forested with northern species such as birches, aspens, fir, cedar and pine, interspersed with stream and river crossings and occasional forays down to lake level to take in scenic attractions like the century-old Split Rock Lighthouse.
Start // Jay Cooke State Park, Minnesota
End // Minnesota/Ontario border
Distance // 310 miles (499km)
More info // www.shta.org

SHIKOKU'S 88 SACRED TEMPLES PILGRIMAGE

A legendary Japanese journey in the footsteps of the great saint Kōbō-daishi, where pilgrims endeavour to attain enlightenment on a 1200-year-old Buddhist pilgrimage.

Everything I needed was at Temple 1, the Ryōzen-ji, the first of 88 little goals on my 870-mile (1400km) journey. Or make that 89, because to do the pilgrimage properly, I'd have to round Shikoku's 88 temples, then walk back to Temple 1 and complete the circle – for a circle is like the search for enlightenment, never-ending. It is said that the great saint and founder of Shingon Buddhism, Kōbō-daishi (AD 774–835), achieved enlightenment on Shikoku and for 1200 years, *henro* (pilgrims) have been striving to attain the same.

I bought a pure white pilgrim shirt emblazoned with the words *Dogyo Ninin* in black on the back: 'We go together'. Pilgrims are not alone, as Kōbō-daishi's spirit walks with them. A wide pilgrim's hat was next, the kind you see farmers wearing in rice paddies, to shield my head from the sun and to keep rain off my face. Then a *tsue*, or pilgrim's staff, to help me climb the mountains – and there would be a lot of mountains. I also purchased a *nokyo-cho*, a book for the 'signatures' of all 88 temples, beautiful black calligraphy over vermilion stamps.

It was time to say my prayers and start my journey. Although not a Buddhist, I was happy to chant *Namu Daishi Henjo Kongo* – 'Homage to the Saint' – at each of the 88 temples. Shikoku pilgrims have searched for enlightenment or wisdom since the 9th century, so I would do the same.

The trail has changed in that time. Until 100 or so years ago, all pilgrims walked and ancient trails connected the temples. Nowadays, fewer than 1% of pilgrims walk, with most of them riding around the 88 temples in cars or buses on sealed roads. Many of the ancient trails can still be walked though, by those willing to search them out. Through the centuries, most pilgrims

headed out with only a vague idea of where they were going – there were no maps, no guidebooks (the first one was published in 1685), no weather forecasts and, of course, no mobile phones to call home when lonely!

The first 10 temples cover about 25 miles (40km) across northern Tokushima prefecture. I powered along and hiked nine of them on my first day, walking on roads and *henro* trails through people's back gardens. 'Not so hard!' I thought. On my second day, a farmer in his field waved me over and presented me with a massive watermelon he'd grown. Very kind, but a heavy watermelon is not much use to a walking *henro*. Later that day, I struck the mountain

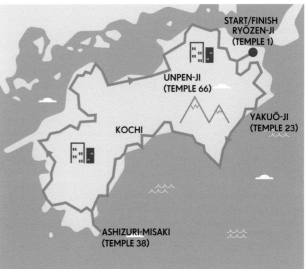

trail from Temple 11 to Temple 12, a climb that is said to be the hardest on the pilgrimage. Temple 19 is a barrier temple, which only those pure of intention may pass. I strode on through. Temple 21 sits high on a mountaintop, testing every walking pilgrim's fortitude, especially when they could simply take a cable car up from the far side of the mountain. The Yakuō-ji, Temple 23, is on the coast in Hiwasa and is a *yakuyoke-dera*, a temple to ward off bad luck for unlucky ages – the worst being 42 for men and 33 for women. Pilgrims put a coin on each of the 42 steps on the men's side and 33 steps on the women's side. I was through Tokushima prefecture in a week.

Known as the pilgrim's testing ground, Kochi prefecture makes up more than a third of the pilgrimage's distance, but has only 16 of its temples. Kochi faces the not-too-aptly named Pacific Ocean and was always regarded as one of the wildest and most remote parts of Japan. Its highlights include Muroto-misaki (Cape Muroto), where it is said that Kōbō-daishi achieved enlightenment, and Ashizuri-misaki (Cape Ashizuri), both of which are weather-

"A millennium of pilgrims has tried to attain enlightenment by completing the Shikoku pilgrimage and that was my goal too"

battered capes hosting spectacular temples. The longest distance between temples on the pilgrimage is the 57 miles (92km) from Temple 37 to Temple 38 at Ashizuri-misaki. I marched through Kochi in 10 days.

Traditionally, pilgrims sigh with relief when they enter Ehime prefecture. I did too, as I realised that the toughest bit of my journey was completed. Ehime has 27 of the 88 temples and is known as the place for attainment of wisdom after overcoming the hardships of Kochi prefecture. Matsuyama, Shikoku's largest city and the prefectural capital, is home to eight of the 88 temples as well as the legendary hot spring of the Dōgo Onsen. I soaked my aching bones in its healing waters before continuing the hike.

WELL-EARNED REST

The good people of Shikoku have been looking after *henro* for 1200 years, so there are many places to stay and eat along the trail. *Henro* stay at *shukubo* (temple lodgings), *minshuku* (family-run B&Bs), *ryokan* (inns), hotels – or they take the option of *nojuku* (sleeping outside). Kōbō-daishi is said to have once slept under a bridge, so pilgrims never tap their staffs on a bridge in case they wake him up!

Clockwise from left: Oboke Gorge; the Chikurin-ji temple; Dōgo Onsen, site of a legendary hot spring; shoes of weary pilgrims hang at Ishite-ji temple. Previous page: the steps to Temple 65

ORIENTATION

Start/End // Ryōzen-ji (Temple 1), Naruto City
Distance // 870 miles (1400km)
Duration // Allow 30 to 60 days
Getting there // Fly, train, ferry or bus to Tokushima City; take a JR Kōtoku Line local train from Tokushima City to Bando (¥260, 25 minutes).
When to go // March to May or September to November.
What to take // Minimal gear, sturdy walking shoes, sleeping bag for *nojuku*. Pilgrim clothing is available at Temple 1, the Ryōzen-ji. If looking like a pilgrim isn't your thing, wear whatever is comfortable.
Things to know // The traditional way to begin is to go to Kōya-san in Wakayama Prefecture, where Kōbō-daishi is interred, and ask for his support on your journey.
More info // www.shikokuhenrotrail.com

The Unpen-ji, Temple 66, at 3000ft (900m) above sea level, is the highest of the temples and the last before entering Kagawa, the fourth of Shikoku's prefectures. *Shi* means 'four' and *koku* means 'country' and this is how the island got its name. The 'place of completion' hosts the last 22 of the temples. I was virtually flying now, at full fitness after nearly four weeks of walking. I rambled down out of the mountains to the Kagawa plains and visited temple after temple.

A millennium of pilgrims has tried to attain enlightenment by completing the Shikoku pilgrimage and that was my goal too. This was more than just a hike – it was something spiritual. As Kōbō-daishi said, 'Do not just walk in the footsteps of the men of old, seek what they sought!' I felt it. I climbed the last steep climb to the Ōkubo-ji, Temple 88, and enjoyed a moment of relief. It wasn't over though. The next day I strode back to Temple 1 and completed the circle. It felt like a major accomplishment – I had walked in their footsteps and sought what they sought – though time will tell if I'm on my way to enlightenment. **CML**

MORE LIKE THIS
JAPANESE JOURNEYS

KUMANO-KODŌ

There are a number of old pilgrimage routes on the Kii Peninsula that were first visited by emperors and nobles, then by *yamabushi* (mountain ascetics) and later by the common people. Now a World Heritage–listed area, these sacred sites and routes are based around Hongū Taisha, Hayatama Taisha and Nachi Taisha 'grand shrines' and the tracks that connect them. The Nakahechi Main Route from Takijiri-ōji to Hongū Taisha, used since the 10th century, is the most popular. There are several places to stay along the way, and in the vicinity of Hongū, some excellent *onsen* (hot springs), including Yunomine and Kawa-yu. The best place to get started is Tanabe, on the peninsula's west coast, easily accessed from Kyoto or Osaka. The Tanabe City Kumano Tourism Bureau is a mine of information.
Start // Takijiri-ōji (Nakahechi Main Route)
End // Hongū Taisha (Nakahechi Main Route)
Distance // 24 miles (38km)
More info // www.tb-kumano.jp/en

TATEYAMA-KAMIKŌCHI HIKE

The classic hike covering the length of the North Alps takes around seven days in the most spectacular alpine scenery Japan has on offer. This hike starts at Murodo (8040ft, 2450m), the high point on the enthralling Tateyama-Kurobe Alpine Route, which links the western and eastern sides of the North Alps with a series of cable cars, buses, trolley buses through tunnels and a walk over the Kurobe Dam. Climb the sacred peak of Tateyama (9890ft, 3015m), then head south to climb spear-like Yarigatake (10,430ft, 3180m) and Oku-Hotaka-dake (10,470ft, 3190m) before dropping into the remote resort village of Kamikōchi (4920ft, 1500m). There are mountain huts with bedding and meals along the way, meaning you can take minimal gear, plus a number of camping areas. In the four days between Tateyama and Yarigatake you'll likely see fewer people than on one Tokyo rush-hour subway carriage!
Start // Murodo
End // Kamikōchi
Distance // 40 miles (65km)
More info // www.alpen-route.com/en; www.kamikochi.org

FUJI-SAN

At 12,388ft (3776m), Fuji-san is a massive stand-alone volcano and Japan's highest mountain. While the panorama from the top is stupendous, the classic views of Fuji are from a distance – the one on the ¥1000 note is from Motosu-ko, the westernmost of Fuji's five lakes. This is a top hike, best when accomplished overnight in time to see the sun rise – after all, Japan is the 'Land of the Rising Sun'. Prepare to join the crowds, especially on weekends, as the official hiking season is short (1 July to 31 August). There are a number of tracks, but the easiest and most accessible is from the Fuji Subaru Line 5th Station (7560ft, 2305m). There are several huts for rest and sleep on the way up and at the top.
Start/End // Fuji Subaru Line 5th Station (Yoshida Trail)
Distance // 12 miles (19km)
More info // www.fujisan-climb.jp/en

Clockwise from top: the mighty Fuji-san; Nachi Taisha grand shrine on the Kumano-Kodō; negotiating Chubu Sangaku National Park in the Northern Alps

VILLAGE TO VILLAGE IN THE MARKHA VALLEY

Possible without backpack or guide, the multi-day Markha Valley trail links Buddhist village homestays in glorious Ladakh, India's top-of-the-world Tibetan-Buddhist kingdom.

Sometimes, trail maps prove wrong. And here, on the banks of the raging Zanskar River, mine has proved exhilaratingly wrong. Where the trek starts it shows a bridge, but there is no bridge. A 2015 flood has left its mangled remnants frothing up waves and the only alternative is a wire series of pulleys and a dangling metal basket.

Surviving this contraption, I walk an hour through semi-desert before oases of emerald-green barley fields start to soothe the starkness of the rocky valley. Small irrigation canals gurgle by, operating little waterwheels that aren't for electricity, but to turn Buddhist prayer wheels fashioned from old tin cans. And their gyrations fill the air with loving kindness...if you believe that sort of thing. Whitewashed stupas and sturdy homesteads appear here and there. Prayer flags flutter clues to the presence of fresh-water springs. Tinkling bells announce occasional trains of small horses laden with goods or with the camping equipment of trekking groups who plan to go beyond the homely comforts of the valley.

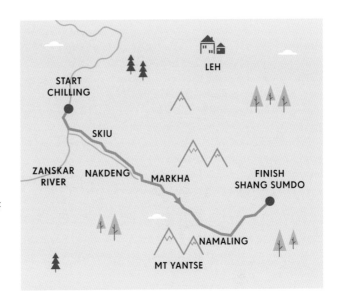

© Fat Jackey | Shutterstock, © Jonathan Tichon / Alamy Stock Photo

But I'm travelling light and am reliant on the homestays that make this route so perfect for casual walkers. Most foreigners sleep first in the villages of Skiu and Markha, but I settle upon a charming little homestead between the two at Nakdeng. Here I'm the only guest, other than the chukars (bar-winged partridges) that scuttle between bushes as I recline in the outdoor dining area shaded by a canopy fashioned from an old parachute.

The second day is a joyful wander between rocky spires and fields full of mustard-yellow flowers. A beautiful viewpoint of the bifurcating valley is blessed by a stack of vermillion-painted cow skulls and an ochre-coloured *latho* (spirit shrine) lavished with votive silk scarves. Ahead are a few minor route dilemmas: the river changes course each year and where the path has been washed away I change into sandals to wade through low rapids. A pair of French hikers try to avoid the trouble by rock hopping – managing successfully until the very last step. And big splash.

Around 3pm a rusty metal sign and donation box indicates the presence of Tacha Gompa, a lonely Buddhist monastery perched almost invisibly on a perilous crag above. I scurry up, but after 15 minutes of panting and sweating I reach a locked door. Defeating disappointment with panoramic views I am suddenly startled by a voice behind me. 'You want coffee? Real good coffee!' Somehow I'd walked straight past a trio of travellers brewing up on a precipitous ledge. But I'm keen to press on. The light is perfect for spectacular afternoon views. And sure enough, beyond Umblung, the twin-peaked monster of the vast 21,000ft (6400m) Kang Yantse reveals its vast snowy flank. Meanwhile, cinematically illuminated by the low sunshine, Hankar's shattered fortress tower lies perfectly framed between barren foothill folds. I gaze in wonder.

After an exploration of magical Upper Hankar, day three climbs more steeply, leaving the 'oasis' villages for barren, arid terrain with crumbling erosion formations and occasional tufts of greenery at streamside meadows. Then, beyond a small lake, spreads an upland plain. At 15,256ft (4650m), the only shelter here is Nimaling, a seasonal camp where pre-erected tents with mats and duvet-blankets provide homestay-trekkers with warmth and sustenance. As it's the only logical place to sleep before the long last day, it's something of a walkers' bottleneck, and there's a mild sense of anxiety amongst unequipped hikers fearing, unnecessarily, that it might prove to be full. By early afternoon the place is already abuzz. Many of my fellow hikers here are now 'friends', or at least nodding acquaintances, that I've passed or been passed by several times en route. There's wise-cracking Tim and Sophie from Belgium; Barnaby, an American Buddhist who seems more frenetic than spiritual; And Lyudmilla, a Russian woman who decides to use the thumb-twiddling afternoon to teach us all 'high-altitude yoga'.

Later the skies darken beneath a battlegroup of naval-grey clouds. Warm afternoon plunges into frigid evening and we scurry back to the dining marquee wrapped in blankets to play cards with a group of cheerful Swedes. Someone orders a bottle of super-

CHILLING IN CHILLING

Accessed by a spectacular 19-mile (30km) jeep-ride down the dramatic Zanskar River canyon, it's worth spending a little pre-trek time in Chilling village. Founded centuries ago by Nepali metalworkers who had been brought to Ladakh to construct a giant Buddha for Shey Palace, Chilling is almost invisible from the road but retains a very special atmosphere, with layered fields, antique houses, mature fruit trees and several coppersmiths still beating out traditional wares at archaic little forges.

Clockwise from top: horses take the load in the Markha Valley; Tibetan copper craftwork; Nimaling campsite. Pevious page: the tents at Nimaling offer shelter; Buddhist Mani stones

"Gaggles of walkers stand dazed by the breathless climb and sublime panorama of partly snow-topped peaks"

© Ana Schleicher | Superstock

strength Godfather beer but it's so distasteful that drinking a glass is reserved as a punishment for losing a hand.

At 6.30 next morning, independent groups are packing up their tents while homestay-trekkers like me grab a quick breakfast and head off – straight up the side of the ridge towards the Kongmaru Pass. Given the remoteness of the location, the sudden mini-swarm of humanity snaking up the trail looks incongruous. But two hours later, there's a great sense of camaraderie. Having reached 16,831ft (5130m), gaggles of walkers congratulate each other or stand dazed by the breathless climb and the sublime panorama of partly snow-topped peaks. Views are framed by colourfully fluttering prayer flags. And there's Barnaby unfurling another long string of such flags as a personal act of devotional piety.

After a lengthy pause it's time to descend into the red-rock landscape below. The path skips to and fro across a stream that rapidly gathers power, creating pretty canyons and vividly coloured micro valleys. Two hours on there's a handy parachute cafe and beyond that the fascinating village of Chokdo, where there are several tempting homestays. But I'm anxious to get back to the Ladakhi capital Leh so I stride on, arriving by 3pm at Shang Sumdo, the trek's traditional endpoint. Gathering a group of fellow travellers at the teahouse, we charter a ride in one of the two vehicles left in the village and drive off. A hasty move, perhaps. I later discovered just how beautiful is the nearby Shang Valley. But it's always great to save something for the next trip. **ME**

ORIENTATION

Start // Chilling
End // Shang Sumdo
Distance // 41–48 miles (67–78km)
Getting there // The nearest airport is at Leh, 36 miles (58km) away. Rent a jeep from there, or pay for a spare seat on the transfer bus of one of the Zanskar River rafting companies to save money.
When to go // July to August is best; June and September are possible, but snow on the Kongmaru Pass can be a worry.
Where to stay // There are homestays in virtually every village and hamlet along the route. At Nimaling there's no village but a seasonal camp provides bedded tents. All provide dinner, breakfast plus a simple packed lunch.
What to take // A few snacks and water bottles to fill at homestays. A water filter saves weight by allowing you to drink water from uncertain streams.

Opposite from top: crossing a suspension bridge on the Himalaya-bound Gochala Trek; Kee Gompa monastery in the Spiti Valley

MORE LIKE THIS
INDIAN HOMESTAY TREKS

LADAKH-ZANSKAR

Ask an old-time adventurer how to cross between these two most archetypally Tibetan regions of northern India and you are likely to be regaled by tales of the fabled Chadar Ice Trek. Only really feasible in February, that route involves gingerly walking down the frozen Zanskar River in dramatic canyons and across teetering snow bridges. However, a recent onslaught of ill-prepared domestic Indian trekking groups along with warmer winter weather (and thus thinner ice) have combined to make the Chadar at once less special and much more dicey than in past years. These days you'd do better to take the mid-summer mountain route, spectacularly roller-coasting up sharp ridges and back down into roaring river valleys. With good route planning it's possible to do the trek with minimal baggage by sleeping in homestays en route. Start from the Photoksar road's southern end, around five hours' walk before Lingshed.
Start // Kyupa La
End // Zangla
Distance // 40 miles (65km)
More info // www.gesar-travel.com

GOCHALA TREK

In the forest-rich former Buddhist Kingdom of Sikkim, October is the ideal month to avoid the leeches and get the clearest skies. The best-known trail here is the stupendous Gochala Trek, a week-long classic whose great prize is staring down the 28,169ft (8585m) of Kanchendzonga, the world's third-highest mountain, and communing with many other Himalayan giants en route. There are no villages so the choice is between camping or bedding down in pretty basic huts. You'll need a guide and a permit too, but arranging either is very easy at short notice in Sikkim's bustling capital Gangtok, or in the charming little 'royal' village of Yuksom, where the trek actually starts. Some hikers are satisfied with a shorter trail to Dzongri, which still serves up sublime views, while if you don't want to pay guides and National Park fees, there are a series of short village-to-village homestay hikes around Yuksom that are, perhaps ironically, less touristy than the far more difficult Gochala.
Start/End // Yuksom, Sikkim
Distance // 54 miles (87km)
More info // www.trekkinginsikkims.com

SPITI HOMESTAY TREK

Huge and varied, Himachal Pradesh is one of India's most fascinating states. And it's at its most appealing in the inaccessible folds of the Spiti Valley. While many of the gem sites here are semi-accessible by jeep roads, traffic is very sparse and a great way to visit is on a multi-day homestay trek short-cutting across panoramic hillsides between traditional villages. The classic route takes in ancient Buddhist monasteries at 11th-century Langza, 10th-century Lhalung and 12th-century Dhankar, along with occasional yak pastures and a wonderful range of mountain panoramas. No permits are required and you'll generally be able to find your way with a basic map, but though days are short (generally less than five hours of walking), beware that virtually the whole route is above 13,100ft (4000m) so, to avoid altitude sickness, you'll need to have a considerable acclimatisation period before setting out.
Start // Langza
End // Dhankar
Distance // 34 miles (55km)
More info // spitiholidayadventure.com

MAMASA TO TANA TORAJA

Hike through two distinct cultural lands, stay in traditional houses with boat-shaped roofs and drink rice wine with locals on this rugged and remote Indonesian adventure.

As we approached the clutch of weathered, arched-roofed homes, five children ran to greet us. Around a dozen houses were scattered over a steep clearing that abutted a shallow winding river. Before them was a view over a patchwork of agricultural fields and mist-tinged mountains. By the time we'd walked a few more minutes towards our rustic home for the night, I was holding hands with two of the children, who gazed up at me with bright smiles.

'Belanda', my travelling companion Emre and I learned (after hearing it cried out at us through the day), means 'Dutch person', but more than 60 years post Dutch colonisation of Indonesia it's used to describe anyone remotely Caucasian looking. Whenever we reached a habitation, a crowd of happy kids followed in our wake, calling us Dutch, sometimes for a half hour or more before turning around and heading home.

Domingus, our Mamasan guide, led the way. Our supplies – sugar and cigarettes for adult gifts, sweets for the children and package noodles plus water for ourselves – were loaded on to a small horse handled by a tiny man with large crooked teeth. The quiet horseman eventually divulged that he'd been working with his beloved and well-cared-for beast for more than 17 years.

The hike had begun in hard-to-reach Mamasa, where simple

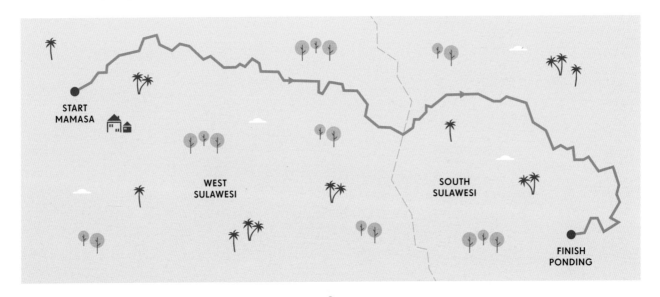

buildings in the flower-filled, buzzing town contrasted with the intricately carved *banua sura* (traditional Mamasan houses) in the bucolic outskirts. Here, we were told, the boat-shaped roofs are less curved, thicker and shorter than the more famous, dramatically arched ones we'd find at our destination, Tana Toraja. The *banua sura* were painted yellow, red, black and sometimes blue and the front and back of each building were bedecked in rows of buffalo horns. As we travelled deeper into the mountains, the walls of the houses lost their paint and the carvings became less intricate but the sloped roof shape and buffalo horns remained.

We spent the first night of our trek in a *banua sura* a short walk from Mamasa town, and there we discovered the reality of what we were in for. Thick quilts on the floor were our mattresses and we only had thin, synthetic blankets to keep us warm. A few hours into the night, Emre and I ended up under our 'mattresses' to keep warm. Dinner was noodle soup with floating chunks of pungent, home-butchered pork. Emre puked hers up in the middle of the night. Dogs howled and a mosquito kept buzzing in my ear.

But rest or no rest, we were up by six and breakfasted on sugary tea and omelettes. We said goodbye to our smiling hosts, assuring them we had slept marvelously, and began to walk uphill, past rice fields, through a summer-dry jungle and into cooler coffee and cacao plantations. After a few hours, we reached a high pass where we could see the green, misty Mamasa Valley in one

"We walked past rice fields, through a jungle and into coffee plantations"

direction and layers of dark ridges to the other, behind which lay the highland region of Tana Toraja.

The path descended over the next few miles through more coffee and cacao plantations and wilder regions where the grass reached our shoulders and almost engulfed the trail. It began to rain slow, heavy droplets, so our guide picked giant, multi-fingered leaves that we used as umbrellas. Shortly after the sun came back out we came to the village in the clearing and the five friendly children calling us 'Belanda'.

Kids came from all around as we arrived at the homestay. Taking our hands, they led us to pools fed by the river where the community raised goldfish. A few children were already plunking pancake-sized fish into buckets for their family's dinner. The children walked to show us the toilet, a bamboo perch over the river, and the shower, which was a small bamboo stall a few feet away. When I went to shower before dark, the kids all followed me and watched as I tried to demurely get clean wearing a sarong.

That night we stayed up till the ungodly hour of 10pm in our one-room shack lit with a hurricane lantern and drank sour-sweet palm wine with Domingus, our horseman, and the smiling couple who

REGIONAL BELIEFS

Hemmed in on all sides by mountains, the people of Mamasa and Tana Toraja were protected and isolated enough that their elaborate cultures could take form. Dutch Christian missionaries arrived in the early 1900s but had better luck in Mamasa than Tana Toraja. Today, the groups are mostly Christian but hold on to many animist beliefs, as seen in funerals that include buffalo sacrifices, dances and feasts.

Clockwise from left: rice fields in Tana Toraja; the vernacular architecture; local girls in traditional dress. Previous page: a Tana Torajan village

owned the house. Then to bed on the same quilt mattresses as the night before but, fortunately, with warmer blankets. We slept well.

Then the next morning we were off again, downhill through rice fields, past tiny one-room churches on ridges and through villages of small wooden shacks on stilts. After several hours, we crossed a bamboo bridge over a river, the border into Tana Toraja. Almost instantly everything felt more prosperous. Traditional houses, now called *tongkonan*, were far grander than what we'd become accustomed to, with larger roofs sweeping higher into the sky. Some roofs were thatched, others had wood shingles and others were corrugated iron. The road grew wider until it could accommodate motorbikes, then cars, and gradually we found ourselves back in a more modern world.

The first town we came to was Ponding, along a dusty road, and here we slept in an unmemorable guesthouse with real, yet lumpy, beds. The next day we caught an early morning jeep to Bittuang and then onwards to Rantepao, the heart of Tana Toraja. This majestic region is surrounded by steep slopes of terraced rice fields, ancient villages of elaborate *tongkonan* and cliffs studded with hanging coffins, and is highlighted by documentary-worthy funeral ceremonies. We were back on a comfortable and spectacular tourist trail, but found ourselves missing the backcountry of Mamasa where each village welcomed us as if we were old friends. **CB**

ORIENTATION

Start // Mamasa
End // Ponding
Distance // 40 miles (65km)
Getting there // Mamasa is 12 hours on public transport from Makassar, while Ponding is reached via Bittuang from Rantepao using jeeps and minivans. There's an international airport in Makassar and a domestic airport in Rantepao.
Tours // Arrange the trek with a local guide. They are found everywhere in Mamasa and Rantepao.
Where to stay // There are plenty of hotels and homestays in Rantepao, and a few homestays are found in Mamasa. En route, you'll be put up in villagers' homes.
What to take // Water purifier; head-lamp; sarong; snacks; gifts of sugar, cigarettes and sweets; rugged clothing for hot-to-cool temperatures and a sense of adventure.

Opposite from top: a Cordillera mountain village in Luzon; in a region famed for its traditional tattoo artists, a Northern Luzon woman takes time out

MORE LIKE THIS
REMOTE CULTURES

KALINGA VILLAGES, PHILIPPINES

Mingle with the Kalinga people of North Luzon, who were still headhunting into the 1960s. The hike starts in the tiny, highway-side town of Tinglayan; from here most people choose to take a motorbike to the trailhead for Buscalan. You'll then hike into and up a river-cut ravine for around an hour to Buscalan village. This village has become famous thanks to Whang-Od, the last *mambataok* (traditional tattoo artist). You can get inked before staying the night in a simple homestay, or continue on through terraced rice fields to villages of rickety wooden homes, wandering pot-bellied pigs, chickens and laughing children. Possible stops for the night include Butbut, Ngibat and Sumadel. All will offer you accommodation in a local home. Expect to drink lots of thick, sweet coffee and dine on rice and beans cooked over a wood fire. If you arrive during a festival, you'll partake in traditional line dancing, sing a song to the whole village and drink lots of rice wine to make your performance a little easier.
Start/End // Tinglayan
Duration // Two days
More info // Find guides in Tinglayan or via the Municipal Tourism Office in Bontoc

SIMIEN MOUNTAINS, ETHIOPIA

Trails opened in 2016 by the African Wildlife Foundation and Ethiopian Wildlife Conservation Authority lead hikers on multiday jaunts through remote areas of the World Heritage-listed Simien Mountains. This community-based tourism venture sets groups up with a guide, a cook and donkeys to carry luggage, through villages set on nearly treeless, steep mountains with spectacular views at every turn. Expect to meet goat herders and lots of children and to sleep in rustic, round thatched huts called *tukuls*. Coffee is served via a ceremony of roasting and grinding the beans then boiling the brew three times. Dine on *injera* (spongy sour bread) and chickpea sauce before huffing and puffing to views of Ras Dashen (14,872ft, 4533m), Ethiopia's highest mountain.
Start // Gondar
End // Limalimo
Duration // Three to seven days
More info // www.tesfatours.com

XELA TO LAKE ATITLÁN, GUATEMALA

This three-day trek leads hikers past pea and corn fields, through coffee plantations and cloud forests to ancient-feeling pueblos often shrouded in fog. The trail wanders through steep ravines and across rickety wooden bridges and in and out of forested canyons. At night, lodging is with village families who welcome you to use their *temazcal* (traditional Mayan saunas) to warm up, relax and soothe hike-weary muscles. You'll eat what the locals eat: rice, beans, chicken or eggs and maybe drink a delicious *licuido* (blended fruit drink). Finish the hike with an early morning start to catch the pink-and-blue sunrise at the edge of Lake Atitlán.
Start // Xela
End // Lake Atitlán
Duration // Three days
More info // www.quetzaltrekkers.com

MT KAILASH PILGRIMAGE CIRCUIT

A pilgrimage to the sacred Mt Kailash in western Tibet is said to erase all the sins of a lifetime. A fresh start has clear appeal.

Mt Kailash (24,980ft, 6714m) rises above the Himalayan steppe, a snow-capped sentinel watching over the dusty, crumpled bottomlands, with their dry valleys and meandering rivers, their Buddhist monasteries balanced on crumbling cliffs, their humans in rubber sandals and woollen robes, herds of baying goats and gemstone lakes cast in blinding hues. Rather small by Himalayan standards, Mt Kailash is nonetheless a symbolic titan, the axis of the world, with faces set in each cardinal direction and glacial waters feeding the major rivers of Asia.

In Buddhist, Hindu, Jain and Bön traditions, completing the 32-mile (52km) *kora* around Mt Kailash earns spiritual merit. Some walk through the night or make prostrations the whole way while others ride horses, hire porters or consume bottled oxygen. Most do it clockwise, though practitioners of Bön, an animist tradition that pre-dates Buddhism, make their pilgrimage in reverse. Its crux is the Drölma-la, an 18,470ft (5630m) pass battered by harsh weather. Attempting the summit would be considered sacrilegious. This is the realm of the gods.

For the more experienced hiker, Mt Kailash has little in common with your average alpine challenge. Even if you are not on a religious mission, the symbolism and devotion shown here is powerful. It is a place where regular people achieve the extraordinary. There is no escaping the sense that your exertion could, in some way, make things right in a larger sense.

Accompanied by a friend and a guide (our mandatory escort in the Tibetan Autonomous Region), we hit the trail on the outskirts of Darchen. With pilgrims, tourists and migrant labour pouring in, Darchen has swollen like a gold-rush town, with half-finished hotels, trinket shops and wild dogs skulking through overflowing refuse. We exit the fray and head west on the sandy Barkha plain. Even this modest ascent tests the lungs. But with brilliant blue skies my steps are buoyant. At 16,240ft (4950m) we hit a cairn, which is festooned with prayer flags and the first views of the snow-packed southern face of Mt Kailash. It's the first of four prostration points. Lobsang, our guide, teaches us the proper form. We bow to the mountain, our hands clasped in prayer, falling to the ground and rising to repeat.

Our path curves northward into the Lha-chu Valley, making a slow, steady ascent through a tawny expanse hemmed by ridges on

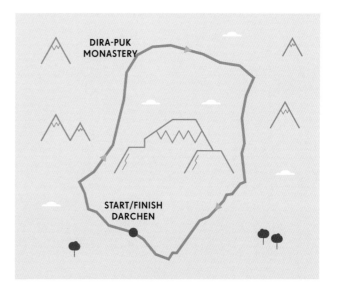

"Even if you are not on a religious mission, the symbolism and devotion shown here is powerful"

each side. We pass other travellers coming from milder climates, in zippered tracksuits or pyjama bottoms, carrying oxygen bottles or cameras. The valley narrows, and we pass landmarks of ruined chortens (shrines), a footprint of the Buddha and the tiny Chuku Monastery, perched high in the rock face.

Herders pasture their yaks along the river here in summer, but it's late spring and the grass has yet to come in. By the time we cross a bridge to our lodging for the night, Dira-puk Monastery, we've gone 12 miles (20km) and ascended 650ft (200m). It has taken seven hours, including a leisurely stop for lunch, banked against the wind. The monastery is regal but bone cold, cast in the yellow glow of flickering candles made of pungent yak butter. We take in the cramped and glowing meditation cave where the saint Gotsangpa was first led by a yak that turned out to be a goddess. Teenage monks slip down the hallways, smiling and evading us.

I wake up in the icy dawn an unwilling pilgrim. Wind heaves and snow obscures the frontal view of Mt Kailash outside our cracked windowpane. After breakfast on the camp stove and reluctant visits to the frozen outhouse, we begin our walk.

We join others in the arduous work of climbing Drölma-chu Valley. Many of these pilgrims are elderly, wearing thick robes and carrying bundles. A pair of grandmothers befriends us, drinking glucose from tiny vials for the sugar rush. The going gets steep, snow swirls and doubts multiply. It's not the snow that worries me, it's what comes next. In the Shiva-tsal, discarded clothing is strewn about, symbolic renunciations of the former self. I add a lock of my own hair to the pile.

Along a glacial ridge a group of men is gathered around a rock. They call us over and egg us on. The Bardo Trang is a test of sorts. Pilgrims must squeeze underneath the boulder and squiggle out the other side. Only the sinners will get stuck, according to the belief. Struggling through the narrow canal over icy ground feels like a second birth. They cheer our success and move on.

On the Drölma-la, the whole mountain pass is draped in a fluttery patchwork of prayer flags. Snow-streaked granite peaks encircle us. The place is crowded with ghosts and good intentions, from the sombre Tibetan portraits to money pegged to boulders. Every scrap of colour speaks to human endeavour. I join a group of strangers sharing chocolate and fermented snacks before the pitched 1970ft (600m) descent.

We reach the valley floor with our feet barking in our boots. A pot of milky tea restores the warmth to my bones. Sun shining, we work our way down the valley alongside the tumbling Dzong-Chu river. Dinner is served from a vat of scalding noodles. Perched high on the slope, I listen to the chanting of the monks of Zutul-puk. I don't know if my sins have really left me, but there's a peace here that logically follows the trials of the trail.

On the final day we travel 9 miles (14km) on a gentle road that leads us back to the sparkling Barkha plain. Our circle nearly completed, we keep a steady onward pace. A human pace. In the distance, trucks whistle across the steppe. **CMC**

DRÖLMA DO

The Drölma Do is a landmark cubic boulder on the Drölma-la pass. It's believed that when Gotsangpa got lost pioneering the route, 21 wolves led him up the pass and merged into one before becoming the boulder itself. They were emanations of Drölma, or Tara, goddess of mercy and protector of the pass. The pass is considered the point of rebirth and forgiveness. Pilgrims circumambulate the boulder and may paste money there or attach prayer flags.

Opposite, clockwise from top: yaks at work on Mt Kailash; Chuku Monastery, one of several that line the route; the land is marked with holy motifs. Previous pages: pilgrims walk the kora; the mountain juts out above the plains

ORIENTATION

Start/End // Darchen
Distance // 32 miles (52km)
Getting there // Ngari Gunsa Airport is about 200 miles (330km) from Darchen.
Tours // Tibet Highland Tours (http://tibethighlandtours.com) offers a 16-day overland tour from Lhasa that includes the Mt Kailash circuit. In Tibet, it is mandatory to travel as part of a guided trip with travel permits.
When to go // Mid-May to mid-October.
Where to stay // Darchen has many hotels. On the trekking route several monasteries offer basic accommodation and meals.
What to take // High-altitude trekking clothes: waterproofs, down jacket, thermals, a fleece and hiking boots. Trekking poles are helpful, sunglasses and sunscreen mandatory.

Mt Kailash

*Opposite from top: in deep
contemplation on the trek to Gaumukh;
Glastonbury Tor, place of legends*

MORE LIKE THIS
WALKING PILGRIMAGES

SOURCE OF THE GANGES, UTTARAKHAND, INDIA

The trek to Gaumukh is undertaken by thousands of Hindu pilgrims en route to the sacred source of the Ganges. For many it is a once-in-a-lifetime opportunity to cleanse the soul where the silent waters flow from under a huge wall of ice. A dip in the bitter waters here is believed to wash away sins. While the company of pilgrims has its own attractions, it is recommended to continue the trek to a camping spot around the magnificent alpine meadow at Tapovan (14,600ft/4450m) on day three. Stay at the sheltered campsite at Chirbasa (11,811ft/3600m) on the first night (and also on the descent), and the rather desolate rest house and shelter at Bhojbasa (12,434ft/3790m) the following evening. This trek across the glacial moraine requires reasonable fitness, and acclimatisation is essential. Before you set out, check if there are any new regulations (permits are mandatory) that may impact on your itinerary.

Start/End // Gangotri
Distance // 32 miles (52km)

CROAGH PATRICK, IRELAND

Croagh Patrick is Ireland's holiest mountain as it's believed that St Patrick fasted here for 40 days and 40 nights, emulating the biblical accounts of Moses and Christ. The chapel at the summit is Ireland's highest church and pilgrims ascend the slopes to perform penance at designated stations along the way. For those not primarily concerned with spiritual enlightenment, superb views over the island-studded inlet of Clew Bay more than reward the effort of the climb. The most frequently travelled route to the top is the wide tourist path, but a less-trodden and wilder one starts quietly at Belclare bridge, following a westerly route to the top (2500ft/764m) and onwards in the same direction to descend via Ben Goram (1830ft/559m). Bear in mind that the national day of pilgrimage is the last Sunday in July, when thousands of the faithful, some in bare feet, climb the mountain from Murrisk.

Start // Belclare bridge
End // GR L875808
Distance // 6.2 miles (10km)

GLASTONBURY TOR, ENGLAND

Degrees of undulation and elevation are how hikers usually rate routes, but the Somerset Levels are epic precisely because they have neither. The once-waterlogged Levels are utterly flat between the Quantocks Hills and the Mendips, with one major exception: the surreal, myth-soaked mound of Glastonbury Tor, associated with everything from Arthurian legends and the Holy Grail to the beginnings of British Christianity. The Mendip Way, a 50-mile (80km) long-distance walking route, skims the Levels, passing through the cathedral city of Wells. From here, follow in the footsteps of druids and festival folk to make a pilgrimage to the enigmatic Tor across Queen's Sedgemoor. If the direct route feels flat and featureless, follow footpaths (including sections of the Monarch's Way, King Charles II's 1651 escape route after the Battle of Worcester) on an arcing adventure through the Polden Hills, across Worminster Down, Launcherley and Pennard hillocks.

Start // Wells
End // Glastonbury Tor
Distance // 6 miles (10km)
More info // www.nationaltrust.org.uk/glastonbury-tor

HUÁNGSHĀN

Like exploring the landscape of a Chinese painting, a hike up Ānhuī's iconic mountain brings wizened peaks and mist-shrouded intrigue, but watch out for those jelly legs!

My uncle and I step gingerly out of our hotel in the ancient Chinese capital of Xī'ān, wondering incredulously how our legs seem even stiffer than yesterday. We go to cross the road. As we approach the curb we turn in unison through 180 degrees, step backwards down on to the road, turn around again, and cross. It's three days since we climbed the 60,000 steps carved into the granite crags of the mighty mountain, Huángshān, and our jelly-like thigh muscles still won't allow us to walk down curbs forwards.

Huángshān is one of China's most celebrated mountains. Its archetypal granite peaks and lonely, twisted pines have inspired poets and painters for generations, and it was the promise of that quintessential ancient-China landscape that had drawn us to its famous rocky slopes a few days earlier. What we hadn't counted on, though, was quite how frazzled our legs would become after climbing up and down 14 miles (22km) of stepped pathways.

Rewind four days and our excitement is palpable. We've read

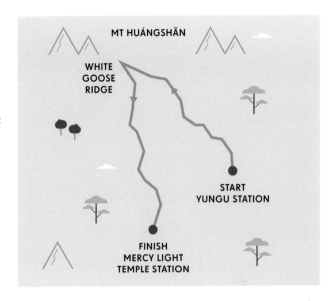

MT HUÁNGSHĀN

WHITE
GOOSE
RIDGE

START
YUNGU STATION

FINISH
MERCY LIGHT
TEMPLE STATION

about it, heard about it and seen photos of it, but now here we are at the foot of the famous Huángshān, about to start our ascent of its Eastern Steps: 5 miles (7km) long, 0.6 miles (1km) up. The crowds are unreal, but the tour groups soon make a beeline for the cable car (cheats), leaving us hikers strung out along the steep mountain pathway. It's still busy, but part of the attraction of being in China is meeting some of its 1.4 billion people.

'Can we take a photo?' ask some university students. We line up for a group shot, as they fire questions at us: 'Where are you from? How is China? How old are you?' My uncle has this one prepared: 'Liu-shi-er sui,' he says in his best Chinese. Sixty-two. The students let out a collective 'wooaaah' then tell him that he is 'so strong' and 'so brave'. Appropriately enough, we soon reach a rock formation called Xianren Zhilu, the Immortal Pointing the Way.

Many features on Huángshān have fantastical names that add mythical backstories to the mountain. In the right light, the Immortal Pointing the Way looks like an old man in a cloak, raising his hand didactically. He was, we're told, a wise teacher who steered a misguided merchant towards the right path in life before turning himself into a stone memorial. Inspired, we walk on.

The steps are starting to hurt now, but porters in baggy blue worker's overalls and flimsy green plimsoles remind us how lucky we are as they stride past carrying heavy supplies – food boxes, drink bottles – on either end of bamboo shoulder poles. Incredibly,

> ## "The granite peaks and twisted pines have inspired generations of poets and painters"

two more approach us carrying a bamboo sedan chair on top of which sits a smiling and rather overweight Chinese tourist. 'Lai, lai, lai!' they shout (coming through!), as they squeeze past without breaking stride. Sweat drips from their hair. Their clothes are sodden. Suddenly our daypacks feel as light as air.

Three hours later we reach White Goose Ridge and the main summit area. After bagging two beds in a guesthouse dorm, we spend the rest of the day grazing on unusual Chinese snacks – shrink-wrapped chicken's feet, anyone? – and marvelling at other-worldly views: Beginning to Believe Peak is decorated with a fine sprinkling of Huángshān's signature pines, while a solitary rock stack – Flower Blooming on a Brush Tip – pokes out from the forest with a single pine sprouting from its top.

After an impromptu game of basketball with some porters (where do they get the energy?), we bed down early, knowing we've got to be up before dawn to have any chance of seeing the famed Yun Hai (Sea of Clouds), a morning mist that fills the valleys with fog and turns distant peaks into floating islands.

It's still pitch black when we're woken by our dorm pals. We put on the heavy, army-surplus overcoats that are rented out to

© VCG | Getty

A CULTURAL ICON

Since AD 747 when its name was changed by imperial decree to honour the mythical Yellow Emperor, Huángshān (Yellow Mountain) has been one of China's most revered geological features, drawing hermits, poets and artists inspired by its dramatic landscape. The Tang Dynasty poet Li Bai dedicated works to the mountain and depictions of Huángshān helped establish the Shan Shui (Mountain and Water) school of landscape painting.

Left: the mountain's many leg-punishing steps; Previous page: dawn breaks over the range

shivering tourists, and follow them into the crisp night air, soon reaching Refreshing Terrace where we wait for the sun to rise. Only it doesn't. Today is too cloudy, so the magical morning mist – that Sea of Clouds – is indistinguishable from the actual clouds that simply envelop us. No mystical floating mountains; just mist.

The expectant crowds grow impatient and start hollering and whooping in an attempt to get some sort of Mexican wave-like echo going. We cut our losses and decide to begin our long descent down the mountain, quickly discovering that yesterday's climb was a doddle.

Today's Western Steps are even longer – 9 miles! (15km) – and the repetitive step-down motion soon has us dreaming of flat ground. Thankfully there's respite along the way, not least when we reach Huángshān's most iconic tree; *Yingke Song* (Greeting Guests Pine). There's a bottleneck of hikers here, but our thighs, now shaking with every downward step, welcome the wait. We've seen a lot of pine trees, but this one's special; perched serenely beside a huge granite rock, with two layers of branches reaching out to the valley below, like arms extending for a hug. We've seen the image on paintings, in photos – how surreal to now have the actual tree right in front of us, while we stand halfway up a misty mountain in central China. We don't yet know that we'll be unable to walk forwards down steps for three days to come, but even if we did, we wouldn't regret being here for a moment. **DMC**

ORIENTATION

Start // Yungu Station (foot of Eastern Steps)
End // Mercy Light Temple Station (foot of Western Steps)
Distance // 14 miles (22.5km)
Altitude // From 2920ft (890m) at Yungu Station to 5807ft (1770m) at White Goose Ridge.
Duration // Two days total; nine hours' hiking.
Getting there // Buses shuttle between Tangkou, Yungu Station and Mercy Light Temple Station. Tangkou is reached by bus from cities including Hángzhōu (3½ hours) and Nánjīng (five hours). Tunxi is an hour by bus from Tangkou.
Where to stay // In Tangkou, hotels cluster on Tiandu Lu. Túnxī is nicer – try Old Street Hostel (http://hiourhostel.com). On Huángshān summit, Shilin Hotel (http://shilin.com) and Beihai Hotel (www.beihaihotelhuangshan.com) have dorms and rooms.

© Thomas Edinger | 500px

MORE LIKE THIS
SACRED CHINESE MOUNTAINS

TÀI SHĀN

The eastern mountain of China's *Wu Yue* (Five Great Mountains), Tài Shān, in Shāndōng Province, is associated with sunrise, birth and renewal and as such is usually regarded as the most revered of all mountains in China. The main route up from Dai Temple (490ft, 150m) to Jade Emperor Peak (5026ft, 1532m) has been used since the 3rd century AD and is strewn with a bewildering number of much-venerated trees, bridges, inscriptions, caves and temples. Largely forested, the route is almost 6 miles (9km) long, and despite being stepped all the way (as all China's sacred mountains are) it still takes around six hours to reach the top, where you can find accommodation before easing your way down one of the other three routes the following day.

Start/End // Dai Temple in Tai'an
Distance // 11 miles (18km) round trip; 4600ft (1400m) climb

ÉMÉI SHĀN

One of China's Four Sacred Mountains of Buddhism, this stunning series of forested peaks rising up from the western rim of the steamy Sìchuān basin is dotted with Buddhist temples and monasteries, many of which have simple guest rooms you can stay in. You could spend two or three days up here, hiking the various routes that criss-cross the landscape. Just be sure to watch out for the armies of cheeky Tibetan macaques that guard some of the pathways. The climb from Baoguo Temple (1800ft, 550m), at the foot of the mountain, to Golden Summit Peak (10,095ft, 3077m) is a monstrous 24 miles (38.5km), so bank on taking around three days to hike up and down. Beware too that altitude plays a role here, with the summit topping out at around 10,000ft (3000m) above sea level.

Start/End // Baoguo Village, 4 miles (6km) from Emei Town
Distance // 48 miles (77km) round trip; 8291ft (2527m) climb

WŬDĀNG SHĀN

The apocryphal birthplace of t'ai chi, Wŭdāng Shān, in Húběi province, is one of China's Four Sacred Mountains of Taoism. It too is dotted with temples that add cultural and historical clout to your hike, and there are martial arts schools on its slopes where you can learn how to cultivate your *qi* (energy). The hike from the 12th-century Purple Cloud Temple (1916ft, 584m) to Heavenly Pillar Peak (5289ft, 1612m) takes at least three hours. En route you'll pass numerous atmospheric temples, including the enchanting red-walled Chaotian Temple with huge tombstones guarding its entrance. Near the summit is the magnificent Forbidden City, with stone walls 8ft (2.4m) thick hugging the mountainside. Just below it is Good Luck Hall (c 1307), thought to be the oldest solid bronze shrine in China.

Start/End // Purple Cloud Temple, a shuttle-bus ride from the entrance to the mountain
Distance // 6 miles (10km) round trip; 3373ft (1028m) climb

Clockwise from top: a golden Buddha
sits atop Mt Éméi; making light work
of the stairway to Tài Shān; Húběi's
Purple Cloud Temple, built c1100

A SUMMIT OF ISLAND PEAK

Dreaming of the next step in your hiking career? Get a surprisingly achievable taste of Himalayan mountaineering on Nepal's Island Peak, in the shadow of Everest.

Here you are reading *Epic Hikes of the World*, so I'm prepared to make two guesses: one, you like hiking. OK, that was easy.

Two: at some point, probably on a Monday afternoon at work after too much lunch, you've allowed yourself a little daydream. You've dreamed of doing something more, somewhere far away. You've dreamed of open space, cold air and freedom. You've had – maybe just for the briefest of moments – that dream of struggling to the top of the world, looking down on humanity, and knowing that...

Sorry, I'm going to interrupt your daydream there.

You don't have the two years to train ceaselessly, the three months off work, and the spare US$35,000 needed to climb Everest. Even if you do, it's really cold, painful and very dangerous.

However, what if you could have just a little taste of what it means to take your love of hiking to the next level, to get a quick blast of real Himalayan mountaineering, on a peak that any fit trekker could try? You need Island Peak.

'Bed-tea, sir.'

It's 1am. A sherpa is waking you with a cup of tea. You struggle into your clothes – lots of clothes – as camp comes to life around you. You don't know what the temperature is, but judging by the sparkle of frost covering the inside of your tent it's somewhere between -10°C (14°F) and -20°(-4°F) . Head-lamp on, you set off with the rest of camp in the thin, dry air towards the summit – the final push. Ahead of you is the glacier, where you'll put your crampons on, rope up, and keep plodding.

Now you're probably thinking, this isn't me. I'm no climber – I couldn't do any of this. But to get here, you've trekked for 12 days in the shadow of Everest. It's not been a walk in the park (actually, it has – Nepal's Sagarmatha National Park – but you know what I mean). You've been sleeping in a tent. You've had the altitude to get used to. And it's been cold at night.

But with yaks carrying your bags, a well-planned acclimatisation programme, and a huge team of sherpas to put up your tent, cook your meals and generally look after your every need, it's not been

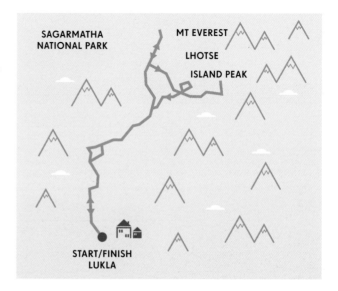

"You feel like a fraud who could be escorted down the mountain for not really belonging. But you do belong. You walked here"

harder than other hikes you've done. The longest day has been six-and-a-half hours of walking. Many have been just three or four – the altitude making the pace slow and rest stops frequent.

And the rewards? People come to the Khumbu region of Nepal expecting to be wowed by the mountains. But they leave just as overwhelmed by Sherpa culture. There are no roads here, so walking the trails is what everyone does – trekkers, builders carrying doors on their heads, gnarly Everest mountaineers, old men ferrying crates of Coke, kids walking to school, grannies picking up yak dung to dry for fuel...everyone. And above it all stands a constant circle of the highest mountains on earth. Everest, the tall kid at the back of the class photo, looms at the back.

Reading this, you probably don't get the sense of how surreal that summit day feels. You start climbing in pitch black. The only sounds are panting and the squeak of plastic boots in cold snow. No one has the energy to talk – it takes all your breath just to put the next foot forward. It's 5am in the freezing morning.

But as you walk out over the glacier, it starts to get light. And as it does, you realise where your days of panting and slogging have got you. Your rope is strung out over a perfect bowl of snow. All around you are ice-fluted Himalayan giants. And now, for the first time, you are looking across at them, not up. It's the kind of view normally reserved for the elite of the mountaineering world, yet here you are enjoying it. There are crevasses to peer down. Snow-bridges to cross. You feel a strange mix of privilege and stuttering confidence, as though you are a fraud who could be found out at any minute and escorted down the mountain for not really belonging.

But you do belong. You walked here.

And slowly, step by breathless step, you reach the top of the glacier and the steep slope above it.

From here to the summit is 820ft (250m) of fixed rope that loops its way along the perfect snaking S of a ridge 3ft (.9m) wide. With a fixed rope to clip into, it's the safest and most exhilarating part of the whole climb.

You put your head down and keep breathing, keep trudging. Then you hear a primal scream of joy from the first of your group to make it. That gives you the push you need and pretty soon you're there too.

You're standing on a platform big enough for five people. All around you, the ground falls steeply away. It might not be the actual top of the world, but it feels close enough. From here you can see why it's called Island Peak – the 20,305ft (6,189m) summit rises jagged from a sea of glaciers. Beyond those glaciers tower some of the biggest mountains in the world: Everest, Makalu, Lhotse, Ama Dablam.

You've made it – your very own Himalayan peak.

You wait for the rest of your group to join you and desperately try to paint the view into that section of your memory labelled 'Special. Do not delete. Ever.'

Monday-afternoon daydreams will never be the same again. **PP**

WHAT'S IN A NAME?

'Sherpa' is the name of the ethnic group that lives in the Everest region, even though it is commonly used to describe any Nepali guide or porter. Sherpa boys are traditionally named for the day of the week they are born on. So Friday is Pasang, Saturday is Pemba, and so on. So if you stand on a busy street corner in Namche Bazaar and shout 'Pasang Sherpa', one in seven of the local men around you should turn.

Opposite from top: summiting in the deep snows of Island Peak; just in case you lose your bearings. Previous page: the mountain looms intimidatingly ahead

ORIENTATION

Start/End // Lukla Airport
Distance // 85 miles (136km)
Duration // 10-12 days of trekking will get you to Base Camp and acclimatised enough for a summit climb. One day of snow climbing.
Getting there // Fly to Lukla from Kathmandu in 25 minutes.
When to go // March to April, October to November.
More info // A good trekking agency will arrange flights, climbing permits and safety gear, as well as supplying a team of sherpas. Book a tour operator in your home country, or search Trekking Agencies' Association of Nepal (www.taan.org.np) for local operators.
Things to know // Basic snow-climbing skills are needed. Guides can teach these at Base Camp. A weekend of instruction before your trip is the best preparation.

*Opposite: the tents of Everest Base
Camp on the Tibetan side*

MORE LIKE THIS
HIMALAYAN HIGH-RISES

EVEREST BASE CAMP, NEPAL

This is the definitive Himalayan trek, flying into Lukla and climbing to the foot of Mt Everest, through breathless mountain landscapes. Your destination is either Everest Base Camp or the stunning viewpoint at Kala Pattar. As you climb through the foothills of the world's highest mountain, the terrain soars on all sides like jagged shards of glass. The trails are steep and the altitude hangs on your muscles like a diving belt, but this is not a mountaineering expedition or a wilderness survival experience. There are trekking lodges every few hundred metres along the trails and tens of thousands of trekkers come here every year. Because of the risk of acute mountain sickness, it takes a minimum of two weeks to climb to Everest Base Camp or Kala Pattar – you should hike for no more than three hours at any one time on the ascent and rest completely on days three, five and seven.

Start/End // Lukla
Maximum elevation // 18,192ft (5545m)

JHOMOLHARI TREK, BHUTAN

The Jhomolhari trek is to Bhutan what the Everest Base Camp route is to Nepal: a trekking pilgrimage. With two different versions, it's one of the most trodden routes in the country, and almost 40% of all trekkers who come to Bhutan end up following one of the Jhomolhari routes. The first two days of the trek follow the Paro Chhu valley to Jangothang, climbing gently, but continually, with a few short, steep climbs over side ridges. It crosses a high pass and visits the remote village of Lingzhi, then crosses another pass before making its way towards Thimphu. The last four days of the trek cover a lot of distance and require many hours of walking. The trek combines some of Bhutan's best high-mountain scenery, with remote villages and excellent opportunities to see yaks.

Start // Sharna Zampa
End // Dodina
Maximum elevation // 16,175ft (4930m)

ANNAPURNA CIRCUIT, NEPAL

For scenery and cultural diversity this has long been considered the best trek in Nepal and one of the world's classic walks. It follows the Marsyangdi Valley to the north of the main Himalayan range and crosses a 17,770ft (5416m) pass to descend into the dramatic desert-like, Tibetan-style scenery of the upper Kali Gandaki Valley. The walk passes picturesque villages home to Gurungs, Manangis and Thakalis, offers spectacular mountain views of the numerous Annapurna peaks and boasts some of the best trekking lodges in Nepal. The circuit is usually walked counterclockwise because the climb to Thorung La from the west side is considered too strenuous.

Start // Besi Sahar or Bhulebule
End // Jomsom or Naya Pul
Maximum elevation // 17,770ft (5416m)

ALONE ON THE GREAT WALL OF CHINA

Soak up centuries of Chinese history as you follow the Great Wall for two days through the misty, forested mountains guarding the borderlands of Běijīng.

t's been a couple of minutes since I veered off the dusty, partly bricked pathway on to this ridge of hard-packed sun-dried earth. Low, scratchy shrubs block sight of the ground under foot, so I just follow the spine of the hill, knowing that both sides drop away sharply into the valley below. Slowly I feel the path becoming rockier, then the shrubs start to thin out and all becomes clear: stretched out in front of me is an exposed ridge of tumbledown rocks, raised a few feet above the natural lie of the land, and clearly forming what was once – long, long ago – a wall. I've found it; an incredibly rare stretch of mountain masonry dating back to the far-off Northern Qi Dynasty. I've been exploring

the Great Wall of China for more than a decade, and this is the oldest section I have ever placed my feet upon.

Though the Great Wall was built, and added to, over the course of six Chinese dynasties, most of what we see today – those beautifully bricked bastions, snaking off into distant misty mountains – hails from the Ming Dynasty (1368–1644). Still very old, but nothing compared to this. The stones I'm now walking along were positioned here, on the hills surrounding the ancient garrison of Gǔběikǒu, some time between AD 550 and 577. It's almost 1500 years old! I crouch down and lay my hands on the stones; feeling the history; soaking it up. My thoughts wander.

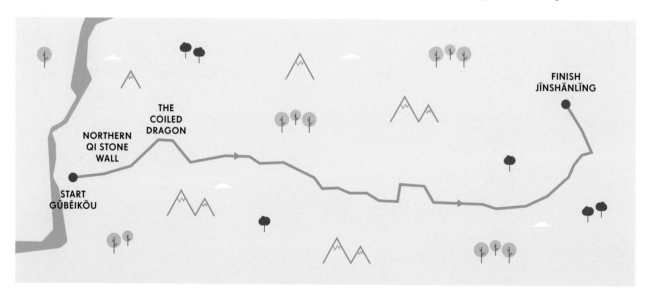

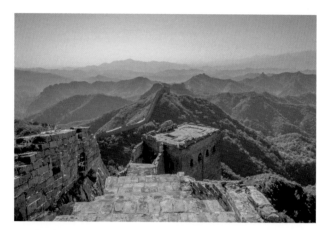

I imagine how it must have looked in its full, stone-wall splendour, stretching across this remote line of hills, and wonder who else's feet it has supported over the centuries: builders, prisoners, soldiers... and now a tourist from a small town in southeast England.

Snapping out of my reverie, I remember that my Great Wall hike has only just begun. There are two more days ahead of me, but it's going to be hard to top this moment.

Gǔběikǒu, these days a quiet rural village about 80 miles (130km) from Běijīng, means 'ancient northern gate', and was once heavily fortified, guarding the main northeast route into the capital. Different branches of the Great Wall converge on the village, creating a kind of Great Wall crossroads; dream territory for history-loving hikers. After spending most of the morning on buses from Běijīng, I know it's too late to make it today to my intended destination – a section of wall known as Jīnshānlǐng, in neighbouring Héběi province – so I've packed a tent and plan to find a suitable camping spot. First, though, I need to negotiate the Coiled Dragon.

The ancient stone section of Great Wall I'm on soon joins up with its younger, bricked, Ming-dynasty brother, and eventually I see *Pan Long* (Coiled Dragon) curled out in front of me. It's an awe-inspiring, sweeping stretch of wall that arcs its way around the lip of a forested depression, and before long I'm on top of it,

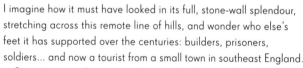

"I haven't seen another person since I set foot on the old, stone section. I seem to have the Great Wall all to myself"

walking along the spine of the sleeping dragon. The views are stunning – folds of mist-shrouded mountains overlap each other in the distance, each a slightly lighter shade of grey than the one before – but I'm forced to keep my eyes on the path. Despite being a thousand years younger than the Northern Qi section I was drooling over an hour ago, this wall is still in ruins – loose bricks wobble under my feet – and alarmingly narrow, with both edges plunging some 100ft (30m) into the valleys below.

The end of the dragon is marked by three turrets, two of which still have parts of their roofs intact – perfect camps for the night. I pitch up, light my stove, and tuck into a large bowl of noodles (what else?). The evening is silent. I haven't seen another person since I set foot on the old, stone section. I seem to have the Great Wall all to myself.

I wake with birdsong at the crack of dawn, and smile, suddenly remembering where I am. A cup of tea later, and I'm off walking again, waving goodbye to the Coiled Dragon, and welcoming in

© Dave Porter Photography | Photoshot, © Horizon Images/Motion | Alamy

CAMPING ON THE GREAT WALL

The half-ruined turrets dotted along the top of the Great Wall built at intervals of 3 miles (5km) and 1.5 miles (2.5km) during the Ming Dynasty are some of the most wonderfully romantic places to camp, but be aware that strictly speaking you're not allowed to camp on top of the Great Wall. In practice, the stretches people camp on are so remote that nobody is around to tell you otherwise, but remember what you're on top of and camp responsibly: take away all your litter, and don't disturb any bricks.

From left: sections of the Wall towards the finish; an arch near the start of the hike; unrestored portions stretch ahead. Previous page: the Great Wall of China

ORIENTATION

Start // Gǔběikōu
End // Jīnshānlǐng
Distance // 4.3 miles (7km)
Duration // Seven hours
Getting there // Take bus 980 from Běiīng's Dongzhimen Bus Station to Miyun, then bus 25 to Gǔběikōu. To return, exit Jīnshānlǐng Great Wall, turn right and walk up to the highway, where you can catch buses back to Běiīng.
Where to stay // In Gǔběikōu: The Great Wall Box House (http://en.greatwallbox.com) has English-speaking owners with a good knowledge of Great Wall hiking.

the warming morning sun. After an hour or so of magical, first-light, wall-top hiking, I reach the striking remains of 24-Eye Tower, unique in that it once spanned three storeys, with three windows, or 'eyes', on each side of the two lower levels. It seems astonishingly well preserved, but I soon realise that the side facing me is the only one fully intact, and that only 15 'eyes' remain.

After a short detour through some farmland, to circumnavigate an off-limits military zone – I'm back on the wall again, but not before negotiating the most unusual of doorways, which is built into the wall itself, allowing me to walk *through* the Great Wall of China to reach the steps up on to it on the other side.

I've now hiked all the way to another Chinese province – Héběi – and am walking on top of the Jīnshānlǐng section of the wall. It's astonishingly handsome, having been renovated in recent years and opened up to tourists, but it still feels very remote, especially at this far end, where the wall dips and rises in and out of foggy valleys, and where day-trippers rarely venture. An old lady sitting alone on a stool in one of the turrets is startled by my 'good morning!', but then sells me a ticket for this section. She is the first person I've seen today. But today, like yesterday, hasn't been about meeting people. It's been about landscapes, about history, and about walking along one of the most epic stretches of Great Wall I've ever visited. **DMC**

The Great Wall of China

Opposite from top: at Old Dragon
Head, the Great Wall meets the Bohai
Sea; its touristy Mùtiányù section
features a toboggan run

MORE LIKE THIS
GREAT WALL HIKES

JIÀNKÒU TO MÙTIÁNYÙ

For a stupefyingly gorgeous hike along arguably the most stunning part of the Great Wall near Běijīng, head to Jiànkòu Great Wall – 60 miles (100km) north of the capital – from where you can hike all the way to the popular Mùtiányù section, which is open for tourism and comes complete with a toboggan ride (you know you want to). Your hike starts in the first hamlet of Xīzhàzi Village and follows a path through farmland up to the wall. Turn left when you hit the wall and you'll soon be scrambling on hands and knees up the very steep stretch of bricks leading to the Ox Horn, where the wall bends through 180 degrees before descending (even more steeply!) to the restored section at Mùtiányù.
Start // Xīzhàzi Village, Hamlet No 1
End // Mùtiányù
Distance // 2 miles (3km)

HORN PEAK TO THE BOHAI SEA

About 125 miles (300km) east of Běijīng, the Great Wall tumbles down Jiǎo Shān (Horn Peak), past the walled town of Shānhǎiguān, to Lao Long Tou (Old Dragon Head) where it dips its toes into the Bohai Sea. Parts of it are missing these days but enough remains to make a rewarding, off-beat Great Wall hike. Start from Dapingding (Big Flat Summit) at the top of Horn Peak then follow the wall down the slopes, past Qixian Temple, to the mountain's main gate. To your left, you'll find a forlorn, earthen section of Great Wall leading to Shānhǎiguān, whose imposing town walls once formed part of the Great Wall. The wall disappears now, so follow roads for the final 3 miles (5km) to Old Dragon Head where a rebuilt section plunges into the sea – a unique opportunity to swim around the Great Wall!
Start // Big Flat Summit on Horn Peak
End // Old Dragon's Head
Distance // 7 miles (12km)

SHĀNXĪ'S WILD EARTHEN WALL

For a more 'out there' Great Wall hike, venture to the dusty loess landscape of Shānxī province to seek out the long-forgotten rammed-earth stretches of wall that sidle their way sporadically across the region. The wall here is less spectacular than the handsome bricked sections that soar up into the mountains around Běijīng, but the remote countryside location makes for fantastic rural-China hiking. Find your way to Weilucun, a village 30 miles (50km) west of Dàtóng. You'll see the wall north of the village; turn left (east) when you hit it, and follow its stumpy beacon towers for around 4 miles (7km) to the village of Bataizi, where a striking church-tower ruin warrants a little of your attention before you grapple with your ropey Chinese to find a taxi to Zuoyun, the nearest town with a bus station.
Start // Weilucun
End // Bataizi
Distance // 4 miles (7km)

THE HONG KONG TRAIL

From the summit of iconic Victoria Peak to the turquoise waters of Big Wave Bay, this is one of the world's truly great urban hikes.

Crunch. Crunch. The sound is coming from the bushes. I swing my torch off the trail for a look, expecting, I don't know, a wayward tourist or a lost poodle from one of the nearby luxury high rises.

It's a porcupine.

A porcupine. On Victoria Peak.

It's 5am and I'm standing atop the mountain in the centre of Hong Kong, one of the densest cities in the world. I've been here dozens of times during daylight hours, when the Peak's lookouts and trails are crowded with visitors carrying selfie sticks and Louis Vuitton shopping bags. It's considered a Hong Kong must-do, and

for good reason: the view down over the northern coast of Hong Kong Island and the Kowloon Peninsula beyond is iconic. From up here, the forest of skyscrapers looks like a Lego city. There's the 108-storey International Commerce Centre, the tallest building in Hong Kong, looking an inch tall. There's the green-and-white Star Ferry, chugging across Victoria Harbour like a child's toy.

But in the predawn hours, the Peak is a different place. There is, for Pete's sake, a *porcupine*, casually chewing twigs not 100 yards from the Häagen-Dazs and Mak's Noodle that, in a few hours, will be lined with throngs of hungry visitors. I've lived in Hong Kong for five years and had no idea we even had porcupines.

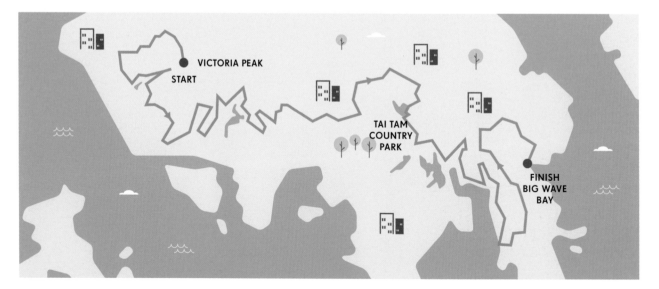

I'm up here before first light with my husband and two friends to begin an assault on the Hong Kong Trail. The 31-mile (50km) hike is broken into eight stages, and Victoria Peak is the start of Stage 1. While I've done many portions of the trail individually, today we're hoping to do the entire hike in one go, hence the early hour.

Stage 1 is a gentle start, circling the slope of the mountain on a wide paved trail. We sip our coffee and enjoy the cool darkness, a rare break from Hong Kong's usual steamy heat. Here and there are signs describing the flora of the dense surrounding forest: the glossy leaved *Pavetta hongkongensis*, thick stands of banana trees and bamboo, the banyan roots branching up the side of the slopes like enormous veins.

Slowly, we descend a narrow path, passing several tiny waterfalls dribbling down mossy rock. Stage 1 ends at Pok Fu Lam Reservoir. We stop for a drink, watching joggers and dog walkers circle the green water in the misty first light. Moving west, we skirt around the hills above Aberdeen, once a fishing village, now home to several yacht clubs and the kitschy-but-beloved Jumbo Kingdom Floating Restaurant. In the middle distance is Lamma, the third-largest of Hong Kong's 260-plus islands, distinguishable by the three skinny smokestacks of its coal power plant.

Concrete gives way to dirt track as we head east along Stage 3 towards Wan Chai Gap. Stage 4 begins at a section of trail named Lady Clementi's Ride, named after the wife of Cecil Clementi, British Governor of Hong Kong in the 1920s. Lady

"From looking down at a concrete jungle, now it's all mountains, clouds and sea"

Clementi's Ride is befitting of a gentlewoman, winding gently uphill through the forest, crossing several small, stone, colonial-era bridges. There are more nature signs here, including some marking the *Aquilaria sinensis*, the incense tree, whose heartwood is the source of the richly scented incense used in traditional Chinese rituals. It was the export of incense tree wood in Aberdeen Harbour that earned the area – and later the whole city – the name Hong Kong, which translates as 'fragrant harbour'.

At Stage 5 we emerge from the woods and follow the vehicular road into Wong Nai Chung Reservoir Park, where we stop for a break. We buy cup noodles and bottles of Pocari Sweat, a popular Japanese grapefruit-flavoured sports drink, and eat while watching couples splash around the lake on rental paddleboats. Fortified, we climb the path to Jardine's Lookout, where British colonists used to watch for clippers coming in with the mail from London. There are no clippers today, but the 1400ft (420m) summit gives sweeping views from the skyscrapers of Causeway Bay all the way to the mountains of the New Territories. The sun is high overhead now, and we're getting sweaty, descending and ascending a series of narrow dirt paths and stone staircases.

UNDEVELOPED HONG KONG

Most people's image of Hong Kong involves skyscrapers and neon. But the city is 75% countryside, much of that contained inside 24 parks and 22 'special areas'. These include mountain forests, rocky foreshores, open grasslands and marine reserves. Developers would love to get their hands on more of the land but much of it is too mountainous or remote to be of that much use.

From left: Tai Long Wan Beach, or Big Wave Bay; a city overlook on the way to Lion Rock; the trail quickly turns a lush shade of green. Previous page: admiring Hong Kong's unparalleled urban vista

ORIENTATION

Start // Victoria Peak
End // Big Wave Bay
Distance // 31 miles (50km)
Geography // The city has three main parts: Hong Kong Island, Kowloon Peninsula and the New Territories. The Hong Kong Trail is on Hong Kong Island.
Getting there // Hong Kong International Airport is on the island of Lantau. From here, take a taxi, bus or Airport Express train to Hong Kong Island. To get to the trailhead, take a taxi, the 15 bus or the Peak Tram to Victoria Peak.
When to go // Late autumn into early winter (Nov–Jan) is generally Hong Kong's pleasantest season, with clear skies and moderate temperatures.
Where to stay // Hong Kong Island has convenient, but expensive, accommodation. You'll find cheaper digs across the water in Kowloon.

Stage 6 comes as a relief, with a paved path wending through the cool forest of Tai Tam Country Park. We walk across the top of the reservoir's dam wall, peering down into the chalky green water at the shadows of fish flickering in the deep. Stage 7 is the least spectacular part of the trail, following a concrete catchment for most of its length.

Finally, we arrive at Stage 8. We've all done this section before, as it's arguably Hong Kong's most famous hike: the Dragon's Back. Though exhausted from the previous 25 miles (40km) or so, the knowledge of what lies ahead gives us a boost. We climb a rocky exposed mountainside for about 20 minutes, and there we are, on the Dragon's Back, the ridge traversing the D'Aguilar Peninsula. On either side is water, glinting aquamarine in the low sunlight of the now late afternoon. It's windy up here, so windy it fills our ears and stops all thought for a moment. Below us, paragliders drift parallel to the mountainside on candy-coloured chutes. Just hours ago, we were looking down at concrete jungle. Now it's nothing but mountains, clouds and sea.

After a final push back down the mountain and through a damp forest we arrive at the end of the trail. Big Wave Bay feels far more like a Hawaiian village than a part of Hong Kong. We've travelled across the city, but it feels like we've gone across the world. We wander through the maze of bungalows and surf shops and emerge at the beach, a glowing crescent of white sand. Gratefully, exhaustedly, we wade into the waves. **EM**

MORE LIKE THIS
HONG KONG HIKES

MACLEHOSE TRAIL

This trail goes east to west across Hong Kong's New Territories, the large, heavily rural district closest to the border of mainland China. It's divided into 10 stages, traversing some of the city's most rugged and varied terrain. Start at the deep-blue High Island Reservoir, on the craggy coast of the Sai Kung Peninsula. Puff your way past atmospheric Hakka villages in the remote uplands, where tea and indigo once grew and wild boar roam. Wind through the rocky outcrops of the Kowloon peaks, including Amah Rock, said to look like a woman with a baby on her back. Watch out for aggressive macaques near the reservoirs, and check out the WWII ruins on Smuggler's Ridge. Tackle Tai Mo Shan, the city's tallest peak, at more than 3000ft (900m), then descend gently through Tai Lam Country Park to the 'village' of Tuen Mun (population half a million).
Start // High Island Reservoir
End // Tuen Mun
Distance // 62 miles (100km)
More info // This hike is usually attempted in stages, except as part of charity endurance races

LANTAU TRAIL

This trail makes a loop around Lantau, the largest of Hong Kong's islands. Though home to the airport and Disneyland, Lantau is largely rural. The 12-stage trail starts and ends in the beach town of Mui Wo, reachable from other parts of Hong Kong by bus or ferry. Early stages summit Lantau Peak and Sunset Peak, the island's highest mountains. Highlights include Ngong Ping, home to the much-visited Big Buddha, a 112ft (34m) statue seated atop a hill, and Tai O, a Tanka fishing village of stilt houses and shrimp drying on bamboo mats. Several temples and WWII ruins along the way make interesting stops.
Start/End // Mui Wo
Distance // 43 miles (70km)
More info // The most accommodating to thru-hiking of the three walks here, with a handful of hotels and campgrounds nearby

WILSON TRAIL

Hopping from Hong Kong Island across the harbour to Kowloon and on nearly to the border of mainland China, the Wilson Trail lies almost entirely within Hong Kong's country park system. It starts with a bang, heading straight uphill on a stone staircase from the colonial village of Stanley, offering dramatic vistas over the island's south side. Across the water, it wends up Devil's Peak, home to an old British fort. It traverses wet forests and deep gullies lush with ferns, past decaying 19th-century villages and jade-watered reservoirs, up mountains with views of dense urban settlements and remote coastline. Keep your eyes open for troops of macaques, who will gladly steal your lunch.
Start // Stanley
End // Nam Chung
Distance // 48 miles (78km)
More info // The Wilson Trail is usually done in stages although camping along the trail is possible

Clockwise from top: taking in Hong Kong's wild side; the starting point of the Maclehose Trail; the view from the Wilson Trail on Kowloon

STEPS AHEAD: MT KINABALU

Incorporating tangled jungle, granite ridges and barren plateaux, traversing Borneo's highest and holiest mountain is a task that requires nerves – and legs – of steel.

Steps. Endless, slippery, winding steps. Steps that are steep and shallow; steps that are deep and broad. Steps formed from intertwining tree roots, gnarled and knotted by centuries of growth. Steps carved into black volcanic rock, slick with moisture. Step after step after step. Countless steps behind; countless steps to come. I've only been on Mt Kinabalu for three hours, but I've already climbed enough steps for several lifetimes, and I'm barely a quarter of the way to the top.

At 13,435ft (4095m), Kinabalu isn't just the highest mountain in Borneo, it's one of the highest mountains in all of Southeast Asia. A great hump of brooding black rock, thrust up by the movement of tectonic plates from Sabah's northern coastline, Kinabalu is a formidable sight: more fortress than mountain, a tower of inky granite, wrapped in mist and shrouded in steaming jungle. To local Dusun people it's known as *Aki Nabalu*, or 'the sacred place of the dead'. It's a holy mountain, haunted by the spirits of their ancestors, and as such, definitely not a place for the living. But ghostly guardians aren't the only obstacle for the 20,000 people or so who set out every year to conquer Borneo's highest mountain. For them, and for me, it's the steps that hold the greatest dread.

Though it's a relatively short climb – from the national park gates to the summit the trail covers little more than 5 miles (8km) – Kinabalu's great challenge is its elevation gain. From start to finish, the trail ascends 7874ft (2400m) – roughly equivalent to scaling seven Eiffel Towers, six Empire State Buildings or three Burj Khalifas. Much of it comes via a punishingly steep staircase that spirals up the mountain; the rest involves climbing over bare, slippery granite or hauling yourself up fixed ropes bolted into the rock. Temperature and humidity levels wouldn't seem out of place

MT KINABALU

START/FINISH
TIMPOHON GATE

in a Swedish sauna. And to cap it all, the mountain is notoriously earthquake-prone – the most recent tremor struck in 2015. In short, Kinabalu is not a mountain to be tackled lightly.

Most people take two days to complete the climb: on day one, a six- to seven-hour trek from the park gates at 6122ft (1866m) to the resthouse at Laban Rata at 10,735ft (3272m) followed on day two by a predawn start and a 2733ft (833m) summit climb to watch the sunrise. The early wake-up call is essential, as the heat of the rising sun causes moisture to boil up from the surrounding jungle; within an hour of dawn, the mountain is frequently swathed in cloud.

For me, though, the summit sunrise is a far-off dream. I've just got to make it through the first day. By lunchtime, I'm drenched with sweat, my leg muscles feel as if they're on fire, and I'm sure someone has surreptitiously replaced the contents of my rucksack with breezeblocks. As I take a breather at one of the *pondoks*, or rest stations, along the trail, I watch the local porters trudge past, carrying supplies up to the guesthouse: oil-drums, sacks of rice, fruit, vegetables. Most are puffing nonchalantly on crooked cheroots as they climb, and nearly all of them are wearing nothing more than a pair of battered flip-flops on their feet. To them, climbing Kinabalu is all in a day's work. Their stamina would put sherpas to shame.

There's no doubt that Kinabalu is a tough mountain, but it's also an astonishingly beautiful one. A Unesco World Heritage Site since 2000, it's celebrated for its biological diversity. As I trudge up the trail, I watch flycatchers, warblers and flowerpeckers blurring through the undergrowth. Creepers tangle around tree trunks. Orchids bloom beside the trail. Pitcher plants sprout amongst the rocks. And, deep in the jungle, some of Borneo's rarest inhabitants hide: endangered animals like the sun bear, ferret-badger, moonrat and orangutan, for whom Kinabalu's forests provide a last, and precious, refuge.

LITTLE STOP OF HORRORS

Like the rest of Borneo, Kinabalu National Park is a treasure trove of biological diversity. It's home to more than 325 bird species, 100 mammals, 600 ferns, 800 orchids and no fewer than 13 types of pitcher plant – but the prize for the weirdest plant has to go to the rafflesia, or corpse flower, which is famous for its repugnant stench, said to be akin to the smell of rotting meat. The foul smell helps attract flies and other pollinating insects to its flower – the largest on earth, known to reach 17in (43cm) in diameter.

Clockwise from top: Kinabalu National Park bathed in morning sunlight; the huge, foul-smelling rafflesia; a hiker at Kinabalu's peak. Previous page: a trail of climbers on Mt Kinabalu's granite summit

© Nora Carol | Getty, © R.M. Nunes | Shutterstock

It's 6pm by the time I finally reach the guesthouse at Laban Rata, relishing the chance to stop, slough off my pack and admire the view. As darkness falls and a chill descends on the mountain, I share curry and cold beers with my fellow hikers, then collapse into my bunk and instantly tumble into a deep, exhausted slumber.

Unfortunately, I barely feel I've drifted off when my guide, Edwin, is shaking me awake to begin the dawn climb. A full moon hangs over the mountain as we set out from the resthouse, glowing in the blackness like a paper lantern. We trudge onwards, then upwards, climbing steps, squeezing through gulleys, scrambling over rocks, hauling ourselves up ropes. Finally, we reach a sprawling granite plateau and glimpse Kinabalu's summit – a pile of sharp, shattered boulders known as Low's Peak. A line of head-torches is bobbing its way slowly across the plateau towards the summit, like a procession of fireflies twinkling in the darkness. I brace myself for the final push. As I climb, the thinness of the air begins to hit me, and by the time I reach the rock pile, I'm gasping for oxygen. Painfully, I haul myself up the boulder heap, step-by-step, hand-over-hand, slowly inching my way towards the mountain's apex.

Then, abruptly, the climb ends. I sit down on the top of Kinabalu just as the sun breaks over the horizon, and the jagged pinnacles around the summit plateau light up like signal towers. The sky shifts through a rainbow of colours – scarlet, purple, pink, tangerine – and mist swirls up from the jungle below, transforming the mountain into an island: a black pyramid floating on a sea of cloud.

Before long, I know the entire summit will be swallowed up by the fog, and soon enough I'll have to face the challenge of somehow getting back down. But for now, the mountain spirits seem content to just let me sit and marvel at the view. I'm more than happy to oblige. **OB**

"Local porters carry supplies up in battered flip-flops. Their stamina would put sherpas to shame"

ORIENTATION

Start/End // Timpohon Gate
Distance // 10 miles (16km) round trip
Getting there // The national park is 55 miles (88km) by road northeast of Kota Kinabalu, linked by daily buses.
When to go // February to April.
Where to stay // Sutera Sanctuary Lodges (www.suterasanctuarylodges.com.my).
What to take // A head-torch, trail snacks, hiking shoes with plenty of grip and a lightweight, waterproof rain jacket. Also pack thermal base-layers as it gets cold at night.
More info // www.sabahparks.org.my.
Things to know // Park entrance RM15, climbing permit RM200, insurance RM7, guide RM230. Guides are compulsory for all climbs, and can be arranged through the national park HQ (www.sabahparks.org.my).

Clockwise from top: Sri Lanka's Adam's Peak, illuminated at night; at base camp, Mt Rinjani, Indonesia

MORE LIKE THIS
SUNRISE HIKES

MT RINJANI, LOMBOK

Looming 12,224ft (3726m) high over Lombok's northern coastline, Mt Rinjani is the second-highest volcano in Indonesia, topped only by Mt Kerinci on Sumatra. It's part of the infamous chain of volcanoes that form the Ring of Fire, where the Eurasian, Pacific and Indo-Australian plates grind together, causing fissures in the earth's crust. It's also one of the toughest hiking challenges in Indonesia, combining forest trails, rocky steps and a night of wild camping on the mountainside before the final exhausting, predawn climb up the flank of the volcano's ashy cone. It's a brutal, leg-sapping challenge, but it's worth it for the chance to watch dawn break over Lombok's coastline – on a clear morning, you'll see all the way to Mt Agung, Bali's highest point.
Start/End // Senaru
Distance // 15 miles (24km) (approx)
More info // www.rinjaninationalpark.com

ADAM'S PEAK, SRI LANKA

In world terms, this conical mountain isn't all that high – only 7360ft (2243m) – but don't let its size fool you. It's a punishing climb, favoured by pilgrims who come to see the Sri Pada, or sacred footprint, said to have been left by either Buddha, Shiva or Adam, depending on which religion you happen to belong to. There are six possible routes to the top, but the one most often used by trekkers is the Hatton Trail, a steep uphill slog involving numerous stairs cut into the mountain. To get there in time for sunrise requires both an early start and a hand from the weather gods: Sri Lanka's jungly terrain means the peak is, unfortunately, often plunged in cloud. But with luck, at the top you'll have a memorable view encompassing the island's west, south and east coasts.
Start/End // Dalhousie
Distance // 9 miles (14km) round trip
More info // www.sripada.org

MT SINAI, EGYPT

Throughout human history, mountains have often been seen as places where ordinary mortals have a chance to commune with the gods – and they don't get much holier than Mt Sinai, where according to the Abrahamic faiths, Moses received the Ten Commandments. Now located in modern Egypt, there are two main paths up the 8625ft (2629m) mountain: the traditional Steps of Penitence, a 3750-step staircase favoured by hardcore pilgrims, or a longer but easier path that's mainly used by camel trekkers. Both start at the 6th-century Monastery of St Catherine, before diverging and converging again on the natural amphitheatre known as Elijah's Hollow, where you can have a cup of tea before tackling the final 750 steps to the summit. Holy revelations might not be guaranteed at the summit, but you will be treated to a cracking sunrise.
Start/End // Monastery of St Catherine
Distance // 9 miles (14km) round trip
More info // www.egypt.travel

COAST TO COAST ON HADRIAN'S WALL

*Through Cumbrian countryside and over Northumbrian crags, this UK cross-country route
follows the remains of the northernmost frontier of the Roman Empire: Hadrian's Wall.*

Sunset. First it is a fading yellow, then a burning orange.
The sun dips below the horizon – a series of grassy
bluffs fronting dolerite crags – and suddenly everything
is a shade of hot pink I've never seen before. I sit at an
outdoor table at the Milecastle Inn (the only building for miles
around) and slowly empty my pint glass of warmish best bitter,
shiver gently into my fleece, stand and employ groaning feet.
Evening falls late and resplendent over Cawfields on day four of
my hike along Hadrian's Wall.

The first three days are a walk out of Bowness-on-Solway – a
tiny village set beside the Solway Firth, an inlet of the Irish Sea

that marks the border between England and Scotland – and into
the undulating green countryside of Cumbria. This is everything
you want a walk in England to be: grass-strewn paths, sometimes
muddy and always sprinkled with daisies and buttercups, fields
full of sheep, teetering farmhouses and hills that seem to roll off
into a dreaming sky. Further on, crossing into Northumberland, the
land becomes less tame, treeless fields climb into craggy cliffs,
above them swirling clouds that might, and very probably will,
keep you gently soaked.

Hadrian's Wall National Trail is an 84-mile (135km) signposted
path that follows alongside the stone and earthen remains of

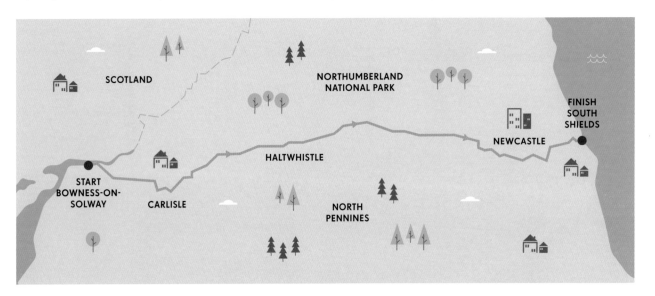

the northernmost frontier of the Roman empire – the emperor Hadrian's final defence against invading northern tribes. Many hikers opt to tackle this route from east to west, primarily because that is the direction in which the wall was built, starting in AD 122. If you want to walk in the footsteps of a Roman foot soldier, you begin at Segedunum, the original fort outside of Newcastle-upon-Tyne, and head west.

I've opted to walk the opposite way to take advantage of prevailing weather patterns. Starting in Bowness-on-Solway and heading east means you'll usually have the wind and rain at your back and you're not squinting into the lowering sun all afternoon. I also have an additional motive: I've decided to make this into a coast-to-coast walk, with the aim of finishing on the sandy shores of the North Sea at South Shields. To splash my aching feet in frigid sea waters at the end of a 97-mile (156km) walking journey is too enticing a prospect to pass up.

It will take me nine days altogether to complete this hike. Though some walkers do it in fewer days, I prefer to go at a leisurely pace and want to explore the incredible wealth of sights along the way, a large portion of which was listed as a Unesco World Heritage Site in 1987. The route is dotted with the ruins of giant forts, such as Housesteads, which at its peak was home to about 800 Roman soldiers. There are some great ancient toilets on display here as well. Eighty smaller fortlets, known as milecastles (literally Roman mile markers) punctuate the distances along the wall, alongside which you stride for much of this hike. And then there is the Vallum – a mound-flanked ditch that provides constant companionship and, in some places, is the only evidence of Roman activity left.

This isn't a camper's walk. Wild camping is illegal in most of England and Hadrian's Wall is an archaeological site, largely unexcavated, that demands to be both respected and preserved. Plus, accommodation is part of the joy of walking in this part of the world. The whole Hadrian's Wall National Trail is well lined with guesthouses, B&Bs and bunkhouses, so all budgets can be catered for. Many hikers also opt to have their luggage transferred from inn to inn each day, carrying only necessaries in a daypack.

On my third night on the wall, I splash out for a well-appointed bed and breakfast in Gilsland, and meet two English brothers and a Canadian couple who are walking in the other direction. Despite a notable age gap (I am the youngest here by 20 years), we all bond over the inn's honesty bar – local craft ales, wine and chocolates are treats for all walkers once boots are off and wet things hung. The atmosphere gets rosy, fish and then sticky toffee pudding are served, another glass of wine, laughter, and finally falling full, happy and a little sore into bed. Later, I creep down creaking stairs wrapped in a blanket and sit on an iron bench in the garden gazing up at the Milky Way's array splashed overhead. Northumberland National Park is a designated dark-sky preserve, and when the clouds part here, the night sky does not disappoint.

It is a strange and wondrous thing to experience a city for the first time by walking into it on foot. Days eight and nine of this walk

THE VALLUM

Along several portions of the trail, the Vallum is the only evidence of the wall's existence that remains. The Romans dug this earthwork, essentially a big ditch with mounds on either side, along the whole length of the wall's south side. In most places, the ditch is about 20ft (6m) wide, while the mounds rise up to 7ft (2m) high. Though the exact purpose of the Vallum remains unclear, many believe it provided a southern military boundary that allowed greater defence of the wall.

Clockwise from top: putting boot to turf at Milecastle 39, or Castle Nick; Northumberland's Sycamore Gap; the Roman fort of Housesteads. Previous page: Hadrian's Wall stretching west from Kings Hill

"To walk Hadrian's Wall is to make a stride-by-stride journey through lands that seem untamed by the march of history"

offer a fascinating, if not jarring, re-entry into urban life, watching the sprawl of Newcastle-upon-Tyne unfold house by house and suburban street by suburban street. The rolling farmland around East Wallhouses gives way to scattered stone villages. The path dips down next to the River Tyne, you start counting the seven bridges that span the river here, and suddenly you are surrounded by zooming cars and hurried workers and hip restaurants. A step-by-step study in human evolution.

On my final day, I spend hours crossing suburban pavements before reaching the Shields Ferry; the seven-minute boat ride across the Tyne is the only non-foot-based transport I take on the whole journey. Then, a final bewildering walk up the busy, pub-lined high street in the seaside suburb of South Shields.

Seawater. A glint off a wave, a shimmering grey undulation. I pound up over a small bank of sand dunes tufted with dry grass and here is the ocean. For days, I have been soaking in endless views of green-meets-cloud, huffing and puffing up rock faces and dodging sheep piles and puddles. Now, I flick off shoes and let foamy waves rush over my feet for an uncountable number of minutes. I crack open a can of Flash House Pale Ale procured in Newcastle's still-working Victorian market a day earlier and breathe in the salt air.

To walk Hadrian's Wall is to make a stride-by-stride journey through lands that somehow seem untamed despite the march of history across them. A chance to walk across England for a glimpse of just how wild yet welcoming this ancient country can be. **ME**

ORIENTATION

Start // Bowness-on-Solway
End // South Shields (coast-to-coast) or Segedunum (official trail)
Distance // 97 miles (156km) coast-to-coast; 84 miles (135km) official trail
Getting there // Carlisle and Newcastle are a three-to-four-hour train journey from London. International flights arrive in Manchester, Glasgow and Edinburgh. Bus 93 and taxis (£30) connect Carlisle to Bowness-on-Solway; Newcastle metro reaches South Shields.
When to go // May to October.
Where to stay // Florrie's Bunkhouse (florriesonthewall. co.uk), the Sill (www.yha.org.uk/hostel/sill-hadrians-wall), Robin Hood Inn (www.robinhoodinnhadrianswall.com).
What to take // Rainproof everything. OS maps 315, OL43 and 316, light snacks, water, blister kit.
More info // www.nationaltrail.co.uk/hadrians-wall-path.

MORE LIKE THIS
COAST-TO-COAST HIKES

WAINWRIGHT'S COAST TO COAST, NORTHERN ENGLAND

This long-distance walking trail was devised by legendary hillwalker Arthur Wainwright in the 1970s and remains the most popular coast-to-coast walk in Britain. Generally hiked in 12–15 days, the trail connects the Irish Sea in the west with the North Sea in the east. It crosses through three national parks – the Lake District, the Yorkshire Dales and the North York Moors – on its journey across England. Though unofficial, the trail is well trodden and generally signposted. The landscapes a walker encounters on this journey are truly epic, from the windswept crags and fells of the Lake District to the upland tarns and waterfalls of the moors and dales and finally the sweeping coast at Robin Hood's Bay.

Start // St Bees
End // Robin Hood's Bay
Distance // 190 miles (305km)

TRANSCONTINENTAL RAINFOREST TREK, COSTA RICA

Making its way from Quepos to Cahuita, this is possibly the only hiking option that allows you to cross the entire North American continent without a truly significant time investment. There are a few different routes that cross Costa Rica's wild interior, generally starting at the Pacific and trekking east to the Caribbean coast. Along the way, you traverse volcanoes, jungle, cloud forests, waterfalls and hidden pools and might spot some of the country's incredible diversity of wildlife, including monkeys, reptiles and exotic insects. This is not a trek that can be undertaken without a guide. In addition to the wild landscapes, several of the routes cross indigenous lands and may require a permit. However, plenty of outfitters offer guided treks that can also incorporate cycling, kayaking, canyoning and other adventurous endeavours.

Start // Quepos
End // Cahuita
Distance // 70 miles (112km)

E4 TRAIL, CYPRUS

The final section of the famous E4 long-distance path, which traverses Europe, crosses the Greek side of Cyprus, taking in much of the island's south. Along the way, the trail passes through some of the most stunning Cypriot landscapes and intriguing historic sites imaginable. Byzantine monasteries nestled in the Troodos Mountains, the island's highest peak – Mt Olympus (not the famous one), the mythic pools where Aphrodite is said to have bathed, the tunnel gorges of the Akamas Peninsula. Due to its length, only extremely fit walkers with an excess of time hike the whole thing in one go, but the fact that the trail is bookended by international airports eases access greatly and allows walkers to dip in and out. Starting from Larnaka in the east, you can spend several days hiking to Larnaka Salt Lake and through the cypress groves of Rizoelia National Forest Park. Or from Pafos in the west, the Akamas sea caves and gorges, and Aphrodite's baths are easily accessible.

Start // Larnaka
End // Pafos
Distance // 397 miles (640km)

*Clockwise from top: Costa Rica's
Arenal volcano; poison dart frogs
inhabit the country's interior; the Rio
Celeste just adds to the fine scenery*

WALKING HISTORY: THE LYCIAN WAY

Linking ruined Mediterranean cities once inhabited by the ancient Lycians, the Lycian Way runs from Turkey's golden beaches and seaside towns to hill villages and mountainous hinterland.

As I wandered out of the fishing village of Üçağız, the locals were just starting to go about their business after their ritual Turkish breakfast. No dallying and just a quick wave to the early birds outside the teahouse, as I was keen to put a few miles of Mediterranean coastline behind me before the freshness of the spring morning melted away. The next village on the Teke Peninsula, the bulge of beaches and holiday towns backed by the olive-grove-dotted foothills of the Western Taurus Mountains, was only accessible by foot or boat. Named after the Byzantine *kale* (castle) overlooking its handful of houses, Kaleköy promised to be well worth the 2.5-mile (4km) walk.

This was a small, but typically scenic, section of the Lycian Way, the 335-mile (540km), 29-day waymarked footpath that follows the Teke Peninsula between the tourist towns of Fethiye and Antalya, skirting the coast and climbing into the rugged back country en route. Ascending a rocky track through the Mediterranean scrub, I was soon overlooking a cerulean bay broken by the undulating outlines of islands and peninsulas. Reaching a boat-building yard, where wooden *gület* yachts were under repair for the coming summer, I climbed a footpath towards the castle and emerged on a ridge studded with towering Lycian tombs, with more emerging from the shallows of the bay below.

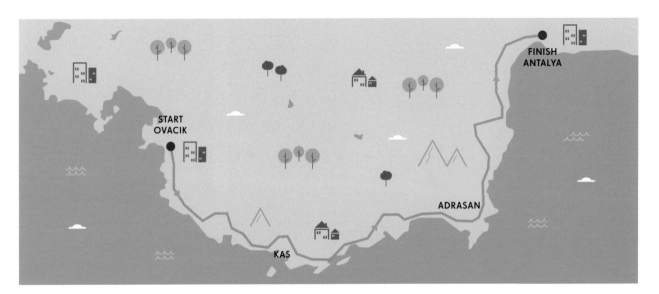

FINISH
ANTALYA

START
OVACIK

ADRASAN

KAS

Across the bay was the island of Kekova, fringed by the underwater ruins of the Lycian city of Simena, which was submerged by earthquakes around two millennia ago. After enjoying a meze lunch on a *pensione* terrace, a local fisherman ferried me across to take a closer look at the Batık Sehir (Sunken City). The smashed amphorae, building foundations and staircases disappearing into the blue depths exemplified the Lycian Way's appeal of discovering spellbinding ancient history in a wild Mediterranean setting.

The footpath was researched, designed and waymarked by British amateur historian Kate Clow in the late 1990s. Aiming to identify and protect Turkey's ancient byways, and to offer a journey back through the millennia to the Mediterranean in the time of Lycia, Clow entered a competition run by a Turkish bank. Winning the competition and a grant, she spent years exploring this sublimely beautiful part of Turkey and bringing local hill farmers round to her envisioned trail and the benefits of tourism. The path is now one of a dozen walking, cycling and horse-riding routes marked and maintained by the Culture Routes Society, and it remains Turkey's original and most popular long-distance trail.

True to the Lycian Way's spirit of discovering this region rather than rigidly following a set route, the trail offers many possible detours, extensions and variations as it crosses the ancient territory of the mysterious Lycians. First mentioned in Homer's *Iliad*, the Lycians inhabited this part of Anatolia from at least three millennia ago, and were likely descended from the Lukka mentioned in ancient Hittite texts. Their high point was the Lycian League, a loose confederation of some 25 city states, often credited with being history's first proto-democratic union. The trail wends its way past the key remnants of the League, which was formed around 165 BC and absorbed by the Roman Empire two centuries later. The moss-covered ancient ruins on the route include Letoön, a religious sanctuary dedicated to Zeus' lover Leto, the national deity of Lycia; the Roman theatre and pillar tombs at Xanthos, the grand Lycian capital until Brutus attacked in 42 BC and the inhabitants committed mass suicide; and Patara, where a meadow strewn with Lycian ruins, including a 5000-seat theatre and a colonnaded street, leads to Turkey's longest interrupted beach. The League debated public issues in Patara's bouleuterion, or council chamber, which is often cited as the world's first parliament.

As much as history, the trail's appeal lies in its mix of romantic ruins and Mediterranean scenery with the comforts of whitewashed harbour towns such as Kas and Kalkan, where hikers enjoy well-earned fish and meze feasts. A favourite chill-out spot along the way was Kabak, another village with limited access, reached only by foot or high-clearance vehicle down steep forest tracks. The valley's traditional industries of farming and bee-keeping have been joined by a handful of new-age retreats offering rustic cabins, morning yoga and terrace restaurants with sea views. It was a wonderful place to relax after braving the rope-assisted path up from the beach at the foot of Butterfly Valley's sheer cliffs.

BURIED TREASURES

The Lycians' distinctive cliff tombs, 'house' tombs, sepulchres and sarcophagi pepper the area's bays, fields and mountainsides, adding further lyricism to the scenery. Good examples include Fethiye's Tomb of Amyntas dating to 350 BC, with its temple facade carved into the cliffs above town; Kaleköy's 'house' tombs rising mythically from the bay; the 4th-century-BC King's Tomb, with two lion heads on its lid, in Kas old town; and Myra's honeycomb of rock tombs, climbing the cliff outside present-day Demre.

Clockwise from top: rocky terrain on the Lycian Way; ancient ruins of Xanthos near Kalkan; contemplating that descent to the beach. Previous page: surveying the coastline en route

© Sevdin | Shutterstock, © Mark Read | Lonely Planet

"The trail's appeal lies in its mix of romantic ruins, Mediterranean scenery and the comforts of whitewashed harbour towns"

Named after its population of colourful Jersey tiger moths, Butterfly Valley is typical of the natural wonders on the trail, which also takes in the legendary Chimaera. This cluster of naturally occurring mountainside flames, attributed by the Lycians to the breath of a terrible lion-goat-snake monster, should be visited after dark for maximum impact. You can easily hike up there from Olympos, where the ruined 2nd-century-BC city leading to the beach was once inhabited by Lycian worshippers of Hephaestus (or Vulcan, god of fire). Today, Olympos is equally famous for its 'tree house' camps, where hikers enjoy hammock time and campfire camaraderie while staying in the misnamed cabins, few of which are above terra firma.

For me, another surprise was Kayaköy, a village marked more by the 20th century than the Lycians, with its ruined 'ghost town' of Levissi created by post-WWI population exchanges between Turkey and Greece. The inspiration for Louis de Bernières' novel *Birds Without Wings*, hillside Levissi was abandoned by its Ottoman Greek inhabitants and never repopulated, leaving eerie streets composed of crumbling stone houses, churches and a castle overlooking modern Kayaköy.

Other walkers I met on the trail enthused about camping in olive groves, sharing their picnic with a Turkish farmer or feasting on a home-cooked meal in a village *pensione* – just a few of the memorable encounters and surprises that await on Turkey's Mediterranean byways. **JB**

ORIENTATION

Start // Ovacık (between Fethiye and Ölüdeniz)
End // Antalya
Distance // 335 miles (540km)
Getting there // Regular buses and local dolmus minibuses ply the coastal D400 highway between Fethiye, 28 miles (45km) east of Dalaman International Airport, and Antalya International Airport.
When to go // Clement temperatures make spring (Mar–May) and autumn (Sep–Nov) the best.
More info // Kate Clow's *Lycian Way* guidebook is available, along with hiking maps, through Trekking in Turkey (http://trekkinginturkey.com). An app can be downloaded from the iTunes Store and you can visit the Culture Routes Society (http://cultureroutesinturkey.com) office in Antalya.
Things to know // Pack light, though helpful guesthouse owners will often drive your bags to your next stop.

Opposite, clockwise from top: the Durdle Door limestone arch on England's Jurassic Coast; a South African dassie; surveying Portugal's wild coastline

MORE LIKE THIS
COASTAL WALKS

OTTER TRAIL, SOUTH AFRICA

South Africa's most famous long-distance hiking trail is a challenging five-day coastal route through the Tsitsikamma section of the Garden Route National Park. Walking up to 9 miles (14km) per day between the frugal huts, hikers cross beaches, ford rivers and climb to the clifftops, with the reward of experiencing Tsitsikamma's pristine coastline, old-growth forests and sightings of whales and dolphins. This is a one-way trail, walked in a westerly direction only, which means that you really get a sense of crossing the finish line when you reach the quaint hamlet and lagoon-backed beach at Nature's Valley. Indeed, it has become a ritual for hikers to hang their smelly boots and champagne empties from the tree in the Nature's Valley Trading Store beer garden.
**Start // Storm's River Mouth Rest Camp
End // Nature's Valley
Distance // 28 miles (45km)
More info // Book with South African National Parks (www.sanparks.org) at least six months ahead. Hiking Trail Transfers (www.ottertrailtransfers. co.za) can ferry you back to your car**

SOUTH WEST COAST PATH, UK

England's longest waymarked footpath, and the longest of the UK's 16 National Routes, follows the beautiful coastline of the island's southwestern-most peninsula. Hikers planning to tackle its entirety, from Minehead in Somerset through the quaint towns and geologically rich coastline of Cornwall and Devon to Poole Harbour in Dorset, are advised to allow at least a month. Twice that time is recommended if you want to walk at a leisurely pace and linger over the views – and cream teas – in spots such as Bigbury-on-Sea, where Agatha Christie penned her crime novels in the art deco hotel on Burgh Island. With 22 miles (35km) of ups and downs, hiking this epic trail is equivalent to scaling Mt Everest four times, and it will eventually form part of the 2700-mile (4345km) England Coast Path, which will be the world's longest coastal footpath.
**Start/End // Minehead, Somerset and Poole Harbour, Dorset
Distance // 630 miles (1014km)
More info // www.southwestcoastpath. org.uk**

ROTA VICENTINA, PORTUGAL

Rota Vicentina is a network of trails, including the Historical Way, the Fishermen's Trail and several circular routes, on Portugal's wild Costa Vicentina, which runs south to Cabo de São Vicente, Europe's southwestern-most point. Offering glimpses of both unspoilt rural Portuguese culture and one of Europe's best-preserved stretches of coastline, the trails cross the Parque Natural do Sudoeste Alentejano e Costa Vicentina with its stratified cliffs and surf beaches. Sticking closest to the coast, the 75-mile (120km) Fishermen's Trail follows the paths used by locals to reach the best beaches and fishing spots, while the 143-mile (230km) Historical Way focuses instead on the region's historical towns and villages.
**Start/End // Santiago do Cacém & Cabo de São Vicente
Distance // 280 miles (450km) (network total)
More info // en.rotavicentina.com**

GODLY WAYS: IL SENTIERO DEGLI DEI

Follow the Path of the Gods along Italy's awesome Amalfi Coast, a cliff-hugging hike via siren-haunted isles, ancient vineyards and glittering sea views.

The limestone crags of the Monti Lattari poke into a deep-blue sky. Sure-footed goats graze on herby pastures, far from bothered by the verdurous, vertiginous valleys on all sides of them. And, over by the side of the kerb, a film crew zooms in on a testosterone-red Ferrari that's noisily negotiating the tarmac curves.

Well, this is the Amalfi Coast, after all. Glamour central. A place of 50s beauties in cats'-eye shades and tanned Adonises all loose trousers and louche charm. An Italian sports car fits right in. But, actually, automobiles of any type are a relatively recent feature here. Until 1815, when Ferdinand II of Bourbon ordered the construction of the Nastro Azzurro (Blue Ribbon), there was no road access to the remote hamlets and tiny fishing villages clinging around these cliffs. Before that, the only way to get between them was to walk. The irony is that, now that human highways have conquered the headlands, what do many of us visitors choose to do? We go old-school and use our feet.

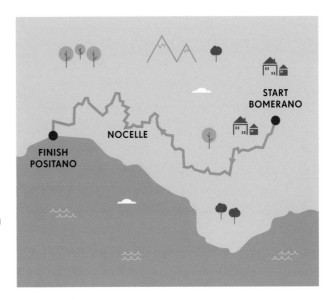

"There's a small, vertigo-inclined part of me that feels an urge to leap for the islands... perhaps the sirens do still sing?"

People have long been drawn to the wildly wonderful Amalfi Coast. Greeks, Romans, Normans, Saracens, Arab-Sicilians and more have left their traces. But for millennia, visitors and settlers alike were reliant on boats or a steep network of footpaths and mule tracks to get around; their grape, olive and lemon harvests had to be hand-carried up staircases hewn from the stone. The Sentiero degli Dei – Path of the Gods – is the most famed of these old farmers' trails, running for around 5 miles (8km) between the hamlets of Bomerano and Nocelle, then onwards to the seaside resort of Positano. And when you don't have to carry a huge basket of fruit on your head, it's the most spectacular of strolls.

Having taken the slow road over the mountains, I arrive in Bomerano. This tiny village sits in Agerola, a district famed for its *fior di latte*, a fresh, sourish mozzarella made from the milk of the local cows. With a short but undulating task ahead, I pop into the little *salumeria* by the church to pick up some fresh focaccia and balls of the smooth white cheese, in case I happen to get peckish.

Leaving the piazza, I weave through the narrow streets to find the trailhead sign: 'Benvenuti sul Sentiero degli Dei'. Immediately ahead the coast unfurls; in both directions great grey dolomitic rock surges up from the dazzling sea. It's rugged and raw, yet somehow has been semi-tamed: farming terraces cut into the sheer slopes, farmhouses perch, paths wriggle. It's an incredible combination of Mother Nature and human tenacity. A case in

point: right here is the Grotta del Biscotto, where strange, rust-like geological formations sit alongside the ruins of ancient dwellings embedded in the walls.

I turn to the west, sun on my back, and let Amalfi work its magic. The trail is mostly downhill in this direction – a descent from Bomerano (at around 1903ft, or 580m) to sea-level Positano – but concentration is required. Some parts are narrow, dropping off to the waves. Some require scrambling. Virtually all is rough and uneven. But the rewards are unending. A peregrine falcon hovers above, trained on some unsuspecting prey; when the raptor finally makes its dive I hear the swoosh of its lightning-quick wings. There are deep-green gullies cloaked in holm oaks, pungent thyme and sweet wild roses. There are teetering vineyards, some cultivating gnarled *ped'e palomma*, Campania's oldest grape variety. And there are farmhouses balanced on improbable precipices, surely reliant on the trail's titular gods for their continued survival.

In the distance, the chi-chi island of Capri provides the dot of the Amalfi Coast's exclamation mark. Nearer though, the glittering blue is broken by a smaller scatter of offshore rocks – the Sirenusas. According to Greek myth, this archipelago was once inhabited by sirens, dangerous bird-women whose beautiful music lured sailors to their deaths. I strain to listen, and do hear a melody. I'm fairly sure it's just the birds, but there's a small, vertigo-inclined part of me that feels an urge to leap for the islands, to

WHEN LIFE GIVES YOU LEMONS

The Amalfi lemon (*Sfusato Amalfitano*) has Protected Geographical Indication status and is known for its flavoursome rind, lack of bitterness and sweet aroma. When scurvy-beating lemons became compulsory for sailors in the late 18th century, Amalfi farmers hacked out cliff terraces to cope with demand. Now, with a decline in the skilled farmers who maintain the groves, the landscape's integrity is at risk.

From left: looking towards Positano and Capri from the Path of the Gods; fishermen discuss the day's catch; famed Amalfi lemons. Previous page: colourful homes on the Positano hillside

dive off this cliff and plummet down into the sea. Perhaps the sirens do still sing?

Far below, the white pumice-stone houses of Praiano are stacked on the slopes. There are trails that detour down there, but I continue over the rock crags, relishing occasional forest shade but largely at the mercy of the Mediterranean sun. There are plenty of other walkers – families, route-marchers, red-faced tourists in inappropriate footwear. We're all equally bewitched by the view.

I pause in Nocelle for my picnic, gazing out to sea just as the coastguards once did. At around 1312ft (400m), the village was an ideal vantage point for spotting pirate ships. Today it passes its time in sleepy fashion; there's little more here than a family trattoria and a muss of broom bushes, vineyards and lemon groves growing the Amalfi citruses craved by chefs worldwide.

Nocelle is technically the end of the Sentiero degli Dei, and you can catch a bus from here to Positano. But, feeling some loyalty to the hardy forebears who had no choice, I walk down instead, a thigh-jellying descent of 1,700 steps to reach the Mediterranean.

Standing in the harbour, I turn to look back at the houses of Positano, themselves rippling wave-like down the cliffs in a palette of lemon-yellow, pale peach and bold terracotta. I shift my gaze further up to pick out the path whence I came. And I raise my eyes higher still, to where the mountaintops meet the sky, and where the gods surely must be smiling down on this walk. **SB**

ORIENTATION

Start // Bomerano
End // Positano (or Nocelle)
Distance // 5 miles (8km)

Getting there // Naples airport is 29 miles (47km) from Bomerano, a hamlet of the Agerola district. Buses run from Amalfi to Agerola; journey time is around two hours. Buses from Positano back to Amalfi take one hour. Private transfers are possible but expensive for individuals.

What to wear // T-shirt, shorts and sensible shoes. A warm layer and waterproof, just in case. A sun hat is essential.

When to go // April to June and September to October are quieter and cooler than peak summer months.

What to take // A head for heights. Sunscreen and water.

Need to know // The route is waymarked by white-and-red '02' signs. A guide is not necessary but can be arranged.

MORE LIKE THIS
ITALIAN COASTAL WALKS

CINQUE TERRE HIGH TRAIL, LIGURIA

The oh-so-picturesque medieval fishing villages of the Cinque Terre ('Five Lands') tumble down the cliffs of the Ligurian Riviera, seemingly detached from the rest of the world. A network of centuries-old coast paths links them, the most popular of which is the 7.5-mile (12km) Sentiero Azzurro (Blue Trail). However, a tougher but less-trodden option is the High Path No1, which takes a loftier route above Monterosso al Mare, Vernazza, Corniglia, Manarola and Riomaggiore, offering sea-glittery views throughout. Going from south to north, the trail starts in the harbour town of Porto Venere and follows the coastal range, running via fragrant pine, leafy vineyards and tiny hamlets to Levanto. A highlight is reaching the Sella di Punta Mesco, from where you can look out over all five villages at once.
Start // Porto Venere
End // Levanto
Distance // 25 miles (40km)

TRAIL OF THE FOUR BEACHES, PUGLIA

The Sentiero delle Quattro Spiagge (Trail of the Four Beaches) traces the edges of the wild Gargano Peninsula, a promontory of limestone cliffs, secret grottoes, aged forests and almond and olive groves protected within a national park in Italy's lesser-visited heel. From the pretty little seaside resort of Mattinata the path leads northwards via bird-rich valleys, high cliffs fuzzed by pungent pine, a 1476ft (450m) lookout and a succession of beautiful coves where it's virtually impossible not to leap into the crystal-clear waters. You'll definitely want to pause at the Baia dei Mergoli, a bay that is sweetly scented by citrus groves and hugged by sheer white cliffs; a precarious-looking rock arch sits just offshore, daring you to swim through...
Start // Mattinata
End // Vignanotica Bay
Distance // 13 miles (21km)

STROMBOLI CLIMB, AEOLIAN ISLANDS, SICILY

Stromboli is like a big black beast breathing fire and fury in the middle of the Tyrrhenian Sea. Indeed, this super-active 3031ft (924m) volcano-island has been erupting almost continuously for around 2000 years. Miraculously, you're still permitted to climb it, as long as you join a guided group. Trips up its ashen flanks usually leave late afternoon or early evening to ensure that you arrive at the summit in time to see a spectacular sunset sinking into the sea. It also means you're in time to appreciate the full effects of Stromboli's impressive red-hot magma-spewing pyrotechnics against the darkening sky. The descent is then completed by head-torch, lunar glow, star twinkle and the lights of the Italian mainland dancing across the waves.
Start/End // Stromboli town
Distance // 5 miles (8km)

From top: Riomaggiore, one of the Cinque Terre; curious coastal rocks in Puglia

THE FOURTEEN PEAKS OF SNOWDONIA

Climbing all of Wales's 3000ft (914m) peaks in a day is an unforgettable challenge, but spreading them over a long weekend reveals the real beauty of Snowdonia.

t's a mountain...it can't just vanish!'

Somewhere behind the inky curtain of night lies the summit of 3090ft (942m) Foel-fras, our finishing line for one of the UK's toughest mountain routes. But after 14 hours of walking, the area of our brains responsible for navigation seem to have entirely shut down.

'We're not lost,' insists one of our trio, 'we're just momentarily misplaced...'

Our day started on Snowdon, Wales's highest mountain, inching along one of its most famous ridges as sunrise turned the sky a succulent crimson. The intervening 23 miles (37km) have been a blur of boulder-strewn plateaux, canyon-like descents and twinkling mountain lakes. We finally stumble into the chest-high plinth that marks the summit of our 14th peak, more by luck than by judgement, as rain starts to fall.

Someone pulls a mini-bottle of champagne from their rucksack, backs are slapped, congratulations offered and we hobble down to the car on legs that have racked up a brutal 11,975ft (3650m) of ascent since dawn. As we are greeted by our 'support team' (Alun's wife, wielding a Thermos flask of hot tea) I'm left with a nagging feeling that mountain athleticism hasn't left a great deal of space for aesthetic appreciation.

But there is a more immersive way to explore the Welsh 3000ers. Spread the route over a long weekend and you can dedicate a day to each of the mountain massifs that make up Snowdonia National Park: the remote peaks of the Carneddau, the mythical granite architecture of the Glyderau and the rock-star appeal of Snowdon.

So one late summer's evening, we spread the map out next to the fire in Rowen Youth Hostel looking for not the fastest, but the

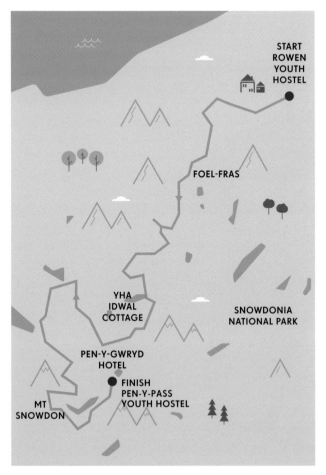

most appealing route across Snowdonia. This time we'd be starting in the north, devoting the whole of our first day to the imposing Carneddau mountains, where Foel-fras would be our first summit.

It's an area rich in wildlife, from dwarf willow (the world's smallest tree) and the carnivorous sundew plant to the wild ponies that graze these isolated hills, and the peregrines flying overhead. But we didn't see a single walker until we were finally climbing the flanks of the 3484ft (1062m) Carnedd Llewelyn. Surrounded by incredible cliff-faces, there are so many possible routes and diversions that you could dedicate an entire weekend to this mountain alone. An out-and-back was required to pick off the shapely summit of 3156ft (962m) Yr Elen, with its grandstand seat of some of the most impressive mountain scenery in North Wales.

The sun was shining as we dropped towards Carnedd Dafydd, with clouds skidding overhead slicing through the clear mountain air. 'Where are all the other walkers?' asked Ben. The Carneddau are almost criminally overlooked, but they deliver a hint of wilderness that's difficult to find in Britain.

By the time we made the summit of 3209ft (978m) Pen yr Ole Wen, our final tick of the day, it was getting dark. We could see Idwal Cottage YHA below us – our stop for the night – and decided to make a direct descent over ankle-busting slopes.

"The ethereal rock formation known as Castell y Gwynt (Castle of the Winds) loomed out of the mist"

Day two started with the shark's-fin peak of 3012ft (918m) Tryfan, an ascent that requires a head for heights and the ability to find your way through maze-like routes to the top. It's a Grade One scramble to the summit, which means you'll need some basic climbing moves to get there. This area is a training route for fighter pilots, and within half an hour we'd gained enough height to look down into their cockpits as they zipped through the Ogwen Valley.

From Tryfan's twin summit rock pillars, known as Adam and Eve, we dropped down its south side to pick up Bristly Ridge, a cavernous, Mordor-like scramble to the top of 3261ft (994m) Glyder Fach, where the ethereal rock formation known as Castell y Gwynt (Castle of the Winds) loomed out of the mist.

At 3284ft (1001m) Glyder Fawr was the highest summit of the day and navigationally our most difficult point. But we were soon basking in the sunlight again as we cruised over the marginally more diminutive 3106ft (947m) Y Garn and 3031ft (924m) 'Electric Mountain' Elidir Fawr, which has a power station below its flanks.

HEADS FOR HEIGHTS

Snowdon was the training ground for the expedition that took Edmund Hillary and Tenzing Norgay to the summit of Mt Everest in 1953. The team stayed in the Pen-y-Gwryd Hotel, which has become a place of pilgrimage for mountaineers. A small glass cabinet in the bar displays memorabilia from their expedition, including climbing rope, boots, oxygen tanks, prayer flags and a Peruvian shrunken head.

From left: setting up shelter for the night in Snowdonia; gazing out from 3261ft (994m) Glyder Fach. Previous page: the mountains of Snowdonia National Park

The crowds were out on our final day as we set out from Pen-y-Pass Youth Hostel to climb to the summit of the big one, 3560ft (1085m) Snowdon. We left the walkers at Bwlch y Moch to climb up Crib Goch – the infamous knife-edge ridge that requires some serious scrambling skills. You can happily bypass it and follow the crowds to the summit, but this ridge offers exposure and excitement for those who have the right experience. The wind was whipping up as we reached the top and shinned across *à cheval* (with legs either side of the ridge); in mountaineering terms it wasn't pretty, but it finally brought us to the path that runs alongside the train line to the top.

After the peace of the Carneddau, the summit crowds on Snowdon – a mixture of walkers and day-trippers clutching return train tickets – came as something of a shock. But by dropping just a few metres from the summit cafe towards Y Lliwedd we found mountain serenity once again on a small rocky ledge.

And although we'd ticked off all the Welsh 3000ers, our day was far from over. By descending over Y Lliwedd we would also complete the Snowdon Horseshoe (one of the UK's favourite routes) and be able to celebrate at the Pen-y-Gwryd, a hotel rich in mountaineering history and the perfect end to our mountain pilgrimage. **MS**

ORIENTATION

Start // Rowen YHA
Finish // Pen-y-Pass YHA
Distance // 33 miles (55km)
Getting there // Trains run to Conwy Rail station, from where the Betws-y-Coed bus runs to Caer Rhun Hall. The Rowen YHA is 2.4 miles (3.9km) from there.
When to go // Summer months when days are long.
Where to stay // Youth Hostels at Rowen, Idwal Cottage and Pen-y-Pass (www.yha.org.uk).
What to wear // Good hill-walking kit including waterproofs, spare food, head-torch, map and compass.
What to take // Lots of food, water, spare gloves and hat.
Things to know // Weather here changes quickly. Check the forecast but be ready for all conditions. This route is unmarked so ensure you're able to navigate in poor visibility.

Fourteen Peaks of Snowdonia

Opposite: catching a breath next to Hound Tor, one of wild Dartmoor's granite formations

MORE LIKE THIS
UK CHALLENGE WALKS

YORKSHIRE THREE PEAKS

There are two walks in the UK that people associate with the term 'three peaks'. One involves climbing the highest summits of each mainland nation: Ben Nevis, Scafell Pike and Snowdon, but it requires almost as much time on the motorway as it does on the peaks. The Yorkshire Three Peaks is a much more wholesome affair: a 23-mile (37km) walk over 2415ft (736m) Whernside, 2372ft (723m) Ingleborough and 2277ft (694m) Pen-y-ghent that allows you to really savour these beautiful and distinctive mountains. The route traditionally starts at Horton-in-Ribblesdale where people can literally clock in at the Pen-y-ghent cafe. The walk is a great way of exploring the Yorkshire Dales, but pedants like to point out that the actual summit of Whernside lies in the neighbouring county of Cumbria. Those who complete the route in under 12 hours are invited to join the 'Three Peaks of Yorkshire' club.
Start/End // Horton-in-Ribblesdale
Distance // 23-26 miles (37.5-42km)

CAIRNGORMS 4000ERS

There are nine mountains higher than 4000ft (1219m) in Scotland and the Cairngorms National Park is home to five of them, two on one side of the Lairig Ghru pass and three on the other. Buses run to the ski centre from nearby Aviemore and from there it's a relatively easy climb up on to the wild arctic plateau that holds the summits of 4085ft (1245m) Cairn Gorm and 4295ft (1309m) Ben MacDui. Dropping down into the Lairig Ghru you then need to climb to the summit of Cairn Toul (4235ft/1291m) for a very different mountain experience that leads you to the 4127ft (1258m) Angel's Peak and the mighty Braeriach (4252ft/1296m). You can split the route into a two-day trip with a free overnight stay in the Corrour Bothy or the far less 'salubrious' Garbh Choire Refuge. Feeling really athletic? Then cycle the 65 miles (105km) to Fort William to walk Scotland's remaining four 4000ft (1219ft) peaks, including 4413ft (1345m) Ben Nevis.
Start/End // Cairngorm ski centre car park
Distance // 21 miles (34km)

TEN TORS, DARTMOOR

Dartmoor is a slice of wilderness tucked into the southwest corner of Great Britain, packed with ancient stone circles, boggy moorland and granite-topped hills. Every year groups of young explorers take on the Ten Tors, a two-day challenge to navigate between 10 of these granite tors. It's the only place in England where you are legally entitled to wildcamp, so you can create your own two-day challenge by unfurling a map and picking 10 tors for your route. The best option is to start at Okehampton, home of the official challenge (which sees groups do routes of 35–55 miles/56–86km), where you can quickly tick off the highest peak, 2037ft (621m) High Willhays. Don't be overly ambitious: walking on Dartmoor can be deceptively demanding, and you should take time to appreciate the different character of each tor, ancient Bronze Age settlements and such magical treasures as Whistman's Wood, just north of Two Bridges.
Start/End // Okehampton camp
Distance // Minimum official route is 35 miles (then 45 or 55 miles) (56km, 72km, 89km)

FOUR DAYS ON THE ALPINE PASS ROUTE

Explore the glorious vistas of Switzerland, a country that's almost a byword for mountains and hiking, and walk in the gravitational pull of some of the world's most famous peaks.

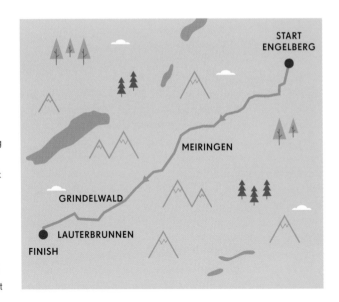

O n the Alpine slopes above Engelberg, the marmots are whistling while they work, but it's a scream that catches my attention. I look up and there, plunging from a gondola towards me, is a woman, her ankles tied to a bungee cord, her scream bouncing between the mountains. Around me, cowbells chime like applause.

As the scream fades away, I walk on. This woman may have fallen for the Alps – literally – in an instant, but I have days rolling on ahead of me.

I'm here to walk across Switzerland, or at least a sizeable chunk of it. I'm hiking on the Alpine Pass Route (APR), a puzzle of trails that cross the entire country – Lake Geneva to Liechtenstein. Broken into 15 stages, it's more than 199 miles (320km) in length and crosses 17 passes, condensing Switzerland into one single glorious journey on foot.

I've come to hike four stages of the APR, covering its finest and most dramatic section, walking through and past some of the most

famous names in the Swiss Alps: the resort towns of Engelberg, Grindelwald and Lauterbrunnen, and mountains such as Titlis, Eiger and Jungfrau.

I've started in Engelberg, climbing first into clouds and then suddenly above clouds as I near 7241ft (2207m) Jochpass. Though it's late summer, fresh snow covers the slopes, and an archipelago of peaks rises from the clouds now beneath me.

The APR has no official status as a hiking route across Switzerland, leaving the way open to individual interpretation. Past Jochpass, paths fray and fray again, and I gravitate towards those that lead higher into the mountains, heading past lakes so still they look painted on to the landscape. At times I'm far from any traditional APR lines, but so long as my feet are pointing west, it doesn't matter because in the town of Meiringen all paths come together again.

It's here, in the town that was the scene of Sherlock Holmes' fictional death, that I'm about to enter one of the most dramatic mountain areas in Europe, rising up past the Wetterhorn, tiptoeing across the waist of the Eiger and plunging into the narrow abyss of the Lauterbrunnen Valley.

Mountains jostle the path as I climb out of Meiringen where, around 1300ft (400m) above the town, the trail detours on to a ledge overhanging Reichenbach Falls. It was from this very ledge that Holmes plunged to his end, duelling with Professor Moriarty.

For five hours, I'll hike relentlessly uphill to Grosse Scheidegg pass, squeezing through a narrow, forested gorge. On one side of the valley, Alpine meadows rise gently up the slopes. On the other side of the valley, the Wetterhorn bristles with rock spires and glaciers fractured with icefalls.

By the time I cross Grosse Scheidegg, grey cloud drapes from the mountains like damp laundry. My greatest hope when starting this hike had been to stand on this pass and eyeball the Eiger – that mightiest of Alpine peaks – but in these conditions even Grindelwald, 3600ft (1100m) below me, is obliterated. As I descend, so do my spirits.

However, there's alchemy in the sky when I wake in Grindelwald the next morning to find the sharp lines of the Eiger sawing at a blue sky. The timing is impeccable because today I have a date with this mountain.

The APR beelines straight out of Grindelwald to Kleine Scheidegg pass, but I've planned a bigger and better day. I will walk 16 miles (25km) and climb around 4900ft (1500m) to take me up to and along the Eiger's famed North Face. It will be one of the finest hiking days I can remember.

From Grindelwald a trail coils tightly through the Eiger's forested lower slopes, rising above the bent and tortured nose of the Lower Grindelwald Glacier. Wild strawberries grow beside the trail, providing grazing fodder. Within an hour, Grindelwald is like an ant farm below and the North Face is near.

The trail crunches across slopes of scree that has crumbled from this mighty rock wall. I peer down on to Grindelwald, across to

EIGER NORTH FACE

It's debatable which climb of the Eiger's North Face is more famous – the first ascent in 1938, or Clint Eastwood's in the 1975 film *The Eiger Sanction* – but we're going with the former. Before that successful climb, most attempts to scale the North Face had ended in death, but finally four members of a German-Austrian team (two independent teams who joined up on the mountain) completed the puzzle of the mighty wall, surviving an avalanche to reach the summit on 24 July 1938.

Clockwise from top: the Bernese Alps seen from Jungfrau; Lauterbrunnen; an Alpine marmot. Previous page: meadows and mountains

© MriraWonderland | Shutterstock

"Fresh snow covers the slopes and an archipelago of peaks rises from the clouds now beneath me"

the Wetterhorn and up – most bizarrely – to a line of holes drilled through the North Face that are windows for the Jungfrau Railway, which travels inside the mountain.

The fact that this wall of rock is one of the touchstones of mountaineering is acknowledged along the trail. Near its end, just a few yards from the path, is the point where the first successful climb of the North Face commenced, as marked by a sign outlining the course of that route. A short distance on, just before the trail reaches its highest point, the clay handprints of famous Eiger climbers are bolted to the rock face.

All that remains of my walk now is a final descent into Lauterbrunnen, but it's no ordinary finish. It will take me 4900ft (1500m) down into one of the most dramatic valleys in the Alps, past the revered Mönch and Jungfrau mountains. Glaciers drape from the so-called 'Young Woman' like a string of pearls, and as I walk, seracs continually shear away, the ice smashing itself apart as it avalanches down the rock faces.

A short distance ahead are the cliffs that enclose Lauterbrunnen, a town huddled in a valley so narrow it's like a paper cut in the Alps. Some of Europe's highest waterfalls plunge over the edges of these 1650ft (500m) cliffs, but they aren't the only things that fall here. Lauterbrunnen is also one of the world's prime BASE-jumping locations, and as I approach the valley I see a handful of people in wingsuits step to the cliff edge and leap. The Swiss Alps ring with screams once again. **AB**

ORIENTATION

Start // Engelberg
End // Lauterbrunnen
Distance // 48 miles (77km)
Getting there // Switzerland's major airports are Zurich, Geneva and Basel. A superbly efficient public transport system makes it easy to access points all along the route.
Tours // Utracks (www.utracks.com) runs a 14-day self-guided Alpine Pass Route trip, beginning in Engelberg and ending in Saanen, covering eight of the route's 14 stages.
When to go // Snow often lingers on high passes into early summer, so its best to hike the route July to September.
Where to stay and eat // This is a civilised trail, passing regularly through towns and mountain huts, providing ample options for sleeping and eating.
More info // For a dedicated guide to the route, pick up a Cicerone's *Alpine Pass Route*, by Kev Reynolds.

Opposite from top; an ibex finds its perch on the Europaweg near Zermatt; a hiker sees the Chamonix Valley stretch before him

MORE LIKE THIS
LONG-DISTANCE ALPINE HIKES

TOUR DU MONT BLANC

Arguably Europe's most famous hike, the TMB passes through three countries as it makes a lap around the highest peak in the European Alps. This circuit of about 110 miles (170km) loops out from Chamonix, crossing into Italy and Switzerland before returning to the ever-popular French Alpine resort town. There are low- and high-route options in many places, and the scenery is sublime, whether it be the Toblerone skyline of the Grand Jorasses or the grandstand final views along the Aiguilles Rouge. For most hikers, it's a journey of 10–11 days (if that seems pedestrian you can always run around it in the annual Ultra-Trail Mont Blanc), and accommodation is plentiful along most stretches, though the popularity of the trail means it can be wise to book ahead during the busy times of July and August. Expect to climb more than 30,000ft (9000m), or about the equivalent of summiting Everest from sea level.

Start/End // Chamonix
Distance // 110 miles (170km)

HAUTE ROUTE

With Mont Blanc as its starting block and the Matterhorn as its finish post, the Haute Route is like a date with the mountain gods. Created originally as a ski-touring route, it quickly also morphed into a summer hiking trail, adopting a slightly different course but sticking to its brief as the 'High Route'. It passes beneath 10 of the 12 highest mountains in the Alps, and though it never rises above 10,000ft (3000m), it's two weeks that'll see you ascend more than 50,000ft (15,000m). The 125-mile (200km) route is dotted with mountain huts, and the safest time to be on the trail is from about mid-July to September – early summer may require crampons. One of the most enticing features of the walk is that it ends in a blaze of glory, finishing along the 21-mile (33km) Europaweg into Zermatt, a trail itself widely regarded as among the most spectacular in Europe.

Start // Chamonix
End // Zermatt
Distance // 125 miles (200km)

EAGLE WALK

One of the Alps' longest hiking trails, the Eagle Walk is a compendium of Austrian Alpine highlights. It begins along the Wilder Kaiser (Wild Emperor) mountains near St Johann in Tirol, and then spools out for more than 250 miles (400km), ending across the slopes of 12,461ft (3798m) Grossglockner, the highest mountain in Austria. The trail is partitioned into 33 stages – 24 in North Tyrol, nine in East Tyrol – and almost traverses Austria north-south. If the idea of hiking in the Austrian Alps lulls you into a fantasy of *Sound of Music-*type strolls, think again – there's more than 10,000ft (30,000m) of ascent along the Eagle Walk, which is exhausting just to write! If you just fancy a few days with the Eagle, it's easy to tap into short sections of the trail, with bus stops and train stations regularly intersecting with the route.

Start // St Johann in Tirol
End // Lucknerhaus
Distance // 257 miles (413km)

MALLORCA'S DRY STONE ROUTE

Taking in sea cliffs, honey-stone villages, isolated coves and the limestone spires of the Tramuntana range, this multiday ramble is a tantalising taste of pre-tourism Mallorca.

Long brushed aside as being a cheap package-break destination in the Med, serious hikers would once have rolled their eyes in disbelief at the mention of Mallorca for a multiday ramble. No more: the biggest and most dramatic of the Balearic Islands is finally being fêted for the phenomenal beauty of its coastline and mountains. And striking out on the Ruta de Pedra en Sec (Dry Stone Route) – or GR221 – gets you to the bits others rarely see. Broken up into eight stages and mostly patched together from old mule tracks, the trail is named after the dry-stone walls that interweave the island's heights, hemming in silver-green olive groves, citrus-laden orchards, terraced vineyards and pine forest.

In staggering contrast to the built-up resorts, the trail, still partly unsigned, leads deep into the island's little-explored hinterland and high into the ragged wilderness and ravines of the Serra de Tramuntana, Mallorca's backbone. Tracing a rough line through the north of the island, this Unesco-listed landscape is ensnared by limestone peaks scarred by the elements. Here, ochre-stone villages cling to hilltops, cliffs drop abruptly to the deep blue sea and terraces march up from the coast. The clang of out-of-tune monastery bells echoes through remote valleys, where nimble-footed goats share the trail.

I begin the Ruta on one of those clear spring days that make you feel glad to be alive. Leaving behind the seaside town of Port d'Andratx, the trail eases me in gently with a four-hour trudge to Sa Trapa, which dips in and out of sun-dappled pinewoods and coastal scrub heavy with the scent of wild rosemary in purple bloom. At Sant Elm, the offshore nature reserve island of Sa Dragonera appears like a reclining dragon. But more arresting

still is the grandstand view of sapphire sea from Sa Trapa and its ruined Trappist monastery.

Cairns and the odd paint splash guide the way on the second leg of the hike from Sa Trapa to Estellencs. I sometimes lose the rocky trail but soon pick it up again, all the while marvelling at the dividing blues of horizon and sea. Onwards and upwards I go to the knobbly summit of Moleta de s'Esclop (3038ft, 926m), where the view of the Tramuntana is out of this world, with fissured peaks rippling into the distance like waves on breaking point. A gravel trail leads down to Estellencs, a laid-back hamlet with honey-hued buildings scattered on the hills below 3363ft (1025m) Puig Galatzò.

© Vulcano | Shutterstock

Day three ramps up the drama on a six-hour trek between Estellencs and Banyalbufar. As I follow quiet trails that occasionally reveal a glimmer of sea, the only sound is that of foot on rock and a distant braying donkey. Looking as if it will topple off the cliff with the merest puff of wind, the Torre des Verger, a 16th-century *talayot*, or watchtower, makes a fine picnic spot before the onward hike to Banyalbufar. The village is tightly laced with pot-plant-lined lanes and combed with dry-stone farming terraces – *ses marjades* – that form a series of steep steps down to the sea. I'd like to linger but I want to make Esporles before nightfall.

The morning sun warms the stone houses of the village, cradled in the foothills of the Tramuntana. It's day four and the path takes me through thick macchia, orchards and shady olive groves. Cresting rises and cutting through woodland, I pretty much have the trail to myself. Not so in Valldemossa, where crowds mill around the Carthusian monastery where composer Frédéric Chopin and his lover, George Sand, sojourned in 1838. After a quick culture fix, it's back on the Camí de s'Arxiduc, a rocky path shimmying high along the coast to Deià. Perched like an eyrie above the blue sea, this is surely one of Mallorca's most romantic hill towns. It's a romance that wasn't lost on poet Robert Graves, who now lies buried under the cypress tree in the churchyard.

From Deià, the onward coastal trail reveals mood-lifting views of the sea and rock formations like holey Sa Fordada, which resembles an elephant from afar. The tentative drone of cicadas tells me that evening is approaching on the dry-stone Camí de Castelló, twisting up through pine and olive groves to the Muleta refuge above Port de Sóller. That night, the starry sky is more brilliant than ever and moonbeams dance on the sea.

Well rested, I brace myself for a nine-hour hut-to-hut hike delving deep into the mountainous backcountry on day six.

TIME AND TIDE

So you fancy tagging on an extra day or two in Mallorca's north? Wise choice. The coastline northeast of Pollença, the island's most dramatic, is reached by a helter-skelter of a road, which you can cycle if you're as fit as a fiddle. En route are lookouts with views of a sea of deepest blue and the cliffs rearing above it like shark fins. Spend some chill time on Platja de Formentor's ribbon of pine-fringed sand or head on to lighthouse-topped Cap de Formentor for a cracking sunset.

Clockwise from top: the rocky path to Deià; a Mallorcan home; Deià; donkeys nibble at a dry-stone wall. Previous page: the village of Soller

"Perched like an eyrie above the blue sea, Deià is surely one of Mallorca's most romantic hill towns"

After a coffee on the plaza in the lovely hill town of Sóller, the trail ambles on through lemon and orange orchards, now billowing with white blossom, climbing steadily to the sweet hamlet of Biniaraix, tucked among gardens and the Tramuntana's grey stone flanks. A stone path wends up the Barranc de Biniaraix ravine and on to the Puig de l'Ofre (3586ft, 1093m), where the puckered, pale-grey peaks stand out against the azure water of the Cúber reservoir. It has been a long day and my legs are thankful when I finally reach the remote mountain hut of Tossals Verds.

As the hike edges east on day seven, it enters high, rocky terrain, making for a scramble up to the fortress-like summit of Coll des Prat (2749ft, 838m), from where it's possible to ascend 4478ft (1365m) Puig de Massanella, Mallorca's second-highest peak, for captivating views over the eroded karst wilderness of the Tramuntana to the sea beyond. Pilgrims and day-trippers mill around the Monestir de Lluc, where I pause to glimpse the late-Renaissance basilica, before heading on to my bed for the night at the tranquil Refugi Son Amer.

The pockmarked heights of the Tramuntana are interspersed with pine forest on the final stretch from the refuge to the hill town of Pollença. It's late afternoon when I arrive and the shuttered houses glow like warm honey. Above the town sits a pilgrimage chapel, reached by a flight of 365 steps – the Calvari. But it's a climb that will have to wait for tomorrow. **KC**

ORIENTATION

Start // Port d'Andratx
End // Pollença
Distance // 103 miles (167km)
Getting there // The trailhead, Port d'Andratx, is a 30-minute drive from Palma de Mallorca airport. Bus 102 runs regularly from central Palma to Port d'Andratx; the journey takes 1¼ hours.
When to go // Sweltering summer weather can make the hike more arduous, so it's better to dodge the heat and crowds and go in spring or autumn instead.
More info // Consell de Mallorca (www.conselldemallorca. net) has detailed trail information, tips on guides/maps and a booking service for *refugi* (refuges).
What to pack // Temperatures are usually mild, so bring light clothes, sturdy boots, sunscreen and insect repellent.

Opposite: flamingoes descend on Las Salinas, on Spain's Cabo de Gata coast

MORE LIKE THIS
EUROPEAN COASTS

PEMBROKESHIRE COAST PATH, WALES

Wales often conjures images of rain-sodden hills and sheep-dotted valleys, but the Pembrokeshire Coast Path is different. Hugging the country's southwestern coast, this is where Wales opens up to the wild Atlantic, creating a starkly eroded coastline of arches, stacks and blowholes. Dipping and rising over bluffs, dune grasslands and wildflower-flecked heathland, the roughly two-week hike leads to bays tucked into the folds of fossil-rich cliffs, ancient standing stones and hill forts. As you stride, look out for porpoises, Risso's dolphins, minke and fin whales out at sea, and Atlantic grey seals basking on rocks closer to shore. Unmissables include cathedral-topped St Davids, Britain's smallest city, Newgale's magnificent sweep of surf and beach and Abereiddy's sheer-sided blue lagoon. Tag on an extra day for the trip over to Skomer island, home to huge puffin and Manx shearwater colonies.

Start // St Dogmaels
End // Amroth
Distance // 186 miles (299km)

CÔTE DE GRANIT ROSE, BRITTANY, FRANCE

This three-day walk follows the coast path roughly eastwards from the town of Trégastel and takes in the best of Brittany's north coast: excellent paths, fantastic groupings of pink granite boulders, sandy beaches and rocky headlands. The most prominent features are the broad, shallow-reefed bay between the town of Perros-Guirec and Pointe du Château, and the long, narrow Jaudy estuary. Although relatively little ascent is involved, some sections of the walk follow rocky paths or shingle banks – not the easiest of surfaces and reminders of the days when smuggling was a popular pastime along this coast. The places to stay are mainly campsites, you could set up a tent at one near the beautiful headland of Port l'Epine on the first night and the fairytale Plougrescant peninsula on the second. This walk runs through four protected nature reserves.

Start // Trégastel Plage
End // Tréguier
Distance // 36 miles (58km)

CABO DE GATA COAST WALK, ANDALUCÍA, SPAIN

This coastal walk runs along southern Spain's most spectacular seaboard; first the promontory's flat, beach-lined western coast; and then on the rugged southern and eastern coasts, strung with secluded beaches and coves. The locations of the places you could stop for the night make it impossible to divide the walk into three equal days, so we suggest a shorter third day, spending the first night in the pleasant resort town of San José and the next at Las Negras, set on a pebbly beach towards an imposing headland of volcanic rock. Along the way, the combination of a dry, desert climate with the cliffs of the Sierra del Cabo de Gata plunging towards the azure-and-turquoise Mediterranean waters produces a landscape of stark, elemental grandeur. Between the cliffs and headlands are strung some of Spain's best and least crowded beaches.

Start // Retamar
End // Agua Amarga
Distance // 38 miles (61km)

© Holbox | Shutterstock

A WALK THROUGH TIME: THE THAMES PATH

Urban, easy, with plenty of concrete. Nevertheless a day spent walking the Thames through central London shows off man-made beauty spanning more than a thousand years.

I hear you: surely *Lonely Planet* is not saying that 5.3 miles (8.54km) of paved riverside path in the middle of Europe's biggest city is one of the epic hikes of the world? Surely?

But yes, that's exactly what we're saying.

For a hike to be truly epic – a real world-class, mind-blowing zinger – what does it need?

Most people would put scenery at the top of the list. You'll want to be blown away by epic views, to round corners and stop with a gasp at the new vista that's suddenly opened up before you. You'll know you're somewhere truly epic when you get that feeling of panic that you can't take it all in – the view overwhelms you. Or that feeling when the view becomes unreal, because it looks like you've entered a filmset.

But walk from Tower Bridge to Lambeth Bridge and you will see some of the finest scenery on earth. You'll start at the oldest palace, fortress and prison in Europe, the Tower of London; then walk across the most famous bridge in the world (sorry San Francisco), Tower Bridge. The views are instantly spectacular – as you get over the water, the river gives you the space you need for long views – one of the reasons this particular route through London is so visually rewarding.

The skyline from here may not be natural, but the pinnacles and spires are every bit as sublime as those above Chamonix or Jackson Hole. There's the Shard, the Gherkin, the Cheese-grater, the Walkie-Talkie – each a gleaming testament to man's capacity to create beauty from glass, steel and concrete...and to Londoners' capacity to give anything a ridiculous nickname.

As you reach the South Bank and stroll along the broad walkway past City Hall, the incongruity of the skyscrapers next to the squat

11th-century Tower and the Victorian Gothic marvel of Tower Bridge becomes apparent. It brings a smile to your face.

But views aren't everything. What about local life? Is this hike epic from a cultural point of view? You betcha. The people watching is as good as the view. The Thames Path is spacious here, especially after the crush on Tower Bridge, so it's easier to excuse the selfie-sticks jammed in your face, the families stopping in your path to pose or point, the teenagers cycling too fast and too close. Enjoy the show. A band is playing in The Scoop, an open amphitheatre. Buskers, floating Yodas and giant bubbles compete for the attentions – and cash – of kids walking past. Mixed in with

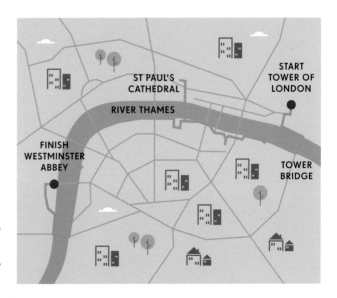

© Tomas Sereda | Getty

the joggers, hand-holding couples, lunching bankers and dog-walkers, you'll see more nationalities here than almost anywhere else on earth. This is, after all, the most visited city on the planet.

Hopefully by now you're feeling hungry. Passing under London Bridge, your nose will start to lead you. Borough Market, under the railway arches, is a 1000-year-old food market where wholesalers supplying restaurants and pubs crowd next to stalls catering for office workers and tourists. Your eyes will be drawn to French pastries, Welsh cheeses and North Sea fish; but your nose will win, tempted by Indian dosa, Dutch pancakes and English bacon. Grab a taste from as many stalls as you can, make your choice, then sit under the spire of Southwark Cathedral to eat. If good food and drink make a hike epic, there would be no competition.

But what about a bit of history, art and culture to add to the all-round epic-ness? Easy. This next stretch of the Thames is historic even by London standards. Whether you choose to stop for a show at Shakespeare's Globe, whisper across the dome of St Paul's, or contemplate the works of Picasso, Rothko and Warhol at Tate Modern, your main problem is getting this tiny hike done in just one day when there's so much to stop you in your tracks.

But as you walk further and become accustomed to the changing views, the mishmash of architecture and the human

> ## "You'll see more nationalities here than almost anywhere else on earth"

wildlife on show, two subtleties of this particular epic hike become apparent. The first is the presence of the river. At the start of the walk it is no more than a handy gap between you and the view, a handrail to stop you getting lost. But spend a few hours in its company and you see the tide change, watch eddies swirl behind the piers of the bridges as the current flows swift. You notice the traffic on the river, not just the roads – pleasure cruises full of tourists, police boats speeding up and down, barges carrying goodness-knows-what. Gulls wheel above, screeching. As the tide goes out, the bridges seem to grow taller, and the riverbanks reveal themselves. A bulldog chases a stick, a couple of amateur archaeologists pick their way along the water's edge. All the while, the river flows by. The Thames isn't big by global standards, but it is the heart of this city today, as it has been for 2000 years.

The second thing you'll notice is that this hike isn't just about landscape. The soundscape is just as varied and interesting. Sure, there's traffic sometimes. But most of the time, there are the sounds of water, boats and gulls to remind you that you're in a port. You hear snatches of conversations in Cockney and Catalan, Arabic and Urdu. Sounds dip in and out. Eaters and drinkers add hubbub, punctuated by raucous laughs. Music undercuts it all.

It may not be natural beauty, but if you want to spend a day marvelling at what man has created, then a stroll along the banks of the Thames is, well...epic. **PP**

ROYAL PERKS

While Tower Bridge to Lambeth Bridge hits the most sights, the section from Hampton Court Bridge to Richmond Bridge is almost as spectacular, but shows a different side to the city. It starts at King Henry VIII's Hampton Court Palace and meanders past stately homes and country parks built as weekend retreats in centuries past. Or the keen can walk the whole 184 miles (296km) from the source of the Thames to the sea.

Opposite, clockwise from top: looking west along the Thames past Tower Bridge; the route starts at the Tower of London; stopping for supplies at Borough Market. Previous page: St Paul's Cathedral

ORIENTATION

Start // Tower Hill Underground station, London
End // Westminster Underground station, London
Distance // 5.3 miles (8.54km)
Duration // Allow at least a full day to visit some of the attractions. This is a route that is worth revisiting.
Getting there // London has four international airports. The nearest stations are Tower Hill and Tower Gateway.
Attractions // Choose just two or three from this list to visit, and try to pre-book online: Tower of London; Tower Bridge Exhibition; HMS *Belfast*; Borough Market; The Clink Prison Museum; Shakespeare's Globe; Tate Modern; St Paul's Cathedral; concerts, theatre and cinema at the South Bank Centre; London Eye; Westminster Abbey.
More info // Detailed route descriptions and maps can be found at https://tfl.gov.uk/modes/walking/thames-path.

*Opposite from top: the grounds of
Ginkaku-ji temple in Kyoto; deer get
curious in Dublin's Phoenix Park*

MORE LIKE THIS
CITY WALKS

YURREBILLA TRAIL, ADELAIDE, SOUTH AUSTRALIA

Completed in 2003, the Yurrebilla Trail provides Adelaide with an asset possessed by few other major cities: a multiday walking track on its doorstep. As you wander through Waite Conservation Reserve on day two – after overnighting at Brownhill Creek Caravan Park – you'll be just 6 miles (10km) from the city, yet you're more likely to see kangaroos than people. The trail traces the line of the Mt Lofty Ranges, linking seven national and conservation parks, including a final day's winding tramp through what is arguably Adelaide's greatest natural asset, Morialta Conservation Park. You can walk the Yurrebilla Trail's entirety or use the suburban bus network to sample it in sections. This can be handy if you want to stop elsewhere than Brownhill Creek and the Crystal Hill Sanctuary Hostel on the second night, as other accommodation options are scarce. Check with South Australia's Visitor Information Centre to see what's around.
Start // Belair railway station
End // Ambers Gully
Distance // 33.5 miles (54km)

DAIMONJI-YAMA, KYOTO, JAPAN

Presenting an epic cityscape, this hike is a great way to see a lot of Kyoto in a short time. It combines temples, enjoyable hiking and outstanding views of the city on a well-used, easy-to-follow track. The walk starts at the Ginkaku-ji Zen temple and ascends the clearing where the *dai* kanji symbol burns during the annual Daimonji-yaki festival on 16 August – one of Kyoto's great sights. The view over the city from the clearing is unparalleled, extending as far as the skyscrapers of Osaka on clear days. It's a one-hour, 1-mile (1.5km) round-trip hike from Ginkaku-ji temple up to the viewpoint, but the trail then continues deeper into the mountains, crossing the summit of Daimonji-yama before heading down to a lovely subtemple of Nanzen-ji, where the *momiji* (maple) trees display their glorious colours in autumn. From there, you return to the starting point via the Tetsugaku-no-michi (Path of Philosophy; stunning during cherry blossom season), passing a variety of shrines and temples along the way.
Start/End // Ginkaku-ji
Distance // 4.3 miles (7km)

PHOENIX PARK AND RIVER LIFFEY, DUBLIN, IRELAND

The 350-year-old Phoenix Park is Europe's largest enclosed park, at 1752 acres (709 hectares). An oval-shaped tract of fields and woodlands, it lies above the north bank of the River Liffey and is surrounded by busy roads and suburbs. It has a network of extensive paths providing a great variety of walks, but we'd plump for a roughly circular route concentrating on the eastern half, diverting to the quiet banks of the River Liffey before returning to the park. Plot your walk via its highlights: the People's Gardens, the All-Ireland Polo Club, the Phoenix Monument and Ashtown Castle; doubling back and diverting to the 1979 Papal Cross before heading for Magazine Fort and the prehistoric burial chamber of Knockmaree Cromlech. Crossing the River Liffey bridge, you'll then turn left towards the Irish National War Memorial Park. Your end point, the 220ft (67m) Wellington Monument, was the world's tallest obelisk in its day.
Start/End // Parkgate St entrance
Distance // 7.9 miles (12.7km)

WILD BLUE YONDER: SELVAGGIO BLU

Those who dare to hike Italy's toughest trek on Sardinia's wild and ravishingly beautiful east coast are rewarded with a taste of an island few ever experience.

'This land resembles no other place. Sardinia is something else. Enchanting spaces and distances to travel – nothing finished, nothing definitive. It is like freedom itself.' So wrote DH Lawrence in his 1921 travelogue *Sea and Sardinia*. Lawrence was bang on, I think, as I inch my way along a limestone cliff that falls abruptly to a sapphire sea. When I dare look over my shoulder, the view is indeed freedom itself: just the Mediterranean, the horizon and the vanishing point between. I feel like a tightrope artist performing a balancing act: placing one foot delicately in front of the other on the narrow ridge. I ponder how clumsy humans are, as two goats hoof it up the rocky ledge, and how ironic it is that life on the edge can feel so liberating.

I'm on the Selvaggio Blu, or Wild Blue, the trek whose name makes even experienced hikers break out in a sweat of fear and anticipation. Billed as Italy's toughest hike – and not, I hasten to add, without reason – this is a four- to five-day tramp into utter coastal wilderness. There are no villages, no roads, no people (bar the occasional fellow hiker) and, most importantly, no signs.

Walking 25–30 miles (40–48km) along the coast might sound like a doddle, but don't be fooled: this is one heck of a hike, geared to the super-fit and sure-footed. You need to have a rope and know how to use one for those instances when the trail ends and you have to grip the rock – either climbing up or abseiling down. Then there's the navigation: a GPS can assist but it's not 100% dependable, so knowing how to use a compass helps. Even then, the trail finding can be bewildering as animals are carving out new tracks all the time that lead hikers astray. Fresh water is difficult to find, too, so everything you need must either be lugged

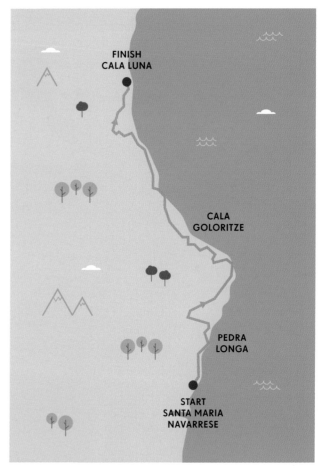

in a heavy backpack or dropped off by boat at designated points.

If the Selvaggio seems indomitable today, it was much more so in the late 1980s, when two Italian climbers, Tuscan Mario Verin and local architect Peppino Cicalò conceived it. Thwacking their way through dense coastal scrub, they pieced together a frail network of old charcoal burner, shepherd and goatherd trails that traced fine lines across the sheer clifftops and deep ravines of the Golfo di Orosei in eastern Sardinia. In so doing they created one of Europe's most epic coastal hikes, taking in rock formations that rise above the sea like fortress ruins and caves as immense and impressive as cathedrals, where kidnappers and bandits once hid. Rivers and creeks snake through woods of gnarled holm oak, juniper, olive and pine. Far below the cliffs are scooped-out coves of smooth white pebbles where people rarely set foot. On the trail, days of backbreaking hiking and mind-blowing coastal beauty slide into moonlit nights around crackling campfires and sleeping on the beach or in caves.

The hike begins near the beach resort of Santa Maria Navarrese at Pedra Longa, a 420ft (128m) spire of rock thrusting up above a sea that fades from pale azure to deep cerulean blue. The start is deceptively easy as I pick my way along the coast, with the hush

"The translucent sea swirls around bizarre limestone formations that soar away from the cliffs"

of the sea below, a light breeze carrying the scent of wild rosemary and thyme, and a peregrine falcon wheeling overhead in an April sky. Some light scrambling brings me to Cala Goloritzè, where the translucent sea swirls around bizarre limestone formations that soar away from the cliffs, including the 485ft (148m) Aguglia, a needle of rock beloved of climbers.

I am under no illusion that the trek will stay this easy for long, and I'm proved right. Soon I find myself clinging to the cracks in the limestone as I edge my way above the overhang, clambering up and over the rocks. I haul myself up a makeshift ladder, its rungs rusty and more than a little precarious. The trail requires maximum concentration, and I am acutely aware of the consequences of one misplaced footstep. When the path levels, there is brief respite and I can survey the view. And what a view! The great arc of the Golfo di Orosei spreading out before me. Cyclamens sprinkle the juniper forest and broom is in golden bloom – spring is coming.

© Olivero Olivieri | robertharding, © Aurora Photos | Alamy

GUIDING STARS

Embarking upon the Selvaggio Blu is easier with a guide – a necessity unless you happen to be remarkably experienced, as they know the terrain, can provide the gear and rework the route. It is as much a mountain expedition as a coastal walk, involving grade IV climbs and some tough inclines. Reliable guides include Corrado Conca, Explorando Supramonte and Guide Star Mountain. Expect to pay around €700–800 per person (£620–£710) in a group of six or more.

Clockwise from left: dealing with the Selvaggio Blu's tricky terrain; rappelling is required; wonderful respite at Cala Luna beach. Previous page: Arco Lupiru rock

ORIENTATION

Start // Santa Maria Navarrese/Pedra Longa
End // Cala Sisine/Cala Luna
Distance // 25-30 miles (40-48km)
Getting there // The closest airports to the trek are in Cagliari and Olbia, both around a 2¼- hour drive (via a private transfer) from Santa Maria Navarrese.
When to go // Avoid the scorching summer weather and tackle the trail in March to May or September to November.
More info // Italian speakers can get the lowdown on the trek at www.selvaggioblu.it. Enrico Spanu's *Book of Selvaggio Blu* is available online or is sold occasionally in local bookstores.
Things to know // If you choose to go it alone, the Lemon House (www.lemonhouse.eu) can arrange the logistics, including backpacks and water drop-offs.

Cala Biriola appears far, far below like a shimmering vision. And after an intense, scrambling descent, I feel I have earned the right to jump into the sea and let the grime slide off me. Dragging myself away from the dreamy cove, the going soon gets tougher. Before long I find myself on a precipice, my heart doing cartwheels at the prospect of rappelling down an almighty cliff. I drop gently into the void and hope for the best. My reward is Grotta del Fico, a yawning sea cave encrusted with stalactites like drip candles.

The next day's hike is to Cala Sisine, the end of the hike proper. It's another tough one, with some cliff climbing on a fixed via ferrata, narrow ridges, ravine traverses and gulp-inducing drops. Abseiling down to the stunning bay sweaty and bedraggled, I draw a few raised eyebrows from the holidaymakers sunning themselves on the beach, who have taken the boat to get here.

After a while, you become accustomed to the Selvaggio Blu and what it can throw at you. By its end I'm eager for a little more, and so continue on to the next bay round, Cala Luna. As I reach the Arco Lupiru, a monumental sea arch high above the coast, I stop for a while as the soft and luminous light of late afternoon softens the contours of the Golfo di Orosei. The bay is like an enormous amphitheatre, where the show is always the sea. **KC**

Opposite from top: Spain's 'Walkway of Death' appears well-named; scaling Half Dome in Yosemite National Park

MORE LIKE THIS
ROPE AND CABLE TRAILS

CAMINITO DEL REY, SPAIN

Do you dare walk a trail once nicknamed the 'Walkway of Death'? The Caminito del Rey (King's Path) near Málaga in southern Spain, which reopened in 2015 with new cables, cliff-hugging boardwalks and a suspension bridge that wobbles with every hesitant step, is still scary – though you'll no longer see your life flash before your eyes. The hike delves into the narrow El Chorro gorge, which is 328ft (100m) deep and a piffling 33ft (10m) wide at certain points. As you teeter along the cliffs wearing a hard hat, there are head-spinning views of the perpendicular rock faces and rushing Gualdalhorce River. Spare a thought for those who risked their lives to hike the old track hacked into the cliffs below – a truly daunting prospect.

Start // Ardales
End // Alora
Distance // 7.7km (4.8 miles)
More info // Reserve permits (€10) online at www.caminitodelrey.info

RAROTONGA CROSS-ISLAND HIKE, COOK ISLANDS

In the midst of the Pacific Ocean, the Cook Islands might be best known for their lovely lagoon-stroked beaches, but inland there are other adventures to be explored. On Rarotonga, an extreme hiking trail crosses the spine of the volcanic isle, taking walkers to Te Rua Manga (The Needle). A colourful character called Pa regularly leads parties along this route, but it's possible to do it independently. Go north–south, from Avatiu Rd following orange markers along a jungle track to Ridge Junction, from where Needle Lookout is another 650m (198m). Fixed chains and ropes lead those brave enough to trust them to the base of the cloud-scraping Needle, which offers eye-popping views across the reef-fringed island. (Don't attempt to touch the 1355ft (413m) point, though, unless you're an experienced climber with your own equipment). Descend via a path that follows Papua Stream.

Start // Avatiu Rd
End // Papua Rd
Distance // 4 miles (6.5km)
More info // www.cookislands.travel

HALF DOME, USA

Yosemite National Park bombards you with sensational mountainscapes on mile after mile of hiking trails into the wild blue yonder. But those hankering after a pulse-racing challenge get their kicks on Half Dome, an 8844ft (2695m) fang of rock. Make sure you begin at sunrise for this awesome 10- to 12-hour hike, leading past tall rock faces, thunderous, rainbow-kissed falls (if you go via the Mist Trail) and forests where black bears hang out. It's a long day's trek, but the real cliffhanger is the final, knuckle-whitening climb up Half Dome's vertical granite eastern slope, a breathtakingly steep cabled ascent that plays out in slow motion. Besides bragging rights, your reward at the summit is the knockout view of Liberty Cap, Yosemite Valley and the High Sierra.

Start/End // Happy Isles (shuttle stop 16), ¾ mile (1.2km) from the trailhead
Distance // 16 miles (26km) round trip
More info // A limited number of permits are available via a lottery system – visit www.nps.gov. Campsites should be booked ahead

GUIDING STARS: TRANSCAUCASIAN TRAIL

This multiday mixture of high passes and magical river-valley trails links some of Georgia's most photogenic tower-house villages – and in the company of local guides it offers even more.

Sometimes laziness pays. Hiking the Omalo-Shatili and Roshka-Juta sections of Georgia's magnificent Transcaucasian Trail is quite feasible alone. But Jane and I don't like carrying bags. Engaging a horseman-guide for each section seems well worth the remarkably modest expense. And we get much more than we bargained for from two remarkable if utterly different characters.

For the first three days our companion is charming, soft-spoken Tedo, who talks to his horses as to close friends. He can talk to dogs too, an essential skill...as we later discover. Clear rolling paths lead us out of Omalo, the tiny summer-only capital

of Tusheti, crowned by a film-set perfect-cluster of *koshkebi* (tower houses). Wide forest vistas reveal an infinity of green mountaintops. In the Tolkienesque hamlet of Dartlo, Tedo has arranged an atmospheric coffee stop at an unmarked local stone house; from here idyllic streamside tracks lead on to Girevi, where our simple homestay is magically illuminated in sunset rays. Day two's narrow, meandering path follows a dancing river, climbing a flower-filled valley dotted with shattered stone ruins including ghost villages Hegho and Chontio. On a beautiful grassy meadow Tedo gets exuberant, standing upright on his horse's back to whoop with delight.

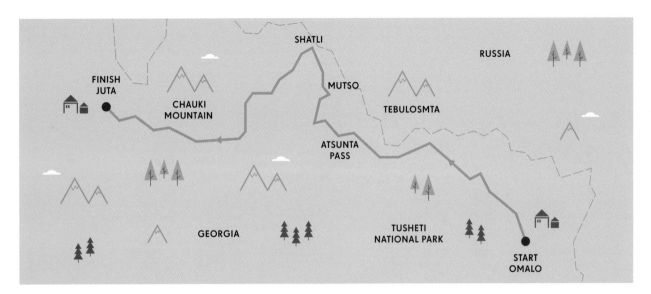

Tonight we're camping on a grassy ledge above a sheep-filled corral. Shepherd Irakli invites us for tea in his rock-walled hovel. Getting there means passing a dangerous canine frenzy of guarding sheepdogs, but at Tedo's firm grunted commands, the dogs fall silent, as though hypnotised. Irakli boils an ash-blackened kettle on smouldering twigs, his poetically wind-sculpted face partially illuminated in the smoky glow. It's a movingly timeless scene and the next morning we return for breakfast. Irakli has slept outside in his thick felt shepherd-gown, a garment so solid and heavy that he can walk out of it and leave it standing. 'The hovel's just for cooking,' he explains. 'If I stayed inside I wouldn't hear the wolves.'

The third day's hike starts with an unbridged river crossing. Most trekkers wade through but we've heard how peak flowing waters drowned a lone Israeli trekker here back in June. For us it's easy – Tedo's horses ferry us across. Dry boots prove a big plus as we zig-zag through piles of broken slates to the bleak 11,257ft (3431m) Atsunta Pass. An impression of desolate moonscape is accentuated by the swirling low clouds. Yet suddenly, out of the mists appears an unlikely sight that our brains struggle to compute: a dozen extreme cyclists carrying bicycles over their shoulders.

There's a joyous feeling of openness as we traverse the Khidotani ridge, despite drizzling rain that obscures views of 14,741ft (4493m) Tebulosmta. Occasional shafts of sunlight still pierce the clouds and an absurd arc of rainbow bridges a side

KOSHKEBI TOWER HOUSES

Many Tushetian villages feature *koshkebi*, spindly stone towers up to five storeys tall. Unlike the better-known *svaneti* towers (also in Georgia), many have pointed roof-caps, but both types are so ancient that even Unesco seems unable to guess exact dates for their construction. It is said that no outsiders ever conquered isolated Tusheti – it simply wasn't worth besieging the hardy populace once they had retreated into their towers. So potential invaders just passed by.

Clockwise from top: the Caucasus; an abandoned village; herded goats. Previous page: mountains of Georgia

> "At Tedo's firm grunted commands, the guarding sheepdogs fall silent, as though hypnotised"

valley beneath us. Bedraggled, we reach a lonely border lookout post where kindly soldiers hand us mugs of coffee. Then, slithering on sodden grass between towering heads of giant hogweed, we descend through the half-abandoned farmsteads of Bakhao, making four stream crossings, one balanced on a narrow metal beam. Finally a semblance of track leads us to the one-family hamlet of Ardoti, where a small, totally unsigned hostel-homestay lies behind thick stone walls incorporating runic petroglyphs.

We're now in Khevsureti, a fabled region whose archaic language is to Georgian what Chaucerian English might sound like to Anglophones. The uninhabited fortified village of Mutso rises in shattered layers above us. Some curious erosion chimneys are followed by thickening woodlands and the spooky 'bone houses' of Anatori, then suddenly civilisation in the form of mystical Shatili. Waving goodbye to Tedo, we explore Shatili's citadel, a Game of Thrones-like cluster of dark stone towers and shadowy gateways. Then we track down the village's only taxi: a popular 'cheat' that shaves a long day's walk off the Omalo-Juta trail via an undulating three-hour drive to Roshka.

© John Grummitt | Shutterstock

Next morning our Roshka homestay has found us a big, brash and boisterous guide who locals nickname 'The Beast'. The morning is freshly fragrant. Patches of blue sky emerge between huge fluffy clouds. Soaring mountains add occasional cameo appearances. While resting at a lovely viewpoint knoll, The Beast pulls out a hip flask. He creates cups by knifing 7-Up bottles. Then it's time to drink. In Georgia it's unthinkable to refuse a round of toasts, even at 10am. Cheers to Georgia. To friendship. To women. To peace. And so on. The copious *chacha* (Georgian grappa) seems to propel us up the steep Chauki Pass (11,256ft/3431m).

On top, The Beast declares 'We must toast to the pass'. He raids a shepherd's 'bad weather' booze stash and we drink yet more. To passes. To shepherds. To life.

Filled with Dutch courage, we forget our near-total lack of equestrian abilities and any sense of peril and mount the packhorses, cantering down from the pass in a giddy blur. By early afternoon we're trotting into Juta. Chauki mountain rises behind us like a gigantic rocky eagle at 11,424ft (3842m), and in the distant valley ahead are hints that the gigantic 16,512ft (5033m) snow cone of Mt Kazbek might be about to materialise. A jolly homestay hostess welcomes us in. 'Before he leaves,' she suggests, 'how about a small vodka for you and your guide? Just one bottle.' And so it continues. **ME**

ORIENTATION

Start // Omalo (Tusheti)
End // Shatili (Khevsureti) or Juta (Kazbegi)
Distance // 47 miles (75km) from Omalo to Shatili; 11 miles (18km) Roshka to Juta
Getting there // Omalo is a five-hour jeep-ride from Alvani in Kakheti, or a day's travel from Tbilisi: change vehicles in Telavi.
When to go // Best in August or early September.
Where to stay // There are good guesthouses in Omalo, a hotel in Juta, and homestays in several villages including Dartlo, Girevi, Ardoti (only one), Shatili, Roshka and Juta.
What to take // Tent for the night between Girevi and Ardoti, water bottles, snacks (food is available at homestays and guides generally bring supplies, including vodka).
More info // Caucasus Trekking (www.caucasus-trekking.com).

Opposite: the Unesco-listed village of Ushguli has as its backdrop Mt Shkhara, Georgia's highest point

MORE LIKE THIS
CAUCASIAN CLASSICS

SVANETI TRAIL, GEORGIA

Yes. Those hills really are alive... Svaneti is true *Sound of Music* country, with blissful meadowlands and soaring Alpine peaks. Yet with its distinctive *koshkebi* tower houses, it trumps Swiss landscapes, offering two particular tower concentrations in the rapidly developing capital of Mestia, and the Unesco-listed gem village of Ushguli. The whole area was virtually inaccessible in the 1990s, but over the last 15 years new roads have turned Svaneti into one of Georgia's prime visitor attractions. Most tourists zip along the Mestia-Ushguli road as a day trip, but walking is far more interesting. A well-trodden four-day trail allows you to sleep each night en route in a village homestay, though consider pre-booking during the peak July–August period especially for Iprali (third night). Also consider leaving spare days to wait it out in case of rain: you won't want to miss those glorious vistas.
Start // Mestia
End // Ushguli
Distance // 36 miles (58km)
More info // www.caucasus-trekking. comi; svanetitrekking.ge.

BABADAĞ PILGRIM TRAIL, AZERBAIJAN

Although it sits at an impressive 11,906ft (3629m) commanding 360-degree views, summiting Azerbaijan's 'holy mountain' is more of a long, steep stroll than a climb – so long as you go on a fine summer's day. It's a thoroughly rewarding experience not just for the views but for the fellow hikers you'll encounter after mid-July. Most will be pilgrims who believe that a medieval Muslim hermit 'disappeared' on these slopes in a kind of mystical ascension that has blessed the peak, making seven pilgrimages here the equivalent in spiritual merit to a full hajj to Mecca. Around halfway, at one of the most breathtaking ridge edges, it's a particularly intriguing sight to witness the ceremonial 'stoning of the devil'. The trail is generally walked up and back in a long day (six hours up, four back), starting well before dawn from Gurbangah, a seasonal camp that's a gruelling two-hour jeep ride from the charming coppersmiths' village of Lahıc.
Start/End // Gurbangah
Distance // 11 miles (17km), with a vertical climb of 4660ft (1420m)

JANAPAR TRAIL, ARMENIA

The Caucasus' longest single hiking trail notionally stretches 310 miles (500km), winding from Vardenis on Armenia's Lake Sevan to Hadrut in the self-declared republic of Nagorno-Karabakh. However, only the main Hadrut-Kolatak section is waymarked with the easy-to-spot yellow-on-blue footprint signs. Handily broken up into village-to-village sections of around five hours' daily walking, this is a hike through remote foothill landscapes where you're highly unlikely to meet any other foreign walkers. Nonetheless, using map-guides on the ViewRanger phone app it should be reasonably easy to find your way to such delights as the Karkar Canyon, the Zontik waterfall, Dadivank and Gtichavank monasteries and the Azokh (Azıx) cave, where archaeologists found the oldest humanoid remains in Eurasia. Beware: although visiting Nagorno Karabakh is straightforward from Armenia, legally speaking the region is an occupied region of Azerbaijan and entering is considered an offence under Azerbaijani law.
Start // Hadrut
End // Kolatak
Distance // 83 miles (134km)
More info // www.janapar.org

EARTH, WIND AND FIRE: LAUGAVEGURINN

Iceland's back country feels like an elemental place ruled by elves and Arctic energy, and a walk between its volcanoes and glaciers is a symphony of wind, stone, fire and ice.

Want to hear every guide's favourite joke to tell visitors to Iceland? Here it is: 'How do you find your way out of an Icelandic forest?' 'Stand up.'

Not the best joke in the world then, but as a guest you're obliged to give it a polite giggle. Every time.

My guide, Siggi, grew up among the island's treeless recesses. His home town, Hvolsvöllur, is known for having the country's biggest abattoir; its backyard the setting of *Njál's Saga*, an epic pre-medieval legends enumerating the Shakespeare-style demise of its leading characters. And while the landscape is as bleak as its reputation, there's an uncanny beauty to the area's wilderness that lures countless travellers from every corner of the globe.

They come to complete the Laugavegurinn, Iceland's premiere hike, which tackles a sequence of lunar landscapes over the course of several days. The name translates into 'Hot Spring Rd,' which seems appropriate, especially at the trailhead, Landmannalauga, where Siggi and I scamper over to soak our legs in a bog-ridden brook gurgling with steaming sulfuric water before setting off on our hike. The first time Siggi and I hiked the trail, we finished the traditional four-day adventure to Thórsmörk in only two, with enough energy to continue on through to the epic portion of Fimmvörðuháls, a volcanic spur leading all the way back to the coast. And to us, the entirety of the course has remained our true version of Laugavegurinn ever since.

Now, 10 years later, Siggi and I wade in the warm swampy waters and continue to reminisce about our first adventure together. I remember the flecks of shimmering pebbles (Siggi called them 'raven stones') at the beginning of the hike; a field of shattered obsidian reflecting and refracting the Arctic sun.

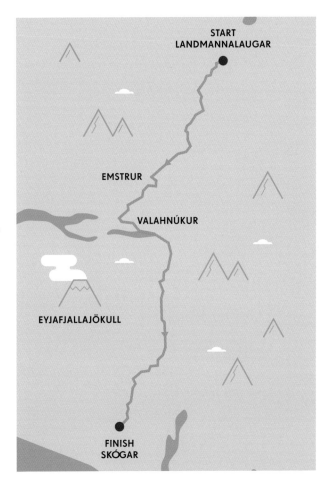

START
LANDMANNALAUGAR

EMSTRUR

VALAHNÚKUR

EYJAFJALLAJÖKULL

FINISH
SKÓGAR

© Pyty | Shutterstock

Over the last decade we've tackled various parts of the hike together in different directions and in different seasons; Siggi often using his Spidey sense to take us off-route to explore the neighbouring hills. But completing the traditional trail from start to finish is an undeniable act of pilgrimage we undertake with a certain amount of reverence. And it's not just us; every person who calls this giant seismic rock home feels the call to complete the journey at some point in their life.

The decision to tackle the hike in a southerly direction may seem rather arbitrary considering there's only a slight descent in elevation throughout, but on the walk towards Álftavatn – as the vista opens up to the looming Tingfjallajökull mountain range – one begins to understand the dramatic reveal of Laugavegurinn's second act.

The Álftavatn hut and its summertime orbit of neon tents mark the halfway point of the traditional trek and is where everyone – regardless of speed or stamina – takes a well-deserved break from the elements. It's like some kind of Nordic Burning Man fuelled by weariness and Snickers bars instead of hallucinogens and ayahuasca.

The walk through the third section, Emstrur, feels like an acid trip unto itself, with ribbons of red, ochre and fluorescent blue scarring the ground and hillside; a reminder of the intense geological activity creeping up from below the planet's surface. As the path

"The Álftavatn hut and its summertime orbit of neon tents are like some kind of Nordic Burning Man fuelled by Snickers bars instead of hallucinogens"

curls down into a valley shot through with fingers of glacial melt, the final leg of the trek comes into view. While most of the journey has followed a more subtle undulation of scorched stone, the rise up on to the volcanic crest at Fimmvörduháls is markedly more dramatic. A series of steps hoists hikers up on to a turfy plateau sprinkled with arctic flowers, and as the trail hugs the mountain's edge, cascading boulders hem the pass like flying buttresses, clerestories, and other architectural elements of gothic brick.

Often thought of as an add-on, the trek through Fimmvörduháls can feel especially challenging after several days on foot, but it's also considered the most rewarding part of the trip. While the walks through Álftavatn and Emstrur will have you wondering what it might have been like to be the first person to find soothing hot springs during Viking times, the basin of ash at the top of the pass is, quite literally, history in the making.

When the slumbering volcano hidden under the Eyjafjallajökull glacier erupted in 2010 it created a mega-geyser that vaporised

KELDUR'S LIVING HISTORY

Iceland's southern swath of moonscape is the backdrop to a Viking saga as brutal as anything in *Game of Thrones. Njál's Saga* is a gruesome story of family rivalry that ends with almost every character in the ground. Remnants of those settlement days still feature on that ground – the most authentic being Keldur, a turf-roofed farm once owned by Ingjaldur Höskuldsson, one of the major players in the saga.

From left: Skógarfoss waterfall; there's only one way to go at the River Krossá. Previous page: crossing the colourful Landmanndaugar

tonnes of frozen water and shot mounds of tar-like, liquefied ash down both the sides of the peak. Born from the embers were two brand new baby mountains, Magni and Módi, which both belch plumes of steam for passers-by to admire. Once you clear the fields of desolation caused by the recent eruption, a mossy carpet unfurls anew. Each step is slightly lower than the last, passing a parade of waterfalls (22, to be exact) that diminuendos down to a final chute – Skógarfoss, plunking you right back on to the country's main drag, the Ring Rd.

But before tackling the last day-long walk back to Route 1, the valley beneath awaits. As we leave the coloured earths of Emstrur behind, Siggi explains that the area below is known as Godaland, or 'Land of the Gods'. Tucked beneath a halo of glacial peaks, the enclave is like some kind of ancient reliquary filled with mounds of shale resembling troll fingers and elven churches. The air is different here, too – calm – guarded from the quixotic elements that wreak havoc on the landscape above.

And without the perilous arctic wind, the valley is also home to a dense thicket; Siggi and his Icelandic brothers call it Thórsmörk – 'Thor's Wood'. It's here, under the shade of a tree in the midnight sun, that we set up camp for the night. 'Turns out not every Icelandic forest is the brunt of a joke,' Siggi mutters as we settle in for the night in this unexpected spot, nestled deep within this divine land. **BP**

ORIENTATION

Start // Landmannalaugar
End // Skógar
Distance // 48 miles (77km)
When to go // July to mid-September
Where to stay // Midgard (www.midgard.is) has comfy rooms, a health-conscious restaurant and plenty of guides. Hike options are camping or reserving a bed in one of the no-frills huts.
What to take // Plastic bags to keep wet and dry clothes separate, a swimsuit for hot springs, and a GPS.
What to wear // 'Cotton is killer' are good words to live by as you dress for your trek. Go for wool layers, and be prepared to encounter all four seasons.
More info // www.fi.is, the homepage for the Iceland Touring Association, which runs the cabins on the trail.

Opposite: dramatic Hornbjarg cliffs at the Hornstrandir reserve

MORE LIKE THIS
ICELANDIC HIKES

HORNSTRANDIR

If it weren't so hard to get to, the protected reserve of Hornstrandir would be Iceland's most popular hiking expanse. Like little lobster claws nipping at the Arctic Circle, the northernmost peninsulas of Iceland's Westfjords are brutally lonely, save for colonies of cawing guillemots and the occasional Arctic fox. In summer (early July–mid-August) the preserve is blanketed in a glittering green carpet as travellers walk from cairn to cairn. For the full experience, take the ferry from the townships of Bolungarvík or Ísafjördur up to Veidileysufjördur, a glacially carved fjord, and spend four or five days hiking up to Hornvík and the bird cliffs at Hornbjarg before venturing down the mountain pass to Hloduvík and on to the cluster of abandoned cottages at Hesteyri to wait for the return ferry.

Start/End // Bolungarvík or Ísafjördur
Distance // Variable

FIMMVÖRDUHÁLS

The more traditional version of the Laugavegurinn hike ends in Thórsmörk; our perfect version continues all the way to Skógar through what we consider the most scenic part of the journey. That final stretch connecting Thorsmörk to the Ring Rd is called Fimmvörduháls, and can be undertaken as its own hike – generally tackled in the reverse direction. The day-long walk is divided into three distinct sections. The first starts at the massive waterfall in the village of Skógar and passes over 20 additional chutes as you make your way to a field of ash – the site of the 2010 Eyjafjallajökull eruption – before descending into a secret valley dotted with wild arctic flowers and hemmed by large cathedral-like rock formations. The terminus of the hike at the Básar site is known to Icelanders as Godaland, or the 'Land of the Gods', for its ethereal terrain – it's the perfect place to base oneself for some quiet camping and going on additional short walks.

Start // Skógar
End // Básar
Distance // 14 miles (23km)

HELLNAR TO ARNARSTAPI

An epically easy walk undertaken at any time of the year, the coastal stroll from the ancient farmstead of Hellnar to the village of Arnarstapi in western Iceland's Snaefellsjokull National Park is especially dramatic on an inclement day when the rock formations act like blowholes, shooting a mix of rain and sea spray into the gusty air. The short walk passes a series of frozen lava flows and eroded stone caves that are, of course, quite pretty on a sun-filled day as well, and columnar basalt, ravines and grottoes ensure plenty of off-trail exploring. Reward yourself afterwards with a steaming bowl of fish soup, which is available at either end of the walk.

Start // Hellnar
End // Arnarstapi
Distance // 1.5 miles (2.5km)

BESIDE THE LAKE IN WORDSWORTH COUNTRY

Contemplate man's place in nature on a short but poetic walk in Britain's busiest and loveliest national park – the Lake District.

There are few things so low, so deplorable and so very morally bankrupt as stealing someone's sandwich. Especially when they have spent the whole morning toiling through steep hills on foot, to finally sit down on a grassy hillside in the sun. And double-especially when that sandwich is poised before their open, expectant mouth. Snap! Jaws come out of nowhere and half the sandwich is gone.

'Pepper!' I yell, startling the other walkers sitting nearby.

To be fair, Pepper didn't want the whole sandwich – she seems quite happy to share. Still, sensing that the deed has not been received so well by the woman holding the remaining half, she

does the only sensible thing in the circumstances and legs it to the lake below, chewing as she runs. After a moment of hesitation, I cut my losses and follow her.

In case you haven't guessed, Pepper is my dog. The two of us are on a pilgrimage. Even though she doesn't know it, she is named after another dog called Pepper whose portrait hangs in a cottage on today's route. That Pepper belonged to William Wordsworth – poet, walker, guidebook writer and hero of mine.

We're in Grasmere in the Lake District, described by Wordsworth as 'the loveliest spot that man hath ever found'. And he should know – he founded the English Romantic movement, changing how

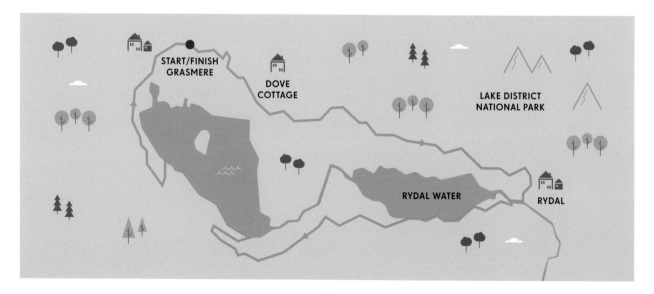

START/FINISH GRASMERE

DOVE COTTAGE

LAKE DISTRICT NATIONAL PARK

RYDAL WATER

RYDAL

© Joe Daniel Price | Getty

we view the natural world and first defining the reasons why, for so many of us, spending time in nature is so enriching.

This landscape was his muse – he spent more than 50 years living in the neighbouring villages of Grasmere and Rydal, filling the valley first with reprobate drug-addled poets, writers and revolutionaries, then with the hordes of tourists who came after reading his work. But on the Monday morning when Pepper and I park in Grasmere, you wouldn't know it. We are one of five cars.

Even though I've been here before, I'm struck by the beauty of the place. The scenery...well, there's a lot of it. Grasmere sits in a bowl. At its bottom, a perfect circle of water, a tree-bristling island and bright green fields of cows and sheep. Surrounding these, steep, craggy hills crowd in, colourful with purple heather, dark trees, browning bracken and pale rough grass. Their diminutive height, combined with their steepness and closeness, means that there's a confusion of hills and valleys, waterfalls and lonely farmhouses in every direction. Wordsworth was right: it is lovely.

We walk down a lane between grey slate houses and pass Dove Cottage, where William lived during his most productive period. I'd like to go in and show Pepper the portrait of her namesake, but she's not allowed – the tiny interior is pretty much as William left it when he moved out in 1808.

Houses behind us, we pass a flat rock beside the trail. A sign tells us that this is a Coffin Stone. In this rocky, steep region, not

> "Man is part of the scenery here, part of nature. Is isn't meant to be an empty wilderness – it's comfortable, lived in"

every village had a graveyard, so the dead had to be carried on the shoulders of their neighbours to those churches that could bury them. Any flat rock along the way was a resting place.

The path is easy (but not so easy I'd want to carry a coffin). On our right is an old, moss-covered stone wall marking the top-most field. On the left, beech and oak trees give way to the open hillside above. The only sounds now are songbirds and the ever-changing sounds of water.

This landscape is green for a reason. In a country famed for its rain, the Lake District is the wettest part. Water is everywhere. It sprinkles down my neck with every gust. The wall drips with mosses. Every two minutes we walk over a gurgling stream. We've been walking barely half an hour, and already the sun has been replaced by rain twice. But the weather isn't to be cursed. Along with the compact complexity of the landscape, it is the other reason this place is so breathtaking.

Each corner we turn, the view is different. One minute a valley is obscured by a distant rain shower, the next it is picked out in

A LAKELAND LEGACY

Lakeland's other famous literary resident was Beatrix Potter, who created Peter Rabbit. In the Lake District she was equally renowned as a farmer and sheep-breeder – despite being raised in London. By the time of her death, Potter had used her wealth to buy 14 Lakeland farms, which she gifted to the National Trust 'for the benefit of the nation', creating the beginnings of today's national park.

From left: Lake Grasmere as seen from Loughrigg Fell; Dove Cottage, once home to William Wordsworth. Previous page: Grasmere in autumn

radiant light. As the hills recede into the distance, one is black with shadow, the next golden in sunshine. And all of it constantly shifting as the clouds gather and break.

After the village of Rydal, where we visit another Wordsworth home, the route becomes busy. We walk back along the shores of two lakes. There are walkers everywhere. On Rydal Water we see orange buoys floating towards us, before I realise they are swimmers in the lake. The sound of their laughter carries over the water. Mountain bikers pass us, braking when they see the dog. We reach a rest stop between the two lakes and it's here, amid about 20 walkers, that Pepper steals the stranger's lunch.

The Lake District is busy. But this isn't meant to be an empty wilderness – it's comfortable, relatable, lived in. Nearby are Victorian villas, 17th-century cottages, Roman forts and Neolithic stone circles. Man is part of the scenery here, part of nature.

When I get back to Grasmere, I linger. There's Wordsworth's grave to visit, gift shops to browse and, just as important as the walk itself, the post-walk visit to a tearoom.

By the time Pepper and I are ready to leave, the tourist coaches have gone and the light is softening. We walk back along the river, enjoying the views, different again in the evening light.

Pepper and I agree – it's like Wordsworth said: 'This circular vale, in the solemnity of a fine evening, will make...an impression that will be scarcely ever effaced.' **PP**

ORIENTATION

Start/End // Stock Lane Car Park, Grasmere
Distance // 6.3 miles (10.2km)
Duration // Allow 2½ hours for the walk, but all day to include visits to Wordsworth's homes at Dove Cottage and Rydal Mt.
Getting there // The 555 bus links Grasmere and Rydal with National Rail services to Lancaster and Windermere.
When to go // The Lake District is accessible and equally beautiful at all times of year – just be prepared for rain.
Where to eat and drink // There are endless options for tearooms, cafes and pubs. Hotel and restaurant The Forest Side (www.theforestside.com) is Michelin-starred.
What to take // Good waterproofs, including waterproof walking shoes or boots.
More info // www.lakedistrict.gov.uk/visiting

*Opposite from top: seeking a spot
to camp around Nada Lake in the
Enchantments; the otherworldly
landscape of Prusik Peak*

MORE LIKE THIS
LAKE WALKS

KARERI LAKE CIRCUIT, INDIA

This accessible trek leads through Hindu
villages to Kareri Lake and the ridges of the
Dhauladhar. The itinerary doesn't cross any
passes and there are no demanding days,
yet you'll ascend relatively remote trails
through magnificent forests to savour the
views across the Kangra Valley and glimpse
the peaks of the Himalaya. September
through October is the ideal time to walk
and you'll need to bring a tent, stove,
cooking gear and enough food to last
the whole trek. Start the six daily stages
in a taxi to Stowari then walk the 9 miles
(15km) to Kareri village. An intermediary
hike from there to Harote on day two allows
acclimatisation. On the third day you'll
reach Kareri Lake by mid-morning, and
thus have ample time to ascend the alpine
meadows beneath the Dhauladhar. From
your campsite return to Kareri village on
day four, then climb to the village of Bal
the next day, before completing the 'half
circuit' back to McLeod Ganj.
Start // Stowari
End // McLeod Ganj
Distance // 40 miles (65km)

ENCHANTMENT LAKES, WASHINGTON, USA

This is a gruelling climb up mountains in
the Alpine Lakes Wilderness, yet it pays off
in an otherworldly realm of granite slabs,
jewel-like tarns and lofty spires. The going
is arduous – the viewless Snow Lake Trail
demands strength and endurance as it
traverses a strand of steep lake basins
partitioned by high granite walls. You'll
appreciate a walking stick or trekking
poles in several places. The clear waters
of Upper Snow Lake provide solace for
weary hikers on the way up, who must
later summon courage for a perilous log
crossing over a waterfall that spills from
the sheer-faced rim of Lake Viviane. This
is the threshold to the sparkling Lower
Enchantments. To the south rises McClellan
Peak (8363ft/2549m) and around the
corner from Sprite Lake is the wedge-like
Prusik Peak. Open late July–October,
the trail should only be attempted by
experienced backpackers.
Start/End // Snow Lake Trailhead
Distance // 20 miles (32.2km)

LAKE ANGELUS TRACK, SOUTH ISLAND, NEW ZEALAND

Despite its relatively short length, this hike
rates as one of the best in New Zealand,
boasting all that's good about Nelson
Lakes National Park. In fine weather, the
walk along Robert Ridge is spectacular –
seldom do hikes afford such an extended
period across open tops. The views will
blow your socks off, and they will again
as you descend into extraordinary Lake
Angelus basin. You'll also positively
enjoy the stopover at the Angelus Hut, a
particularly fine specimen built in 2010.
Perched on the edge of the lake 5413ft
(1650m) above sea level among golden
tussock, it has insulated walls, a capacious
common area and a large sunny deck.
Many walkers choose to spend two nights
at Angelus Hut, allowing them a whole day
to explore the beguiling environment of the
'glowing white lake', as the Maori call it.
Start // Mt Robert car park
End // Coldwater Hut
Distance // 13.4 miles (21.5km)

ACROSS THE BALKANS ON THE VIA DINARICA TRAIL

The Via Dinarica Trail stretches across the Western Balkans, giving hikers access to ancient paths, soaring mountaintops and some of Europe's last Old-World communities.

It was still dark when the smell of coffee filled our log-cabin mountain hut on the Via Dinarica Trail, a hiking route that traverses the western half of the Balkan Peninsula in southeastern Europe. We were in Bosnia and Herzegovina's Sutjeska National Park, two days into a week-long, cross-border trek. The country's tallest peak, the 7828ft (2386m) Mt Maglic, and dense forests separated us from Montenegro. As the aroma of the roasted beans reached our bunks, the world here – the valleys, rivers, chamois, goats, villages, sheep, atonal cowbells, farms, vineyards, roosters, olive groves and kaleidoscopic wildflower meadows crowding the landscape – also seemed to spring to life like a Balkans-wide alarm clock clanging on a bedside table.

Morning coffee on the trail is sacred everywhere, but nowhere so much as the Balkans and the Via Dinarica, which links summits and the most isolated pockets of Slovenia, Croatia, Bosnia and Herzegovina, Montenegro, Albania, Kosovo and Macedonia. Regardless of where you trek along this nearly 1200-mile (1931km)

route, which crosses the Dinaric Alps and Šar Mountain Range, the thick, stove-cooked, liquid blackness is more than an addictive wake-up remedy; its consumption here, where the East meets the West, is a metaphor for life. Your dented metal camping mug holds history. It holds the dawn. It holds promise. It holds centuries of gossip and compromise. It is a cup full of empires: Greek, Roman, Byzantine, Ottoman, Austro-Hungarian. It brims with drawn-out tales, secret strategy sessions and comrades sitting around a rough-sawn table. *Kafa* (coffee) is to be enjoyed with a hand-rolled cigarette and tumbler of local schnapps. In the Balkans, it is a hard-working and multi-purpose ritual as well as a caffeinated elixir.

Hard-working and multi-purpose are also apt descriptors for the Via Dinarica Trail, which offers both easy-to-moderate walking stages and sections that demand technical prowess. It links seven countries, dozens of national parks and Unesco sites, and many of the region's highest mountaintops. Trekkers can tackle it with hardcore adrenaline. But the trail is more than that: it is a cultural corridor to be embraced by time travellers and history buffs for three months or three days. The path is a lens on to some of the last remaining Old-World, authentic communities in Europe. Mornings here mean trekkers rustle out of sleeping bags, affix headlamps, pull on trousers and lace up boots – to be sure. Sunrise also means it's time for village farmers to coax and stoke embers in iron woodstoves. When light cracks the horizon, herders step out of dirt-floor lean-tos in nomadic camps and survey their flocks amid dew-covered rolling hills, as they have done since time immemorial.

The Via Dinarica concept is a decade old. However, the route's building blocks date back centuries and, in some cases, are prehistoric. The concept, which stitches together shepherds' transversals, ancient trading roads, military trails and mountaineering paths, became official in 2010. In 2013, a project tracked and recorded much of the trek's length. Since, the Via

> *"Recent tourism trends are for 'real experiences'. Well, we've hundreds of years of real experiences to be discovered here"*

Dinarica has become a cross-border, collaborative chorus for the countries of former Yugoslavia and Albania – a unified way to promote this previously unheralded adventure-travel playground.

'One powerful aspect of the Via Dinarica is its value as an adventure tourism tool to bring travellers to places most people don't know exist', says Aleksandar Donev, the Director of the Agency for Promotion and Support of Tourism in Macedonia. 'But another great aspect is the trail's ability to give locals – from Slovenia to Macedonia – a way to share traditions they've been perfecting for generations. The recent trend in tourism is "real experiences". Well, we have hundreds and hundreds of years of real experiences to be discovered here.'

GOURMET DELIGHTS

You'll enjoy the coffee, but that's not the only gourmet pleasure on the Via Dinarica. Stopping in villages along the route is like a progressive meal with fresh meats and vegetables from beginning to end. Each country is proud of its gastronomy, which was Slow Food long before the term existed. Try to buy any of the farm-fresh and homemade bread, cheeses, greens, honey and liqueurs you can manage to get your hands on along the path.

Clockwise from top: Church of St John at Kaneo, Macedonia; a shepherd boy and his charge; on the approach to Mt Sneznik in Slovenia
Previous page: hiking in the Maglic massive, Bosnia and Herzegovina

© Elma Okic

After coffee and reorganising gear into backpacks – carefully jiggering wedges of cheese, sausages and packets of peanuts among foul-weather gear and layers – we set out from the hut for the craggy climb up Mt Maglic, the top of Bosnia and Herzegovina. It was slow going, a vertical crawl: handholds and careful foot placements. When we reached the summit, I caught up with Thierry Joubert, a regular hiking companion who has trekked nearly every section of the Via Dinarica with me over three years of piecing together stages when schedules allowed.

'There are wonderful similarities across the Via Dinarica, but it's always different because there are so many interpretations of landscape, culture and history', said Joubert, who is the director of Green Visions, an adventure-travel operator based in Sarajevo. 'When you walk through Croatia, you parallel the Adriatic Sea. In Albania, you are under soaring peaks. In Macedonia, you straddle a ridgeline border with Kosovo. This trail gives hikers a route to untouched mountaintops. It gives hikers a way to see villages and shepherd communities that may not be here in 10 years.'

We descended the other side of the mountain into Montenegro and stood on a ridge, resting on our hiking sticks, looking down at the heart-shaped, glacial Trnovacko Lake – a calling-card photo-op along this section of the trail. After several minutes, we started again. The border crossing and a new country seemed to give Joubert an extra pop to his step. When he was several yards ahead of me he looked back over his shoulder. 'At this next clearing, let's take a break', he said. 'I'll pull out the stove and we can make some coffee.' **AC**

ORIENTATION

Start // Postojna, Slovenia
End // Ohrid, Macedonia
Distance // 1199 miles (1930km)
Getting there // Fly into Ljubljana, Slovenia, an hour's bus ride from the trailhead. Depart from Skopje, Macedonia, about 2½ hours by car from Lake Ohrid.
When to go // The best Balkans hiking is in late spring (May and Jun) and autumn (Sep and Oct).
Where to stay // Manned mountain huts, unmanned shelters and homestays abound. Packing a tent widens options.
What to take // A sleeping bag, foul-weather gear, layers and sunscreen should be in your backpack. Broken-in, high-quality hiking boots are a must.
More info // For guided information, contact the Via Dinarica Alliance (www.via-dinarica.org): a cooperative of adventure operators committed to the trail. For questions about accommodation, route and conditions, check out the Via Dinarica project site (https://trail.viadinarica.com).

© Ivan Vukelic | Getty, © Elma Okic

*Opposite: on the Via Alpina through
the Wetterstein range in Germany*

MORE LIKE THIS
CROSS-BORDER EUROPE

VIA EGNATIA

Paved between 146 and 120 BC, the Via
Egnatia (VE) connected Rome to Istanbul
(then Byzantium), and thus the Western
Roman and Eastern Roman Empires. 'In its
long history, VE has been used intensely,
decayed, was restored several times and
decayed again', states *Via Egnatia on Foot*,
a guidebook published by the Via Egnatia
Foundation. After centuries of relative
dormancy, the trail – running through
Albania, Macedonia and Greece – has
been resurrected with 301 miles (485km) of
the original 684 miles (1100km; to Turkey)
described and marked with GPS tracks.
Once used for travel, trade and military
movements, today the route combines
cities, ancient ruins, mountain views and
rural expanses. If you prefer to go guided,
the Albania-based Our Own Expeditions
takes walkers from Durres, Albania, to
Thessaloniki, Greece.
Start // Durres, Albania
End // Thessaloniki, Greece
Distance // 301 miles (485km)
More info // www.viaegnatiafoundation.
eu; ourownexpeditions.com

NORDKALOTTLEDEN TRAIL

Also known as the Arctic Trail, the
Nordkalottleden Trail runs 497 miles
(800km) and crosses borders 15 times as
it snakes through Norway, Sweden and
Finland. Described as the most northerly
long-distance hike in Europe, the entirety
of the route sits within the Arctic Circle.
This is, not surprisingly, not a path for the
winter months. Trekking should be done
from July to September, which will allow
expeditions sufficient time – around 45
days of moderate backpack walking – to
complete. The well-marked track, which
also boasts a solid hut system from end to
end, was proposed in 1977 and supported
by all three countries. The Nordkalottleden
was realised in 1993 and takes adventurers
through wide-open expanses and giant
skies and along lakes, glaciers and gorges.
Start/End // There are three starting
and ending points: Kautokeino, Norway
(north); Sulitjelma, Norway (south);
Kvikkjokk, Sweden
Distance // 497 miles (800km)
More info // www.nationalparks.fi;
www.traildino.com

VIA ALPINA

In 2005, the Alpine Convention completed
the markings and signage creating,
officially, the first trans-Alps trail: the Via
Alpina. There are five routes that make up
this system of tracks, which connects the
countries and already well-established
paths of the Western Alps. However, the
spine of this network is the Red Trail, which
runs from Trieste, Italy, to Monaco, and
links eight nations: Italy, Slovenia, Austria,
Germany, Liechtenstein, Switzerland,
France and Monaco. This hike covers
approximately 1500 miles (2414km) over
161 stages, and crosses country borders
a whopping 44 times. Along the way,
mountaineers walk within a stone's throw
of the continent's highest peaks, trek
through hidden villages, stay in huts and
learn more about honest European life and
gastronomy than they would ever imagine.
Start // Trieste, Italy
End // Monaco
Distance // Approximately 1500 miles
(2414km)
More info // www.via-alpina.org

CAMINO DE SANTIAGO

Join hikers from all over the world on this ancient pilgrimage across northern Spain from the French Pyrenees to Santiago de Compostela in Galicia.

Walking alongside rows of neat grapevines in the late-morning sun, I felt a dryness in my throat and my thoughts drifted to the glass of Rioja from this very region that I vowed to search out once I reached the *albergue* (hostel) that afternoon. There was no one ahead of me on the dusty path and as I walked I listened to the thud of my boots on the hard ground, my rucksack swishing against my shorts and the distant rumble of traffic on the highway.

Turning a corner, I saw Clara and Silvia, two Italian pilgrims (people walking the Camino), sitting under a tree and sharing a huge bunch of grapes. 'Want some? A farmer gave them to us',

Clara called out. I threw down my rucksack, sat down beside them, took off my walking boots and massaged my hot, aching feet.

One week into the month-long 490-mile (790km) walk from Saint-Jean-Pied-de-Port in the French Pyrenees across northern Spain to Santiago de Compostela in Galicia, the days had developed a familiar rhythm.

Mornings started early, waking in a bunkbed to the sound of rustling plastic, backpack zipping and heavy footsteps as the first pilgrims headed out at sunrise. Throwing my pyjamas into my rucksack, I would follow the yellow arrow waymarkers out of town, walking for an hour or so until I saw somewhere to stop for coffee

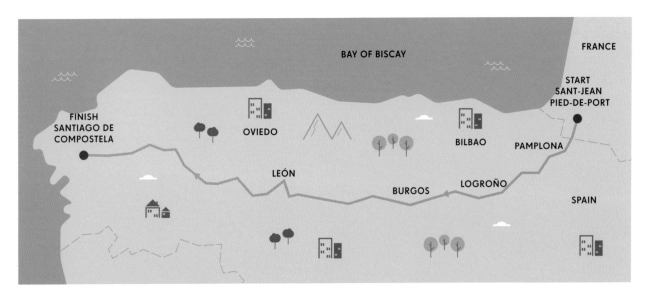

BAY OF BISCAY

FRANCE

START
SANT-JEAN
PIED-DE-PORT

FINISH
SANTIAGO DE
COMPOSTELA

OVIEDO

BILBAO

PAMPLONA

LEÓN

BURGOS

LOGROÑO

SPAIN

and tortilla. Usually, I would pass the same people at around the same time each morning, walkers with enough patience to pause and take in the scenery around them. That first week I was too focused on reaching the next destination to stop and explore the pretty villages I passed through. I would keep walking with as few breaks as possible until I reached the town where I planned to spend the night, hiking for about 16–20 miles (25–35km) a day.

Sometime in the early afternoon I would reach an *albergue*, one of the hostels along the Camino that provide accommodation for pilgrims. The most memorable were atmospheric places in ancient parochial buildings, with dinners eaten at communal tables and bunks up in the rafters. Other places had swimming pools; in the hot summer weather the cool relief of a dip in a river or pool was the refreshing highlight of the day.

Often I would get the heads-up about a good *albergue* from one of the pilgrims who had walked the Camino before. Stefan and Carina, a German couple in their twenties who had met on the Camino and were re-walking the route on their honeymoon, were a good source of information.

It was Stefan who told me about Anya's house in the village of Ages. The timber-framed house with pink exterior walls looked like it belonged in a fairy tale, as did Anya herself, a Norwegian woman in her sixties with long grey hair. There was room in her loft for eight people.

"For four weeks I travelled only by foot — no cars, buses or trains — moving slowly allowed me to notice what was around me"

In the morning, over breakfast by the range cooker in her cluttered kitchen, Anya told us that we were now a third of the way along the Camino. The first third, she said, was physically challenging: dealing with blisters and getting used to walking through varied landscapes.

I thought back to the Pyrenees, where I had set out on that first damp day in thick fog, struggling to see the path ahead of me, accompanied by a chorus of bells hanging from the necks of cows I could barely make out in the mist and my pulsing anxiety at the thought of the vast distance that lay between me and Santiago de Compostela. Shrouded with clouds, the forests took on an enchanted air. In Navarra and Rioja, the landscape had changed to gentle hills and fields of sunflowers, scattered with picturesque villages. In Puente la Reina, my arrival coincided with a local fiesta, with street parties and bull running.

The next third of the walk, between the cathedral cities of Burgos and León across a largely flat, arid landscape, was where the spiritual work would begin, Anya explained. With fewer

For over 1000 years pilgrims have followed the path to Santiago de Compostela to visit the tomb of St James, thought to have brought Christianity to the region. But the route dates back to pre-Christian times, when Celts would follow the Milky Way west to Finisterre (land's end). Today, pilgrims walk for a range of reasons. Many tie a scallop shell – a symbol of the pilgrimage – to their rucksacks.

From left: another pilgrim on the Camino; the scallop shell is the symbol of the route; the trail passes through town as well as country. Previous page: the way to Santiago de Compostela is well trodden

distractions, the monotony of walking every day would become meditative. Now was the time to think about why we were walking the Camino.

Why are you walking the Camino? It was a question everybody asked. The answers were often deeply personal: dealing with grief or illness or a sense of religious obligation. Some people returned to walk the Camino for a second or third time with their families or partners. I could only mutter that I had a month free with nothing better to do; the truth was I wasn't sure why I was there.

By the time I reached León, two-thirds of the way to Santiago, I had had plenty of time to think. For four weeks I had travelled only by foot – no cars, buses or trains – and moving slowly allowed me to notice what was around me, to chat about everything and nothing with other pilgrims and snack on blackberries along the way. I had relaxed into the routine of walking every day with everything I needed in my small backpack, with nothing to think about except arriving in the next place. After walking all morning, the simple pleasures of taking off my walking boots, a hot shower and a cold beer were intensified.

About 60 miles (100km) from Santiago, the Galician mountains stood between me and my destination; the demanding climbs came with breathtaking views. Finally arriving in a rainy Santiago a month after setting out from Saint-Jean-Pied-de-Port, I felt a true sense of accomplishment when I thought of how far I had come. **IA**

ORIENTATION

Start // The full Camino Francés route of the Camino de Santiago starts in Saint-Jean-Pied-de-Port, but you can start walking anywhere along the way.
End // Santiago de Compostela
Distance // 491 miles (790km)
Duration // 30–34 days
Getting there // The nearest airport to Saint-Jean-Pied-de-Port is Biarritz. The nearest airport to Santiago de Compostela is 8.7 miles (14km) east of the city centre.
Things to know // The route is waymarked with yellow arrows. Register at the pilgrim's office in Saint-Jean-Pied-de-Port to get a *credencial* (pilgrim's passport), stamped at each *albergue* (hostel) on route. You must walk at least the final 62 miles (100km) to Santiago to earn the *compostela*, a certificate of having completed the pilgrimage.

MORE LIKE THIS
SPANISH TREKS

LA SENDA PIRENAICA (GR 11)

Dividing France from Spain, the Pyrenees may not be as lofty as the Alps (the tallest summit is Pico de Aneto, at 11,168ft (3,404m), but they're arguably even more gorgeous, blessed with diverse landscapes and abundant wildlife. The GR 11, traversing the Spanish slopes, is one of three long-distance trails tracing the range. And what a trek. From the Basque Country in the west, this extremely demanding but rewarding 45-stage beauty takes in craggy gorges, wildflower-strewn meadows and medieval villages to reach mainland Spain's easternmost point in Catalunya. Highlights include Aigüestortes i Estany de Sant Maurici National Park, which is studded with gem-like tarns, and the dramatic karst canyons of Ordesa y Monte Perdido National Park – watch for magnificent, rare bearded vultures dropping sheep bones to smash on rocks before gulping down the pieces.
Start // Cape Higuer
End // Cap de Creus
Distance // 522 miles (840km)
More info // www.cicerone.co.uk

CALDERA DE TABURIENTE, LA PALMA

The northwesternmost of the Canaries, La Palma is, it's claimed, the world's steepest island. This volcanic speck soaring from the Atlantic Ocean is also a verdant dream for hikers, laced with some 620 miles (1000km) of waymarked trails. In its centre rises Caldera de Taburiente National Park, dominated by its namesake crater – a 5-mile (8km) wide cauldron filled with Canarian pines, laurels, flowers and birds, venue for La Palma's most memorable hike. From the viewpoint at Mirador de los Brecitos, the trail curls around the crater's inner rim, delving into a spectacular ravine past a once-sacred rock outcrop; a worthy detour accesses the bijou multi-hued waterfall known as the Cascada de Colores.
Start // Mirador de los Brecitos
End // Las Viñas car park
Distance // 9 miles (14km)
More info // Book a taxi to the Mirador from the nearby town of Los Llanos de Aridane

PICOS DE EUROPA CIRCUIT

The unforgettable nine-day circuit of the Picos de Europa covers the range's extraordinary river gorges, alpine lakes, depressions, dense beech woods, narrow canals, cliff-hanging trails and peaks with breathtaking views. For reasons of ease and safety – some sections should not be attempted in reverse – this hike is done in a clockwise direction from and to Lago de la Ercina, incorporating Vega de Ario, the villages of Caín and Bulnes La Villa, the glacial Vega Urriellu, Refugio Diego Mella/ Collado Jermoso, Cordiñanes village, the campsite at the Vega Huerta and the Refugio Vegarredonda. Bring a map and compass as it's easy to get disoriented if fog settles, be aware that rain sometimes makes steep sections too dangerous to tackle and *refugios* are often full in August, so carry a tent with you. It'll be worth it as you visit national park villages, explore the Garganta del Cares gorge and walk through high green pastures against a backdrop of stunning mountains.
Start/End // Lago de la Ercina
Distance // 65 miles (104km)

Clockwise from top: high in the Picos de Europa; corn drying by the road; greeted by an Iberian goat

WALKING ON THE TROLL'S TONGUE

*A spur of rock projecting out above a glacial blue lake, Trolltunga
is one of Norway's most legendary, and legend-laden, hikes.*

It's a grey autumn morning in the mountains of western Norway. A shroud of cloud is suspended over the black peaks above Lake Ringedalsvatnet as I strap up my boots and begin to climb. It's early, and the forest is quiet. Morning dew glitters on the mossy boulders, and mist filters between the trees, tinting everything in a silky smoke-glow, as though the world's being viewed through a pane of frosted glass. The only sounds are water running over rocks, and a crow croaking among the treetops. It feels like wandering into a fairytale. And in a way, I have.

Norway's hills, fjords and forests are rich with fairy stories. According to legend, they're home to a menagerie of fantastical creatures: mischievous gnomes, irascible dwarves, ethereal elves, wicked water spirits known as *nøkken* and seductive forest sprites called *huldra*. But the mountains are the land of the trolls, and I'm on my way to visit their most famous haunt of all: Trolltunga, the Troll's Tongue, a shard of rock poking out from the black mountainside high above Lake Ringedalsvatnet. If you believe the folklore, it was formed when a dim-witted troll was caught poking his tongue out at the sunrise, and turned to stone. And even if you don't, it's equally well known for having one of Norway's most legendary views – a cliff-edge, sheer-drop, heart-in-the-mouth panorama that's the stuff of acrophobic nightmares.

START/FINISH
SKJEGGEDAL

TROLLTUNGA

LAKE
RINGEDALSVATNET

Unfortunately, getting into troll country isn't easy. Trolls being naturally reclusive creatures, they prefer to live in remote caves and valleys hidden amongst the mountaintops, so it takes effort to reach their domain – and Trolltunga is no exception. From the trailhead at Skjeggedal, it's a there-and-back hike of at least eight hours, traversing forest trails, rocky plateaus and granite ridges, many of which stay snow-covered for at least half the year.

It takes around an hour to climb the first section, a leg-sapping slog up a staircase cut into the wooded mountainside, emerging on to a mountain plateau sprinkled with pools formed by summer snowmelt. By the time I reach the plateau and push on to the next climb, the mist is burning off, and streaks of blue are breaking through overhead. Peaks appear behind the cloud, lined up like guards manning a castle watchtower. Lakes sparkle in the morning light, and a carpet of tundra stretches up the mountain, sprinkled with wildflowers. I refill my water bottle from a cold stream, breathing in the crisp mountain air before continuing the ascent.

The trail dips into a grassy valley, then climbs, and suddenly, the blue sweep of Lake Ringdalsvatnet appears, a curve of turquoise backed by sheer, black slopes, still topped by a dusting of snow. It's a cinematic view that stays in focus for much of the remaining climb to the troll's lair.

> *"Lakes sparkle in the morning light, and a carpet of tundra stretches up the mountain, sprinkled with wildflowers"*

I pass a couple of wild campers, and stop for a cup of coffee, brewed over a whistling camp kettle. They've been up here for a couple of days, they tell me, exploring the landscape and photographing the sunsets. We're nearly a kilometre up, so it's cold and windy at night, they say – but it's worth the hardships for the chance to experience Trolltunga without any crowds. I feel a pang of envy, and resolve to return with my own tent when I can.

The last section of the trail climbs along the ridgeline, unfurling fresh views of Ringdalsvatnet as it creeps up the rocky boulders to Trolltunga itself. By now the cloud has evaporated, and a clear canopy of blue stretches overhead. In the distance, I catch a metallic glint on the horizon, and I wonder if it could be the distant glaciers of Folgefonna, Norway's third-largest icecap – remnants of the mighty ice sheets that once covered all of northern Europe, and carved out Norway's jagged topography of lakes, mountains, valleys and fjords.

POWER RANGER

As you follow the shores of the fjord north from Odda towards the Trolltunga turn-off, you'll pass through Tyssedal, home to one of Norway's most historic hydro-electric power stations, a masterpiece of early 20th-century industrial design by the pioneering architect Thorvald Astrup. You can take a guided tour of the power station, and high above the fjord, follow the clifftop path once used by engineers, which has been turned into a thrilling via ferrata.

From left: the monstrously good view from Trolltunga; a reminder that it's a long way down. Previous page: the Troll's Tongue itself

I round a final corner and suddenly it's there: Trolltunga itself, jutting out from the sheer cliff-face, a granite promontory perched 2296ft (700m) above the valley below. Even though I've been hiking for four hours and it's only mid-morning, there are still a few hikers here already to share the view. Carefully, they creep down the rockface and inch on to the troll's tongue itself, matchstick figures dwarfed by the scale of the landscape, and the sheer drop below. Contrary to appearances, the tongue itself is actually surprisingly wide, at least a few metres across. That said it pays to keep well away from the edge; fatalities have happened here. I watch as the group snap selfies, smiling and seemingly oblivious to their position on a slip of rock dangling over the void.

And then it's my turn. Gingerly, I walk on to the precipice, like a diver edging out on to the high board. The wind rushes past, plucking at my jacket. Empty space engulfs me, and the yawning blue chasm opens up below. Clouds race past, and for a moment, I feel the rock drop away, a figure suspended between earth and sky. And then the moment's gone, and I'm inching my way back on to the cliff edge, and the safety of bare rock and terra firma.

I take a last look at the view and a swig from my water bottle, then begin the long trudge home. I may not have seen a troll today – but I feel like I've glimpsed some magic all the same. **OB**

ORIENTATION

Start/End // Skjeggedal
Distance // 14 miles (23km) return
Duration // Nine to ten hours
Getting there // Odda train station is 8 miles (13km) from Skjeggedal. Bergen airport is about 80 miles (130km) to the west of Odda. Public transport to the trailhead is limited. A bus runs in July and August, and taxis can be hired at Odda train station. Some hotels and hostels also offer transport.
When to go // June to September.
Where to stay // Hardanger Hotel (www.hotelsinodda.com).
More info // Trolltunga Active (www.trolltunga-active.com) run a range of guided hikes, including snowshoe walks in winter. Good walking boots and waterproof clothing are essential, and it's wise to leave the hike for clear weather, as trailfinding can be tricky in heavy cloud and fog.

Opposite: giving praise to the amazing
vista on Norway's Pulpit Rock

MORE LIKE THIS
LOOKOUT POINTS

PREIKESTOLEN, NORWAY

Arguably the most famous hike in the whole of Norway, Preikestolen – the Pulpit Rock – gets its name from its resemblance to a priest's lectern. It's a shelf of rock framed on three sides by sheer cliff walls, plummeting down 1981ft (604m) into the waters of Lysefjord. While the walk up is steep in places, it's not too challenging – just a couple of hours each way – and the challenge is far outstripped by the epic views on offer at the top. It's a very famous sight, and a favourite of Instagrammers, which also means it's popular – so this is one hike that's well worth reserving for spring (March to May) or autumn (September to November) if you can, when the crowds will be thinner and you'll be able to admire the view in a little more tranquility.
Start/End // Preikestolen Mountain Lodge
Distance // 3.7 miles (6km) return
More info // www.visitnorway.com

FAIRVIEW MOUNTAIN, CANADA

On nearly any hike through the Canadian Rockies, you'll be treated to some stunning lookouts, but this challenging trail in Banff National Park offers perhaps one of the best wraparound panoramas in the entire mountain range. Switchbacking 3 miles (5km) up the mountainside from the turquoise shoreline of Lake Louise, the trail emerges at the mountain summit at 3323ft (1013m) after three or four hours of tough climbing. Thankfully, Fairview turns out to be an entirely fitting name: from the top, you'll get an incredible overview of the lake itself, as well as a host of glaciers, forest and spiky summits along the green Paradise Valley. It was a favourite of the Swiss mountaineering guides who pioneered many of summit routes in this part of Canada, and it's not hard to understand why.
Start/End // Lake Louise
Distance //6.5 miles (10.6km) return
More info // www.pc.gc.ca

DESOLATION PEAK, WASHINGTON, USA

In 1956, Beat writer Jack Kerouac famously spent two months alone while manning a fire lookout at the top of this wild, airy summit in the North Cascades. Kerouac's stay prompted numerous poems, essays and prose experiments, and you'd have to be made of stone not to be at least a little inspired by the view from the top, which takes in the peak of Hozomeen Mountain, the shores of Lake Ross and the snow-capped mountains of the North Cascades. Unfortunately, you won't get to see it without putting in some effort: first you need to cross Lake Ross to reach the trailhead, then clamber up the punishingly steep trail, which ascends more than 4265ft (1300m) of altitude in a little under 5 miles (8km). Unfortunately, the lookout tower itself isn't open to the public, so Kerouac fans will have to make do with paying their respects outside.
Start/End // Lake Ross
Distance // 10 miles (16km) return
More info // www.nps.gov

A WINTER TRAVERSE OF THE GREAT ST BERNARD PASS

Don snowshoes to cross one of the most storied mountain passes in Europe, and meet the brave souls who watch over travellers on the road.

It takes around five minutes to drive through the Great St Bernard Tunnel. Five minutes to drive 3 miles (5km) underneath the Alps and cross the border between Switzerland and Italy as you go – piazzas and pizzerias on one side, timber chalets and watch emporiums on the other. It is just about enough time for a motorist to hum along to Puccini's *Nessun Dorma*, or attempt some light yodelling.

However, there is an older route that runs directly over the heads of motorists in the tunnel: up above the sunroof, up above the strata of metamorphic rocks and a crust of ice and snow, high among the summits where the air is thin and the passing airliners don't seem so very far away. This route is the Great St Bernard Pass, a frozen highway counting as one of the most treacherous and storied trails in Europe.

'Summer and winter are two different worlds up there,' explains Eric Berclaz, leaning on his ski poles at the foot of the pass. 'Summer is not a problem. In winter, you need to know what you are doing.'

Eric is my guide for the ascent, and it is also his job to help decide when the Great St Bernard Pass is able to open to motorists for the summer season. 'Summer' in the loosest sense of the word. For just two or three months of the year, the snow melts enough for tourists to drive to the top, admire the view and maybe buy a souvenir fridge magnet from a kiosk. From September to June, the Great St Bernard Pass is plunged into a near-permanent state of Narnia: the road buried deep in snow, shivering in temperatures that sink to -30°C (-22°F) while holidaymakers on the Mediterranean siesta on the beach not so far away. During this time, the only way to cross the pass is on skis or snowshoes.

I strap into my snowshoes for the three-hour hike to the top. It soon feels like an exercise in time travel. In the valley below, spring is arriving: wildflowers grow in the meadows and people are wearing shorts. The Great St Bernard Pass, meanwhile, is lagging a few months behind in bleak midwinter. The snowdrifts become deeper with every step. Everything is still, but for the croak of ravens and the hum of overhead power cables. A few skiers and snowboarders whoosh past.

Today, like much of the Alps, the Great St Bernard Pass is a place for recreation. But before the tunnel was built in the 1960s, travellers between the Italian plains and northern Europe had

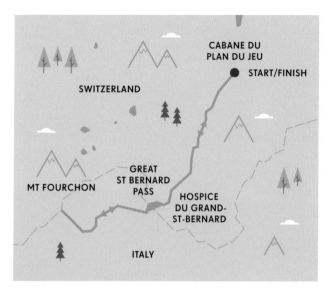

© Justin Foulkes | Lonely Planet

little choice but to come this way. Pilgrims on the Via Francigena crossed on their way from Canterbury to Rome. Napoleon led a 40,000-strong army over the mountains, the soldiers hauling their cannons up the mountainside (the man himself sliding down on his tiny backside). Everyone from Roman legions to counterfeit cigarette smugglers traversed the Great St Bernard Pass. And there were also wayfarers who climbed into the mountain mists, and never came back down again.

Snowflakes glide through the air as Eric and I arrive at the top of the pass. Out of the wilderness there emerges a grand doorway hung with icicles, and windows half-submerged in the drifts. We have arrived at the Hospice du Grand-St-Bernard, a religious hostel that has stood at the highest point of the pass since the 11th century. Its robe-clad holy men and gigantic St Bernard dogs gained fame as a mountain-rescue double act: fishing passers-by out of avalanches, guiding them through fog to the safety of the hospice. Still run by the Catholic Church, the institution exists for the same purpose today: to welcome and protect passers-by.

Today, the St Bernard dogs live in an institute on the floor of the valley, but the two-legged community still thrives at the top of the pass. Three canons and several housekeeping volunteers supply about 50 visitors with clean beds and three generous meals a day

"The A-listers of the Alps assemble on the horizon...the ridge of Gran Paradiso; the perfect pyramid of the Matterhorn"

LEGACY OF ST BERNARD

St Bernard de Menthon (c 1020–1081) was a medieval priest who built a stone shelter for travellers in the Alps. In time, this shelter grew into a small community, with no members more famous than the giant St Bernard dogs, whose thick fur, large paws, strong limbs and sensitive smell made them ideal for rescue missions. St Bernards were used to uncover lost souls in the snow until the 1950s, when helicopters replaced the doe-eyed woofers.

Clockwise from top: up and over the border; essential kit; plaque at the hospice; a guide points the way. Previous page: the beauty of the pass

© Justin Foulkes | Lonely Planet

in one of the most hostile wildernesses in Europe. The front door is open to everyone, regardless of their religion. In 1000 years the door has never been locked.

Packing a sandwich and an apple, I set out on a day trip to Mt Fourchon, the shark-fin-shaped peak that's visible from the kitchen window of the hospice. The trail leads across the Italian border, past sentry posts locked for the winter, and little road signs peeking above the snowline: 'STOP' and 'PASSPORTS'. Hours pass. A northerly wind gathers strength. Distant walkers shrink to tiny dots. As I draw closer to Fourchon, the A-listers of the Alps assemble on the horizon. To the south is the ridge of Gran Paradiso – the tallest peak entirely within Italy, where a little statue of the Virgin Mary stands on the summit praying to the sky. To the east the mass of Grand Combin and the perfect pyramid of the Matterhorn. Back to the north is the beginning of the pass; once the site of a temple to Jupiter, where Romans came to worship the god of lightning.

And beside it is a vast statue of St Bernard himself, his back turned to the mountains and his outstretched bronze hand pointing travellers home to the hospice. Guests return one by one as the sun sinks over the Mont Blanc massif, colouring the snow rosy pink on its way.

Since the building of a tunnel, the hospice is no longer a necessary staging post, and yet thousands of visitors still make the journey every winter. Some people come to conquer a mountain, a few to look for Jesus Christ walking barefoot in the snowdrifts. Many come to be above the world below, here where the air is crisp and the views stretch forever. **OS**

ORIENTATION

Start/End // Bourg St Pierre
Distance // About 5 miles (8km) one way
Getting there // The closest airport is Geneva. From here it's a two-hour drive to the northern limit of the pass.
Tours // www.swissmountainleader.com and www.alpinetreks. com offer two-day treks, overnighting at the Hospice du Grand-St-Bernard.
Where to stay // Before the ascent, at Cabane du Plan du Jeu (cabaneplandujeu.ch), or luxurious options in Marigny.
When to go // Snow is on the ground from December to May.
What to take // Snowshoes lock around walking boots; winter boots will be comfier, but sturdy three-season boots are sufficient. Pack robust waterproof clothing, sunglasses and high-factor sun cream, with avalanche transmitters advisable.
More info // www.saint-bernard.ch
Things to know // Check your travel insurance covers you for Alpine snowshoeing – Swiss mountain-rescue services charge (a lot) for call-outs.

Opposite: wild ibex in the Gran
Paradiso National Park, Italy

MORE LIKE THIS
TECHNICAL WINTER HIKES

BEN MACDUI, SCOTLAND

Crowning the Cairngorms, Britain's highest national park, is Ben Macdui, the UK's second-tallest peak, just 115ft (35m) shorter than big Ben (Nevis). All Highland hikes are epic, but a winter ascent of 4295ft (1309m) Macdui promises extra excitement – especially if you overnight in a snowhole en route (with expert guidance from someone who knows one end of an avalanche probe from t'other). From Cairngorm ski centre, creep through the cauldron of Coire an t-Sneachda, spying snow buntings and grouse-like ptarmigans, and climbers clinging to ice-encrusted cliffs above. When required, don crampons, grip an ice axe, and ascend to the plateau proper, where five of Scotland's six highest Munros (mountains higher than 3000ft/914m) stand, and Am Fear Liath Mòr (the Big Grey Man of Ben Macdui, a Yeti-like monster) is rumoured to roam. After standing atop Macdui, return via Shelter Stone rock, Cairn Gorm and Fiacaill a' Choire Chais.
Start/End // Cairngorm ski centre car park
Distance // 11-mile (18km) round trip
More info // www.munrocentral.co.uk

GRAN PARADISO, ITALY

An ascent of Italy's highest peak (excluding Mont Blanc, which has its head and one foot in France) begins with a hike through the country's oldest National Park. It's not a super-technical climb, but you do require technical equipment (rope, crampons, helmet, ice axe) and a guide if inexperienced in the mountains. The path wends through woodlands before emerging from the trees and gaining height via a series of steep switchbacks, washed by waterfalls and populated by mischievous marmots. At the snowline at 8973ft (2735m) you reach Rifugio Vittorio Emanuele II, your overnight nest. The hard hike to the 13,323ft (4061m) summit begins under torchlight after a 4.30am breakfast. Several routes, one involving via ferrata, lead to the top, where, attached to your guide/climbing buddy by an umbilicus of rope, you squirm towards the apex of Italy and a meeting with Madonna (Virgin Mary statue, not the pop star).
Start/End // Gran Paradiso National Park
More info // www.parks.it

TWO THUMBS RANGE, NEW ZEALAND

Within the extraordinary expanse of Te Kahui Kaupeka Conservation Park, near Lake Tekapo in the middle of the South Island, the wide glaciated valleys and ice-numbed peaks of the Two Thumbs Range offer off-piste adventures aplenty for ski mountaineers during winter. For cold-play seeking wanderers happier hiking than sliding, however, guided snowshoeing escapades offer an excellent alternative. Owned by local family-run Alpine Recreation, Rex Simpson Hut, a 4265ft (1300m) eyrie on the edge of the range, makes a magical base for such missions. From here, slip on snowshoes and stomp along sinuous Snake Ridge to beautiful Beuzenberg Peak 6791ft (2070m), absorbing the surrounding Southern Alps, a twinkling tiara of peaks topped by not-too-distant Aoraki/Mt Cook. Outside of winter (June–August), green-season hiking here is sensational too.
Start/End // Coal River Bridge car park, off Lilybank Rd (near Lake Tekapo)
Distance // 7 miles (11km) one way to Beuzenberg Peak, via Rex Simpson Hut
More info // www.alpinerecreation.com

THE RING OF STEALL

With a blistering series of 3000ft (914m) peaks, astounding views and a delicious hint of exposure, this is a serious candidate for Scotland's finest hill day.

The Devil may have all the best tunes, but in the UK he also seems to have a monopoly on exquisite geology. You can climb the Devil's Kitchen in Snowdonia, Wales, stand on the Devil's Point in Scotland's Cairngorms, descend into the 100ft (30m) gorge of the Devil's Pulpit in the same country's Finnich Glen, and even clamber up the Devil's nostrils in the Shetland Islands. And just a short distance from Fort William, you can cross the Devil's Ridge, a highlight of The Ring of Steall and one of the best mountain day hikes in the country.

This 10-mile (16km) walk across muscular mountain terrain attracts a tiny fraction of the footfall of neighbouring Ben Nevis; while Scotland's highest peak draws an estimated 150,000 people to its 4413ft (1345m) summit each year, we met just one solitary walker during our long day on this incredible route. He had driven overnight from London to climb four of the mountains that make up the Ring of Steall, each of them a Munro: a Scottish mountain over 3000ft (914m). There are 282 of these summits dotted around

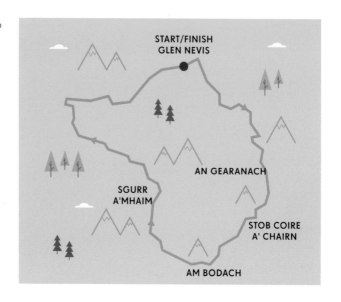

the country and climbing them all is a challenge that takes some people a lifetime to complete, although the fastest-ever circuit is an incredible 40 days.

But this is a walk that's made to be savoured rather than sped through. For us, it began with a stroll through deciduous woodland, with its cacophony of bird life and the River Steall crashing through a deep boulder-strewn canyon below us. As it opened out the river broadened and slowed, and the early morning sunlight sent biblical shafts of light across Glen Nevis.

Our first challenge was to tightrope across the river on a three-wire bridge – one for your feet, two for your hands. Loaded down with walking gear we inched our way across one by one the base of the 393ft (120m) Steall Falls. It was a dramatic Cirque du Soleil start to our ascent of An Gearanach, which at 3221ft (982m) was our first Munro of the day. It's a demanding climb, made more palatable thanks to beautiful views of Ben Nevis and neighbouring Aonach mountain range. As you near the top, the ridge starts to narrow and you can see the entire route laid out in front of you in a spectacularly undulating horseshoe.

The Ring of Steall sits in the centre of the Mamores mountain range, and tackling it in early spring meant there was still plenty of snow underfoot. There were sections of the walk where we would need to kick secure steps into the snow with our boots or where we'd require the stability that comes with an ice axe.

"The summit is the perfect place to quietly contemplate the hordes on the zig-zagging tourist path up Ben Nevis"

The ridge of An Gearanach finally meets the main bulk of the Mamores at the second Munro of the day, Stob Coire a'Chairn (3218ft/981m). For the ultra-fit mountaineer a complete traverse of the Mamores in under 24 hours is the ultimate challenge. It involves eight Munros, with two out-and-back sections to pick off the mountains at either end of our walk. On just our second summit of the day, we were happy to drop our packs for a while and breathe in the unexpectedly clear views. Good visibility can feel like a lottery win in the Scottish hills. From here we could see hundreds of summits on all points of the compass, fanning out across the Highlands, revealing how mountainous this country is.

The clear skies weren't to last. By the time we'd climbed the 3386ft (1032m) Am Bodach (Munro number three), the mist had descended and visibility had dropped to a few feet. Weather changes fast in the mountains so you need to pack spare clothes, extra food, a map and compass, and have good navigational skills.

'Hold on, let's take a bearing off this summit,' said Jeremy, as I shouldered my pack and started to amble down what seemed like

BECOME A MUNRO BAGGER

The Munros are a list of Scottish mountains over 3000ft (914m), compiled by Sir Hugh Munro in 1891. Those aiming to climb all 282 peaks are called baggers. Ben Nevis is many people's first (and only) Munro, but accessible peaks like Ben Lomond (3195ft/974m) are good starting points. Many finish on Ben More, on the Isle of Mull, dipping their boots in the sea before walking the entire 3069ft (966m) to the summit.

From left: the snowy slopes of An Gearanach; treading carefully on Devils' Ridge. Previous page: the Ring of Steall atop the scenic Mamores

the right path. My intuition was proved entirely wrong. I'm not sure how long it would have taken me to realise my mistake, but a little compass work had just saved me the humiliation of a big ascent to get back to square one.

Before we hit our final summit, we climbed to the top of Sgor an Iubhair, which despite its height of 3284ft (1001m) holds the record for having been a Munro for just 16 years; there's a subjective element to this mountain compendium, and this former Munro was demoted to join the 227 subsidiary tops in 1997.

It is the prelude to the Devil's Ridge, an airy section of the route at its most exposed along a broad arete. Blessed with a calm day we sauntered across with hands in pockets, but I can imagine this being dicey when the winds are whipping up or if there's ice underfoot. For those who love climbing over rock there were sections of scrambling to add to the excitement, while nervous members of our group could opt for the grassy path to the side.

That delicious hint of exposure led to the final Munro of our day, the 3606ft (1099m) Sgurr a'Mhaim. The descent from here is tough and the long trek back along the tarmac to pick up our car was gruelling. So we'll finish sitting on top of the final summit. It's the perfect place to quietly contemplate the hordes on the zig-zagging tourist path up Ben Nevis. Few of them realise that they are within easy reach of the Ring of Steall: a connoisseur's mountain route that deserves to be on everyone's must-do list. **MS**

ORIENTATION

Start/Finish // Car park at the end of the Glen Nevis road
Distance // 10 miles (16km)
Ascent // 5499ft (1676m)
Duration // 10-12 hours
Getting there // Train to Fort William and then bus service runs as far as the bridge at Polldubh Falls.
Where to stay // Glen Nevis Youth Hostel www.syha.org.uk
Pack // Waterproofs, warm clothes, good hiking boots, water and spare food all vital, as are map, compass, head-torch and sound navigational skills.
Safety // This is a demanding day over serious terrain for experienced mountain walkers.
When to go // Summer months when days are long and snow is off the ground.

Opposite from top: the view from Pen y Fan in the Welsh Brecon Beacons; the An Steall Ban waterfall and the path through Nevis Gorge

MORE LIKE THIS
BRITISH HORSESHOE ROUTES

COLEDALE ROUND, LAKE DISTRICT

While many tourists are drawn to the Lake District by the collective magnetism of Beatrix Potter and Wordsworth (see pp218–221), it's the fells that are the real attraction. If you're looking for a walk that's worthy of your boot leather, the often overlooked Coledale Round is bristling with incredible summits and littered with relics of Cumbria's industrial past. Starting and finishing in the village of Braithwaite, it takes you over the pyramidal 2595ft (791m) peak of Grisedale Pike and the spectacular Hopegill Head (2526ft/770m). There's an optional out-and-back to Grasmoor (2795ft/852m) and Wandope (2532ft/772m), before a finale of Crag Hill (2752ft/839m) and Causey Pike (2090ft/637m). There are shorter variants that provide an easier but still-dramatic day out. Whichever option you choose, you'll be rewarded with some steep climbs, rocky summit approaches and one of the best routes in the Lakes.
Start/End // Braithwaite
Distance // 11.5 miles (18km)

BEN NEVIS VIA THE CARN MOR DEARG ARETE, SCOTLAND

Climbing Ben Nevis is an essential tick for anyone heading to Fort William, and while the tourist path to the top is a trudge, an ascent via the Carn Mor Dearg Arete is an exciting route for experienced walkers. On a fine day it delivers some of the best views of the North Face of The Ben, host to scores of classic mountaineering routes. Parking at the North Face car park you walk towards the Ben, turning left to climb Carn Mor Dearg. The ridge itself is a long scything approach that steepens sharply as it reaches the top. Take time to explore the observatory ruins and memorials on the summit before taking the tourist path down. In poor visibility you need to follow a bearing of 231° for 492ft (150m) and then a bearing of 281° off the summit to avoid a dangerous section between Gardyloo and Five Finger Gully.
Start/End // North Face car park
Distance // 11 miles (17km)

PEN Y FAN HORSESHOE, BRECON BEACONS, WALES

Wales's Brecon Beacon National Park comes into its own in the low, golden sun of autumn, when the distinctive rocky strata of Pen y Fan's northern face casts a corduroy shadow across mountain. Just a short drive from Cardiff, this is a great day out, starting from the Forestry car park just south of the town of Brecon. You hang a left at the Neuadd Reservoir and begin the climb on to the Craig Fan Ddu ridge. This leads you up to Corn Du (2864ft/873m) and then north along the ridge, offering incredible views of glacial valleys. British Special Forces are based locally and train on this mountain and you'll see evidence of shooting ranges as you continue on to your high point for the day: Pen y Fan (2907ft/886m), the highest peak in the Brecon Beacons. A steep descent from the summit takes you over the 2608ft (795m) Cribyn and the gloriously named 2359ft (719m) Fan y Big.
Start/End // Forestry car park, near Brecon
Distance // 9 miles (14km)

HAPPY FAMILIES: A DONKEY HIKE IN THE FRENCH PYRENEES

Enjoy wildlife-rich pine forests and breathtaking views of craggy peaks in the Val D'Azun, where a Pyrenean donkey will provide the perfect distraction for younger hikers.

The summer that our children turned four and six we made the decision to leave our lovely French coastal campsite, with its fun adventure playground and four-slide mega-swimming pool, and take them hiking up steep hills in the Pyrenees for two days instead.

I didn't expect it to go well. Especially as back then walking for any decent distance would often be met by whining. Yet it became the hands-down holiday highlight of that year, thanks almost entirely to a pure-bred Pyrenean donkey named Lazou.

On the first morning of our hike we met Lazou and her owner Marie at Bernicaze Farm, not far from Arras-en-Lavedan, near Lourdes, in southwest France's Hautes-Pyrénées. It was clear she was a well-loved donkey with shining eyes and a healthy coat, and nothing like the ragtag flea-ridden mule stereotypes you used to see at the seaside.

So it felt like a great privilege when we were entrusted to lead her away from the farm and into the wilderness shortly afterwards. Particularly as we had no phone reception or concrete idea of where we were going. Luckily Marie had equipped us with paper maps and some meticulously detailed instructions, my favourite of which was 'follow [the path] for 800m until you find three unusual fir trees, planted in a triangle'.

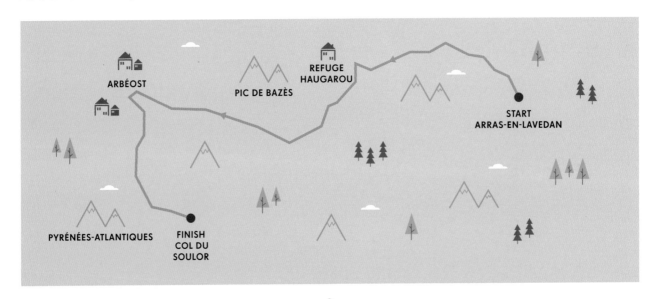

ARBÉOST

PIC DE BAZÈS

REFUGE HAUGAROU

START
ARRAS-EN-LAVEDAN

PYRÉNÉES-ATLANTIQUES

FINISH
COL DU
SOULOR

While the grown-ups got their heads around a trip without GPS, our kids wasted no time in getting to know Lazou, who helpfully also seemed to know exactly where she was going. They each held a section of her lead rope, and took turns in gently stroking her fur while babbling merry strings of nonsense into her ears. Such was the power of donkey distraction that the first hour of walking, through a stunning pine forest, passed in a blur without them noticing the forward motion at all.

We stopped off for a picnic lunch of rock-hard, in the best possible way, mountain bread, cheese and sausage by an actual babbling brook. Meanwhile Lazou munched on some thistles, which seemed to be her favourite snack, much to our childrens' delight and fascination.

We skirted around the edge of this Eden-esque woodland enjoying all manner of giant butterflies, bees, birds and beetles in shades we'd never seen before. However, when we went back into the deep forest the incline sharpened a little and some low-level grumbling began to emerge from the kids. Fortunately we had a trump card – they were allowed to ride Lazou, who was also carrying our overnight bag – so they did that in rotation for the remainder of the day's hike, sitting bolt upright on her back like proud princes in a storybook.

After three hours of pleasant pine-scented and wildlife-rich hiking, during which we hadn't seen a single other human being, we popped out of the trees on to a road just below the Refuge Haugarou, which was to be our base for the night. While Lazou gorged on the long grass and yet more thistles, our kids rarely

"Regardless of how Instagram-worthy the view was, our focus was here; it was pure family time"

far from her side, we relaxed while watching the sun slip down the edge of the tree-green valley below.

Our second day started off with the steepest section of the trip, which wound up through a switchback-style forest trail. But as ever Lazou was a calm and reassuring presence, even if there was some mild bickering between the boys over whose turn it was to ride on her back, forcing us to time their stints in the spirit of fairness (although we secretly gave the younger one a little longer from time to time).

Before long we stepped out from the trees to an amazing high-mountain panorama. The craggy 5919ft (1804m) Pic de Bazès towered to our right, while the Pyrénées-Atlantiques range of mountains stretched off to the horizon in every other direction. Our path was now flat and wide, with plenty of blackberry bushes dotted along the way, so our kids' spirits soon returned to the high levels of the previous day.

We walked side by side on the springy mountain grass and had the kind of enjoyable and meandering chats you only seem to

PYRENEAN DONKEYS

A mix of the tall Catalan and rounder Gascon breeds, Pyrenean donkeys are fit, strong and sure-footed, which makes them particularly suited to the steep and winding hiking trails found in this rocky region. Traditionally used for farm labour and transportation of goods up and down the mountains, their numbers dwindled when car use became widespread, but their decline has slowed since the 1990s and they're increasingly settling into their new role as trekking companions for visitors to the Pyrenees.

Clockwise from top: the Pyrenees offers plenty of wildlife-spotting options, such as bearded vultures; orange butterflies; and, of course, donkeys. Previous page: the Unesco-listed Cirque de Gavarnie in the Parc National des Pyrénées

© Artur Debat | Getty

have with your children on long walks, when phones and all other distractions are out of sight. Along with the donkey, the lack of mobile signal was the unexpected highlight of the trip. Regardless of how Instagram-worthy the view was, our focus was here; it was pure family time.

We picnicked by a lake to a soundtrack of clanging cowbells, watching herds drink at the waterhole and munch on the lush grass around it. We then started to make our way down the valley through the giant glacial scree of the Cap d'Aout. En route we passed springs in the hillside and stone barns by the pathways while vultures circled in the sky, and although we encountered a few more hillwalkers than we'd seen on the first day, we still saw no more than 10 people in total by the time we reached our end point at the Col du Soulor.

We live in the city, so to be that immersed in nature and away from crowds of people felt incredibly mentally refreshing. And although the second day's walking had lasted for close to four hours, it had nonetheless been wholly manageable even for our sons' young legs, thanks, of course, to the steady yet exciting presence of Lazou.

Our youngest was almost inconsolable when it was time to say goodbye to her, and a year on from the trip he still remembers the hike vividly and loves talking about Lazou, wondering what she's up to now. It had clearly been a win-win experience for all of us; a relatively tough walk in a remote setting, yes, but one that we'd all come through smiling, leaving us with the most cherished memories a family can have. **SH**

ORIENTATION

Start // Bernicaze Farm
End // Col du Soulor
Distance // Around 15.5 miles (25km)
Duration // Two days
Getting there // The closest airport is Tarbes-Lourdes, about 30 minutes away. The nearest international airports are Biarritz and Toulouse, each about two hours' drive away.
Where to stay // Refuge Haugarou (www.haugarou.com).
More info // www.tourism-occitania.co.uk; www.labalaguere.co.uk/tour-val-dazun-donkey.html
What to wear // Shorts and T-shirts, but carry waterproofs and warm clothes as it's a high mountain area and the weather can change at any time.
What to take // Sun hats, sunscreen, snacks and water.
Things to know // We had no mobile phone reception for much of this hike, so we had to rely on the basic instructions provided. However, more nervy folk might want to take a hand-held GPS.

*Opposite: a pair of Saint Bernards,
once the mountain rescue dogs of
Switzerland*

MORE LIKE THIS
FAMILY-FRIENDLY
WILDLIFE HIKES

LLAMA TREKKING IN YELLOWSTONE NATIONAL PARK, USA

Llamas are perfect hiking companions for Yellowstone, as they're sure-footed, at home on mountainous terrain, and they leave virtually no impact on the park's fragile trails. Your kids will love their long ears and lolloping style, while you'll be glad of their tent- and bag-carrying capacity. Yellowstone Llamas offers a range of family-friendly pack trips, including the three-day hike and camping along the Slough Creek Trail, which winds through magnificent mountain scenery but isn't too challenging beyond its initial climb. If you're lucky you may spot a bear or hear wolves howling at night, and there are ample meadow-grazing opportunities for your llamas along the way. Back at the riverside campsite, kids will enjoy playing on the rocks around the camp and in the river, which is also a great spot for fishing.
Start/End // Slough Creek
Distance // About 9 miles (15km)
More info // www.yellowstone llamas.com

WALKING WITH ST BERNARD DOGS, MARTIGNY, SWITZERLAND

St Bernards have been the quintessential mountain rescue dog since the early 19th century, when they guided lost travellers through the snow and mist at the Grand St Bernard Pass in Switzerland, where they were housed at a monastery and bred by monks. In 2005 the Barry Foundation took over the breeding of the original dogs from the monastery. Though no longer used in rescues, you can still hear about their fascinating history, including the story of the eponymous Barry, who saved more than 40 people in his life, on guided walks organised by the foundation. The 90-minute walks take place in pretty woodland around Martigny along a route that's flat and suitable for young children, who will love holding the dogs' leads and giving them a good cuddle at the end of the walk.
Start/End // Barry Foundation Museum
Distance // Around 1.3 miles (2km)
More info // www.fondation-barry.ch

HIKING AMID HIGHLAND COWS, PENTLAND HILLS, SCOTLAND

Highland cows are thought to have roamed the rugged Scottish landscape since the 6th century. With their shaggy coats, long horns and long eyelashes, they're everyone's favourite cattle breed and are especially popular with young children. Swanston Farm in the Pentland Hills near Edinburgh is a great place for kids to spot them. The herd roams the hills above the thatched cottages of the farm, which has been a conservation area since the 1970s. From the hills you can enjoy wonderful views of Edinburgh, the Lothians and the Firth of Forth, and there's also a good chance of spying some of the other farm residents, including badgers, foxes, red kites and barn owls, plus the unusual collection of moss, lichen and fungi, including the brilliantly named Candle Snuff Fungus and Scurfy Deceiver.
Start/End // Swanston Farm
Distance // Around 4 miles (6.4km)
More info // swanston.co.uk/activities

ENCHANTED FOREST: THE WESTWEG

Get your fill of Germany's bewitching Black Forest on this challenging multiday trek to dark woods, deep valleys, mountains of myth and lakes of lore.

Early morning and the Black Forest is shaking off its dewy slumber. There's a wonderful stillness at this hour and an almost visible sensation of everything coming back to life. Ferns are lazily uncoiling their fronds, tall firs and pines are stretching towards the light, the day's first rays of sun are raking through the treetops. It's silent but for the tentative hammering of a woodpecker and the occasional crack of a branch underfoot. I'm totally alone. I take a deep breath and inhale the freshness of a golden autumn day. The mist draping the valley is lifting and I can make out a cluster of dark-timber farmhouses and a slender church steeple in the valley below. The pleats and folds of the forest rise above it like multi-layered curtains.

Of all the hikes that dip into Germany's remaining pockets of true wilderness, the Westweg is one of the most celebrated. Running the rolling length of the Schwarzwald from top to bottom, the trek is a serious undertaking, involving two solid weeks of moderately challenging, high-altitude hiking. But boy are the blisters worth it. The waymarked trail heads to off-the-radar viewpoints and cascading waterfalls, half-timbered hamlets, post-glacial lakes and mountaintops that peer across to the not-so-distant Alps – and, *natürlich*, deep into those necks of the woods that are inaccessible to cars. This is a hike through a forest straight from the pages of a Grimm bedtime story, steeped in legends of lake nymphs, witches and paths easily strayed from.

The Westweg takes in the best of the Black Forest's crochet of tightly woven valleys and sharply rising hills, allowing moments of quiet contemplation in among the spruces, where moss grows thick like the plushest of carpets. Some might find the loneliness disconcerting, but I've always found solace in its darkest depths.

John Muir once said that 'the clearest way into the universe is through a forest wilderness' and he had a point. In the protective embrace of the trees, it is easy to unplug from the world and get that bit closer to nature. As my hike begins, I feel a near-meditative sense of calm. Everything becomes more intuitive: the gentle stirring of trees, the profile of a startled deer, the play of light as day turns to dusk, the rhythm of my own stride.

Pforzheim is the gateway town to the trail, but I do not linger. I'm too eager to strike out into the heart of the forest. And so I walk through the upland moors of the Enz Valley, where medieval Schloss Neuenbürg stands high on a hill, and on to the plateau

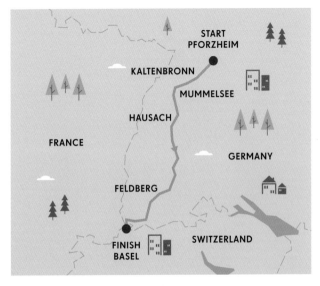

*Opposite: Tasmanian devils are among
the many wild animals residing in the
Tarkine Wilderness Area*

MORE LIKE THIS
FOREST FROLICS

GREENSTONE AND CAPLES, NEW ZEALAND

Lesser-known than many of New Zealand's Great Walks, you'll often have the trail all to yourself on this four-day circular tramp through South Island's backcountry. It's a moderately challenging ramble taking in two World Heritage valleys, sub-alpine passes, glacier-fed rivers, waterfalls and sunlit, lichen-swathed beech forests that look freshly minted for Middle Earth. Have your camera handy for photogenic moments like the view of Lake McKellar against a backdrop of oft-snowcapped peaks from the route's high point – the 3100ft (945m) McKellar Saddle. Nights are spent camping in the wild or staying at basic huts, where you might share a bunk with a local deerstalker or trout fisherman. The area is steeped in Maori heritage, as the sacred *pounamu*, or greenstone, glitters in these rivers.
Start/End // Divide (West) or Greenstone Shelter (East)
Distance // 38 miles (61km)
More info // DOC huts should be booked in advance. Camping is permitted on the bush edge, 164ft (50m) back from the track.
www.doc.govt.nz

KARHUNKIERROS TRAIL, FINLAND

Finland's Bear's Ring trail is the ultimate way to tiptoe away from civilisation and back to nature. The moderately challenging three- to four-day jaunt delves deep into the berry-filled *taiga* (boreal) forest of spruce, pine, birch and larch in the Oulanka National Park, just south of the Arctic Circle. In this corner of Lapland, sidling along the Russian border, the silence is only interrupted by the rush of the Oulankajoki, the Kiutaköngäs Rapids and the Jyrävä Falls. As you walk the park's gorges, primordial forest and lakeshores, look out for glimpses of wolves, reindeer and brown bears. Come in autumn for a glorious kaleidoscope of colours.
Start // Salla
End // Kuusamo
Distance // 50 miles (82km)
More info // www.nationalparks.fi/ karhunkierros

TARKINE WILDERNESS AREA, AUSTRALIA

Although the name is absent from most maps, and its borders are not well defined, the 1350-sq-mile (3500-sq-km) Tarkine Wilderness Area in northwest Tasmania contains Australia's largest tract of cool temperate rainforest. Roughly bounded between the Pieman and Arthur rivers, 'Australia's last great wilderness' is home to towering Huon pine trees, sheltering Tasmanian devils, quolls, platypus, echidnas, wombats, bandicoots and wedge-tailed eagles. If the Tasmania tiger – 'presumed extinct' in 1986 – survives anywhere, it's most likely here, perhaps within the ultra-remote 70-sq-mile (180-sq-km) Savage River National Park. Trails are rough and tough, but they exist. One option leaves Corinna and combines the Huon Pine Trail and the Savage River walk to trace the banks of the Pieman River to the mouth of the Savage River. A link trail then segues to Savage River Bridge and the Mt Donaldson walk, to make a truly epic adventure in a properly primeval place.
Start // Corinna
End // Savage River Bridge
Distance // 9 miles (14km)
More info // www.discovertasmania. com.au

THE
ROUTEBURN TRACK

Follow ancient Maori paths through New Zealand's Southern Alps, where huge flightless birds once roamed and the rivers sparkled with sacred jade.

A late morning sun appears and disappears through a patchwork of high clouds, revealing a huge bushy expanse stretching hundreds of miles over hilltops and shaded valleys, surrounded by jutting peaks of grey rock. This is the tail of New Zealand's mighty Southern Alps, a vast spine of sandstone and granite reaching nearly 300 miles (483km) along the South Island's western coast. It is remarkably isolated. No roads connect the mountains ahead to the rest of the world. Instead, to explore the peaks, lakes and river valleys that stretch from here in the Fiordland National Park to Mt Aspiring in the west, I must make my way on foot via a thin, winding hiking trail known as the Routeburn Track – a 20-mile (32km), three-day journey through some of New Zealand's most spectacular landscapes.

In a sloping green valley known as The Divide, the track begins. I set off with boots crunching into skittering gravel and packed earth. The path leads through thick stands of beech trees swathed in drooping moss, crowded in by the outstretched fingers of fern

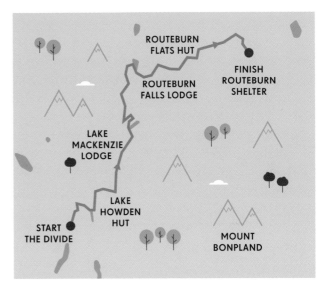

© Philip Lee Harvey | Lonely Planet

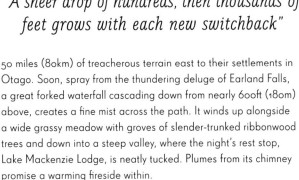

fronds that grasp softly at my knees. The forest is quiet, save for the rhythm of footsteps, my blue waterproof jacket providing a bobbing spot of bright colour in a setting of endless green.

The track traces slowly around the northern lip of the Livingstone Mountains and climbs upwards, higher and higher, twisting with the curves of the terrain, to reach the crest of Key Summit. The wind, held at bay until now by the forested slopes, here whips around a broad grassy mountaintop, grabbing handfuls of my hair and buffeting against my eardrums.

It was along routes like this, climbing high mountain passes and detouring through the surrounding valleys, that the ancient people of this land walked hundreds of years ago. Hardy Maori hunters forged paths through the thick foliage in search of great boulders of pounamu – known as greenstone or New Zealand jade – lying like forgotten jewels at the bottom of the rivers and lakes stretching from here to the west coast.

Great ridges of snow-topped mountains fill the horizon before me, framing three of these great river valleys, stretching off in different directions – Hollyford to the north, Eglinton to the southwest and the bushy green slopes of the appropriately named Greenstone Valley to the southeast. All are shaped by shifting tectonic plates and the inexorable grinding of colossal glaciers.

I trace along the western flank of the Ailsa Mountains, the path growing steeper with every step. The Maori walked these paths in sandals made of woven cabbage leaves, making their way across

"A sheer drop of hundreds, then thousands of feet grows with each new switchback"

50 miles (80km) of treacherous terrain east to their settlements in Otago. Soon, spray from the thundering deluge of Earland Falls, a great forked waterfall cascading down from nearly 600ft (180m) above, creates a fine mist across the path. It winds up alongside a wide grassy meadow with groves of slender-trunked ribbonwood trees and down into a steep valley, where the night's rest stop, Lake Mackenzie Lodge, is neatly tucked. Plumes from its chimney promise a warming fireside within.

The next morning I pick up the track with a steep climb up a narrow, zig-zagging path. Alongside, a sheer drop of hundreds, then thousands of feet grows with each new switchback, until I reach a rocky open area overlooking the Hollyford Valley. The near-perpendicular granite slopes of the Darran Mountains line up before me. Sir Edmund Hillary cut his teeth here before making his attempt on Everest in 1953.

For early European settlers, these westernmost reaches were a dark, forbidding place, unmapped and unknown. Today, as I walk up to the grassy hilltop of Harris Saddle, I look out into the rumpled green distance, and it's clear that great areas of dense forest and scrubland remain as they were hundreds of years ago, still rarely, if ever, visited by humans.

POUNAMU

The moss-green pounamu found here was prized by Maori tribes up and down the country, crafted into jewellery or simply used as currency. Harder than steel, it was also handy for creating the deadliest of weapons, such as razor-sharp axes and broad-bladed clubs called meres, which hung from the wrist with plaited twine and could be used to wrench open an opponent's skull. It was more valuable than gold.

Left to right: Lake Mackenzie; crossing a walk bridge on the Routeburn Track; a giant sculpture of a takahē stalks the streets of the Fiordland town of Te Anau; New Zealand is home to some 550 species of moss. Previous page: a hiker admires the view

It was in remote areas like this that the last of New Zealand's giant flightless birds, the legendary moa, most likely clung on before succumbing to extinction. With some species growing close to 10ft (3m) tall, like a Jurassic-sized ostrich without wings, moa were considered imaginary – a fanciful story of the Maoris – until discovery in the mid-19th century of their long-necked skeletons up and down the country proved their existence beyond doubt.

I round the ridge overlooking Lake Harris, surrounded by snow-dusted peaks, and past the thundering cascade of Routeburn Falls before coming to the evening's rest stop at Routeburn Falls Lodge.

Routeburn Falls marks the edge of the treeline at more than 2400ft (750m). When morning light spills over the mountainside and into the valley, it reveals the undefined border where the craggy grey outcroppings of the mountains descend into forest. From here, the track winds alongside shaggy alpine pastures, over springy suspension bridges and through thick green bush, the downward path encouraging a light step after two days of uphill endeavour.

Before long, a strange noise is heard on the breeze – the rumbling motor of a bus in a nearby car park, sounding rough and foreign to the ears after three days spent isolated in nature – and soon, the Routeburn Track has come to an end.

After a journey of 20 miles (32km), I arrive down on the valley floor, and the soaring highlands above, with all their legends, mysteries and fantastical creatures, are once again out of sight beyond the trees. **CL**

ORIENTATION

Start // The Divide
End // Routeburn Shelter
Distance // 20 miles (32km)
Duration // Three days
Getting there // The nearest airport is in Queenstown, which is just over an hour from the Routeburn Shelter. Note: most hikers use a drop-off service such as Kiwi Discovery.
When to go // Late October to April.
Where to stay // There are four huts on the track. Book all accommodation passes for huts and campsites in advance.
Where to eat // Take food with you. The huts have basic cooking equipment.
What to take // Sturdy boots, waterproofs, lots of layers, a first-aid kit, food and water are the basics: plan carefully.
More info // www.doc.govt.nz. Lonely Planet's *Hiking & Tramping in New Zealand* is also an excellent resource.

Opposite: Mitre Peak rising from the Milford Sound fiord in Fiordland National Park. Previous pages: Earland Falls on the Routeburn Track; the protected kea, the world's only alpine parrot

MORE LIKE THIS
NEW ZEALAND GREAT WALKS

MILFORD TRACK, SOUTH ISLAND

The best-known track in NZ – with its towering peaks, glaciated valleys, rainforests, alpine meadows and spectacular waterfalls – is very popular. That it is not overrun, despite attracting more than 7000 independent hikers every year, is down to a regulation system that keeps people moving while ensuring some level of tranquillity. During the Milford tramping season, from late October to late April, it can only be walked in one direction, from Glade Wharf. Additionally, hikers must stay at Clinton Hut on the first night (even though it's only an hour from the start) and the trip has to be completed in three nights and four days. All restrictions will pale as you clap eyes on the views towards Mt Fisher, for example, or branch off to take in the awesome Sutherland Falls, or scrabble into the tiny cave under Bell Rock – just a few of the many highlights along the route.

Start // Glade Wharf
End // Sandfly Point
Distance // 53.5km (33 miles)
Duration // Four days

KEPLER TRACK

One of three Great Walks within Fiordland, the Kepler was built to take pressure off the Milford and Routeburn. Many trampers say it rivals them both. This alpine crossing takes you from the peaceful, beech-forested shores of lakes Te Anau and Manapouri to high tussock-lands and over Mt Luxmore. The route can be covered in four days, spending a night at each of the three huts. Eye-popping sights include towering limestone bluffs, razor-edged ridges, panoramas galore and crazy caves. The Kepler is a truly spectacular way to appreciate the grandeur of NZ's finest and most vast wilderness.

Start/End // Lake Te Anau control gates
Distance // 37 miles (60km)
Duration // Four days

LAKE WAIKAREMOANA TRACK

Remote, immense and shrouded in mist, Te Urewara National Park encompasses the largest tract of virgin forest on the North Island. The park's highlight is Lake Waikaremoana ('Sea of Rippling Waters'), a deep, 55-sq-km (21-sq-mile) crucible of water encircled by the Lake Waikaremoana Track. Along the way it passes through ancient rainforest and reedy inlets, and traverses gnarly ridges, including the famous Panekiri Bluff, from where there are stupendous views of the lake and endless forested peaks and valleys. Due to increasing popularity, in 2001 the track was designated a Great Walk requiring advance bookings.

Start // Onepoto
End // Hopuruahine Landing
Distance // 28.6 miles (46km)
Duration // Four days

SYDNEY'S SEVEN BRIDGES

Circle shimmering Sydney Harbour in a 17-mile (27km) loop, crossing iconic Sydney Harbour Bridge (and six others), taking in historic urban areas, beaches, bush and more.

I've been a bit of a bridge geek ever since building one out of popsicle sticks in grade school science class, so getting to see seven up close is more thrilling than I'd like to admit. This hike is best known as part of a yearly event called the Sydney Seven Bridges Walk, which raises money for cancer research. But my husband and I have decided to tackle it on an ordinary Tuesday in November.

We live near Sydney's CBD (Central Business District), so we decide to start the hike at its southeastern point, Pyrmont Bridge. Crossing Cockle Bay in the shiny entertainment district of Darling Harbour, the pedestrian-only Pyrmont, festively decked in coloured flags, looks more like a wide beach pier than a traditional urban bridge. Opened in 1902, it's one of the oldest working examples of an electric swing bridge, which means its middle chunk swings open to allow tall boats to pass. We don't get to see that in action today, but we do get a good eyeful of the pleasure yachts that moor here in the shadow of the CBD's modern skyscrapers. Crossing the bridge, we edge around the top of Pyrmont peninsula, passing wharves that once smelled of fish and reverberated with the sounds of shipbuilding. Today they're upmarket apartments and cafes, and many of the adjacent warehouses have been razed and replaced with waterfront green space.

Turning the bend to the western side of Pyrmont, we see it in all its glory: the Anzac Bridge. The Sydney Harbour Bridge may be the city's most famous, but true bridge geeks dig the Anzac more, with its cables like strings on a massive harp. The 2640ft (805m) bridge honours the Australian and New Zealand Army Corps (ANZAC), which fought WWI's Battle of Gallipoli. Far above our heads, an Australian flag flutters against the clear blue sky on the bridge's eastern pylon, while a New Zealand flag ripples on the western pylon. Walking on the pedestrian lane beside eight lanes of Sydney morning traffic, we have views over the disused Glebe Island Bridge, which has sat rusting at the mouth of Rozelle Bay for more than two decades.

We exit the Anzac and we're in Rozelle. We wander the residential backstreets of this rapidly gentrifying neighbourhood, where traditional brick bungalows and wooden cottages sit cheek-to-jowl with modernist boxes of glass and concrete. At the peninsula's western edge, we enter Callan Park. Here, a complex

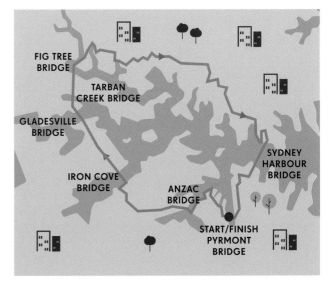

of neoclassical sandstone buildings sits eerily quiet amid lush, slightly gone-to-seed parkland. Once the Callan Park Hospital for the Insane, the buildings are now home to an arts college. People say the area is haunted, and it's easy to believe. Somewhere in the distance, an ice-cream truck plays a tinny version of 'Greensleeves' over and over. I shudder slightly and wipe sweat from my face. It's midday now, and getting hot.

Next up is the Iron Cove Bridge, a mid-century art deco beauty. A second Iron Cove Bridge, opened in 2011, runs parallel. We choose to cross the older bridge, huffing up the stairs and on to the pedestrian walkway. Exiting into the upscale residential neighbourhood of Drummoyne, we stop for flat whites at a cafe in a shopping complex overlooking the Parramatta River. The water is dotted with tiny islands, including Cockatoo Island, home to a 19th-century prison, and Spectacle Island, once used for manufacturing naval explosives.

The next bridge, the tall, graceful Gladesville, offers even more spectacular views (and quite a quad burn too). The afternoon is clear enough for us to see all the way down to the Sydney Harbour Bridge and the CBD some 4 miles (6km) away. The bridge itself is a 1900ft (579m) concrete arch, once the longest of its kind. Elegant white sailing boats glide through the deep blue waters below and ferries chug along, carrying passengers from one suburb to the next.

In quick succession we zip across the Tarban Creek Bridge and the Fig Tree Bridge, a span bridge and a girder bridge respectively.

> *"The mighty steel arch stretches across the harbour between pylons of Australian granite"*

PORT JACKSON

Sydney Harbour is part of a larger body of water known as Port Jackson (though the entire area is often referred to colloquially as Sydney Harbour). It's 12 miles (19km) long, extending from its western tributary, the Parramatta River, to the Sydney Heads, where it opens into the Tasman Sea. Geologically, it's a 'ria', a river valley flooded thousands of years ago. Much of Sydney's colonial history took place along its banks, which are now home to the most densely settled parts of the city.

Clockwise from above: Luna Park and Sydney's north shore; a kookaburra sits on a suburban gate post; enjoying the shade from palm trees. Previous page: the opera house peeks from below Sydney Harbour Bridge

From the footpath we goggle at the real estate of Sydney's North Shore – multimillion-dollar houses tucked into hillsides of gum trees and jacarandas, paths leading to docks where sailing boats and speedboats bob patiently. Just beneath the Fig Tree Bridge is Fig Tree House, a turreted yellow cottage built in the 1830s by Mary Reibey, who arrived in Australia as a convict in 1792 and made her fortune in shipping (you can see her picture on the AU$20 note).

The next two hours are bridge-less, as we traverse the neighbourhoods of the North Shore. There's a lot more real-estate gawking to be done here as we wind through well-heeled streets overlooking the harbour. The highlight of this section is a bushwalk beneath a canopy of gnarled gum trees along Tambourine Bay.

Finally, we drop down through North Sydney to Milson's Point and the star of the show comes into view: the Sydney Harbour Bridge. The mighty steel arch stretches across the harbour between pylons of Australian granite, a testament to the power of engineering. It opened in 1932 to great fanfare, with as many as a million Australians gathering to watch flotillas and sing specially composed bridge anthems. From up here it's a feast of iconic Sydney landmarks: the Opera House just to the east, the vintage carnival lights of Luna Park below, the ferries of Circular Quay across the water.

Coming full circle with a stroll among the 19th-century terrace houses of The Rocks, we sit down at a local pizzeria to revel in our achievement over pizza with pumpkin and sausage. First, a toast: to bridges, to engineering, to the glorious city of Sydney. **EM**

ORIENTATION

Start/End // Pyrmont Bridge (or anywhere along the loop)
Distance // 17 miles (27km)
Getting there // Sydney International Airport is about 4 miles (7km) south of the city centre, connected by bus and rail.
When to go // Sydney is generally pleasant year-round, but its mild winters (Jun–Aug) are especially nice for hiking.
Where to stay // If you plan on starting the walk at the Sydney Harbour Bridge or Pyrmont Bridge, staying in or near the CBD would be most convenient.
What to take // Wear long sleeves and a floppy hat. And as any Sydneysider will tell you, it pays to carry sunscreen.
More info // Cancer Council NSW hosts a Seven Bridges Walk to raise money for cancer research each spring. Their website (www.7bridgeswalk.com.au) has a detailed map of the trail. If you're in town for the actual event, sign up!

Opposite from top: rowing on the Yarra River, Melbourne; hanging at Bronte Beach, Sydney

MORE LIKE THIS
AUSTRALIAN CITY HIKES

BONDI TO COOGEE WALK, SYDNEY

Explore two of Sydney's most famous beaches on this beloved 4-mile (6km) paved urban trail. Start in Bondi, the pin-up model of Sydney beaches, with a bracing swim in the blue-green surf and an exploration of the tidal pools on the northeastern rocks. From here you'll wind south along a clifftop path edging Sydney's posh eastern suburbs. Heading out of Bondi, don't miss the Aboriginal rock carving of a shark or whale on your left. About 15 minutes later you'll hit the beach town of Tamarama, home to the tanned and toned surf set. A bit further on, at Bronte, check out the 'bogey hole' (rock pool) on the beach's south end. Ramble another mile or so along the rocky, scrub-covered cliffs to Clovelly Beach, working up a bit of a sweat on the steep stairs, then on to busy Coogee. Celebrate with a dip in one of the beach's aqua rock pools and a beer at one of the cafes set back from the sand.

Start // Bondi Beach
End // Coogee Beach
Distance // 4 miles (6km)

CAPITAL CITY TRAIL, MELBOURNE

This 18-mile (29km) loop circles central Melbourne, running along the Yarra River and Merri Creek much of the way. It's an urban trail, which means walking under highways and over bridges, following train tracks and passing walls covered in graffiti. It's all part of the charm. You'll pass directly by or near many of Melbourne's top sights, including the Royal Botanic Gardens, the Melbourne Zoo and the Abbotsford Convent complex, an imposing former convent turned mixed-use arts and entertainment centre with an adjacent children's farm.

Start/End // Princes Bridge near Flinders St Station (this is a popular and convenient starting point, but you can start wherever you'd like)
Distance // 18 miles (29km)

DARWIN CITY TRAIL

Languorously located on the shores of the tropical Timor Sea, Darwin has a frontier feel that's only enhanced by knowledge that dinosaur-proportioned saltwater crocodiles inhabit the creeks and sometimes sunbathe on the city's beaches. Built on a headland, it's ideal for foot-based exploration. After hand-feeding wild fish at Doctors Gully, wander east through Bicentennial Park to tunnels built into Darwin's cliffs during WWII. At the Waterfront, plunge into a croc-free saltwater lagoon or surf some breaks in the wave pool. Continue around the headland and bear east to Charles Darwin National Park, adding a bushwalk to this urban adventure, before cutting back across towards Fannie Bay to the Museum and Art Gallery, where fascinating exhibits include a terrifying immersive experience about Cyclone Tracy, which flattened the city over Christmas 1974. End your mooch at Mindil Market, where Darwin's melange of cultures and cuisines fuse together in a spectacular fashion.

Start // Doctors Gully
End // Mindil Beach
Distance // 12.4 miles (20km) or more
More info // www.northernterritory.com

THE GREAT SOUTH WEST WALK

Lose yourself to Australia's natural world and find wildlife wonders aplenty in this multiday hike through southwest Victoria's lush landscapes of forest, river, beach and bush.

After stretching my legs and lungs along the clifftops and beaches of Portland Bay, I turn into the lush greenery of Cobboboonee National Park. At first all I hear is the leafy shuffle of my feet on the path, but gradually the quiet of the bush envelops me with rustling and soft calls. And then I hear something scary...the sound of padding feet and a soft drumming behind me. Carefully turning around I lock eyes with a tall, elegant and beautifully clad local – an emu, making a weird noise in its throat! Head cocked to the side, checking me out, it seems quite unconcerned about sharing the track. So I move on slowly until I find an open space where I can stand aside, then watch as it saunters

slowly by, giving me a cursory glance as only a real local would. This was just the start of a walk that would sharpen my senses to the 'sounds of silence' and give me time to reflect on my place in a world that already seemed far away.

The Great South West Walk is a 155-mile (250km) loop in Victoria state's southwest corner. It unwinds through breathtaking landscapes of towering gum trees, a river of untouched beauty, magnificent ocean beaches and cliffs, and a magical world of flowering native bush. It also offers numerous shorter walks, so you can walk as little or as much as you like. At a gentle pace, the whole hike takes between 11 and 14 days, and most of it is easy going.

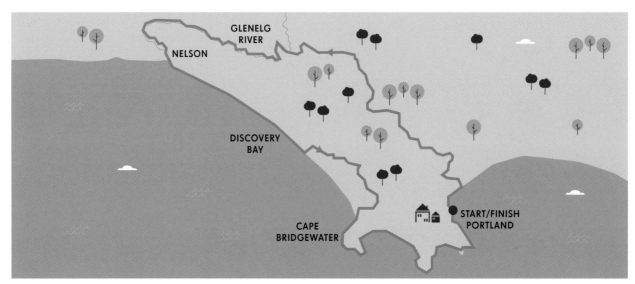

© Sandy Goddard

I wasn't sure when I set out if I was going to do the whole walk, but now that I'm here, I just want to keep going. I feel like I'm connecting with nature; walking, sleeping and waking with it all around me. And as I blend into the natural world around me, I become more aware of the animals, birds and insects everywhere; this walk is famous for its wildlife and I'm seeing dozens of emus and countless wallabies, kangaroos, echidnas and koalas, and none of them seem worried by my presence. And the shuffling and hooting of possums and owls are guaranteed night-time sound effects. I even start to feel a bit like an animal myself, moving quietly through the bush, sneaking up on fellow creatures to see how close I can get to them.

Soon I find myself alongside the serenity of the wide Glenelg River as it winds its way through gleaming limestone cliffs and enormous gorges. I'm having trouble keeping up with the birdwatching – so many sounds and sightings...wrens, robins, ducks, egrets, wedge-tailed eagles, friendly bristlebirds, and a rare sighting of the endangered red-tailed black cockatoo, to name just a few. I'm not keeping count but I've heard that serious birdwatchers have noted 110 different bird species along this walk.

I watch groups in canoes gliding by in this beautiful riverscape and feel a stab of envy; another perfect way of being alone among nature. Some of the river campsites are only accessible by walking or water, which makes this river trek section even more exotic. After a night at the historic Pattersons Canoe Camp, established in the 1920s by the Patterson family of Warrock Station, I head into the small town of Nelson to stock up on supplies and overnight with a hot shower at the local campsite.

Next morning I'm up early and on my way along Discovery Bay beach, with crashing waves, flocks of seabirds, and a salty wind providing an exhilarating soundscape. This is a beachcomber's paradise, and I see lots of curios among the flotilla of whale bones and exotic debris. There are remnants of other life too; walking through huge coastal dunes, some up to 230ft (70m) high, I spy an ancient Aboriginal midden site with scattered shells and pieces of flint from toolmaking, reminding me of the rich cultural history here.

ANCIENT LANDSCAPE

As you walk through the colossal sand dunes near Swan Lake, on Discovery Bay, you will pass flat beds of grey soil that have been exposed by the moving sand. These are actually the remains of ash from local volcanic eruptions that happened more than 5000 yeas ago. Middens of shells and flint chips, found near these deposits and along the clifftops, show that Gunditjmara Aboriginal people were living in this area over 11,000 years ago. If you happen to come across one of these middens, don't disturb it.

Clockwise from above: capes and cliffs of Discovery Bay; meet New Holland honeyeaters and wild emus; the petrified forest. Previous page: the winding Glenelg River

"I feel like I'm connecting with nature; walking, sleeping and waking with it all around me"

ORIENTATION

Start/End // Portland – you can walk in either direction.
Distance // 155 miles (250km), but with the option of lots of shorter 6–13-mile (10–22km) walks too.
Getting there // Portland is 222 miles (357km) southwest of Melbourne. You can fly or there's a daily train service to Warrnambool, with connecting coach to Portland.
When to go // September to March.
What to take // Binoculars, sturdy walking boots, camping supplies, insect repellent, sunscreen.
Where to stay // There are 14 well-kept campsites along the trail that come with shelter, picnic table, eco toilet, fresh rainwater tank and a fire pit.
More info // Friends of the GSWW (www.greatsouthwestwalk.com) for general information, links and helpful phone numbers for planning.
Things to know // Most campsites are in state or national parks and require bookings and payment through the Parks Victoria website at www.parkstay.vic.gov.au/gsww

Halfway along Discovery Bay I have the choice of continuing on the coastal trail or heading inland; I choose the latter, and am soon surrounded by massive gum trees and the fabulous flora of Mt Richmond National Park, where one minute I'm staring up at two koalas in a eucalyptus tree, the next spotting a flock of New Holland honeyeaters feasting on the enormous flowering spikes of grass trees. As I'm absorbing the colours and shapes of some beautiful wildflowers, I notice a tiny, exquisite native orchid at my feet.

This wonderland of bush botany and wildlife gives way to rolling grasslands as I head towards the rugged cliffs of Cape Bridgewater. The views of the wild southern ocean are spectacular from these huge volcanic cliffs, and equally intriging are the pumping blowholes, a petrified forest and the noisy but cute seal colony that has both Australian and New Zealand residents.

My return to the real world starts via the small but lovely Bridgewater Bay village, before heading out along the clifftops to Cape Nelson and the welcome smells of coffee and food from the cafe at the base of an historic lighthouse. It's here that I learn how work started on the GSWW in 1981, and for the past 35 years has been maintained by a group of local volunteers. The Friends of the Great South West Walk are mainly retired men who travel out to do track maintenance on a weekly basis. And at the time of writing this, one of its original founders, Bill Golding, is still pulling on his boots and gloves as part of this dedicated team.

Finally, I'm strolling along the last part of my journey – heading to Portland on a coastal track, watching for whales, surfers and diving gannets. I'm almost at the end of this wonderful walk, and feeling like a different person. There's no doubt that losing myself among the nature here has refreshed my body, mind and soul. **SN**

*Opposite: autumn colours in the
Australian alps; Sealers Cove*

MORE LIKE THIS
VICTORIAN HIKES

DESERT DISCOVERY WALK

This four-day walk is through surprising landscapes in the semi-arid Mallee region of western Victoria. Despite the semi-aridity, the Little Desert National Park is anything but barren, with vast areas of native wildflowers, Flame heath and woodlands of yellow gum and slender cypress found in its heathlands, salt lakes, rolling dunes, dry woodlands and river red gum forests. The range of birdlife is amazing too; from the tiny blue wren, exotic gang-gang cockatoos and honeyeaters to the fascinating mound-building malleefowl. You literally wake and retire to birdsong. The full 52-mile (84km) trek is best suited to experienced walkers, but there are options for one- to four-day hikes, and two campsites along the way. Avoid the summer, which gets very hot.
Start/End // Horseshoe Bend camping ground, Kiata
Distance // 52 miles (84km)

CROSSCUT SAW AND MT SPECULATION

This is one of the must-do hikes in the scenic Alpine National Park. Starting at Upper Howqua Camping Area, it crosses the Howqua River several times, before a challenging climb up Howitt Spur to Mt Howitt. The trail then traverses the jagged angles of the Crosscut Saw, which include the interestingly named Mt Buggery and Horrible Gap, then a steep hike up to Mt Speculation. The breathtaking panoramas of the Australian Alps and the remote and spectacular Razor Viking Wilderness are unforgettable. The return is back across the Crosscut Saw to Mt Howitt and then either down Thorn Range or via Howitt Spur back to the Upper Howqua Camping Area. Walkers usually overnight at the two campsites, the first at Macalister Springs, and the other at Mt Speculation. Best done over three days in November to April.
Start/End // Upper Howqua Camping Area
Distance // Approx 24 miles (38km)

SEALERS COVE

The Prom, at the southernmost tip of Australia, has spectacular scenery of all kinds; huge granite mountains, pristine rainforest, sweeping beaches and coastlines. There are some great walks from the Tidal River campground, and Sealers Cove is one of the best, often described as a 'walker's paradise.' That's partly because it's accessible only by boat or on foot, but also because it boasts clear turquoise waters, golden sand, a shady idyllic campsite and arresting wildlife. On the upward walk there are spectacular views and lush rainforest before heading downhill to the coast. It's about three hours each way, but birdwatchers and plant lovers will want to do it at a more leisurely pace to make time for all the photos. The track is good year round, with boardwalks across winter streams, but the best walking weather is spring and autumn.
Start // Tidal River
End // Sealers Cove
Distance // 8 miles (12.5km)

TASMANIA'S
THREE CAPES TRACK

Weave through dense forest above pounding surf and soaring dolerite cliffs to taste the wilderness of Australia's Tasman Peninsula on an epic but achievable four-day trek.

The welcoming committee on the Three Capes Track was quite something. Tree martins swooped in salute, gobbling kelp flies alongside towering cliffs. New Zealand fur seals bobbed in the coves, waving hind flippers above the waves. And a juvenile sea eagle stood to attention on a stump, peering along its fearsome bill as stern as any royal sentry.

It was a dramatic transition from the bustling precincts of Port Arthur Historic Site. At that atmospheric spot, a Victorian-era penal colony where the most hardened convicts once toiled, I joined hikers boarding a small boat for the 75-minute voyage to the trail's official start. Easing away from the looming penitentiary, we rounded the eerie Isle of the Dead – where more than 1200 transportees lie buried, thousands of miles from home – and admired those birds and seals before being dropped alongside the cobalt waters of Denmans Cove.

Here begins one of Tasmania's newest and most alluring treks. The Three Capes Track is an accessible introduction to wilderness

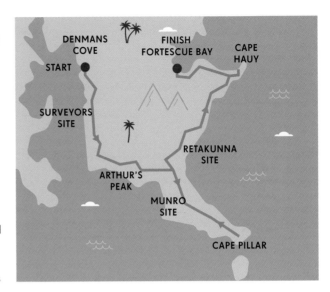

walking, somewhere between rufty-tufty camping trails and the gourmet lodge-to-lodge packages such as those on Maria Island and the Bay of Fires. Over 29 miles (46km) and four days, walkers encounter sea cliffs, aromatic eucalypt forest and leech-infested rainforest, windswept heath and two of the three titular capes (the other, Cape Raoul, is visible but not visited, though it will be included in a mooted route extension). Accommodation is in three custom-built cabin sites, with simple, comfy bunkrooms and well-equipped kitchen and toilet blocks – bring a sleeping bag and food, but none of the other paraphernalia required on a hardcore plunge into Tasmania's more-remote wildernesses.

The walking and landscapes, though, are epic enough from the off. From gorgeous Denmans Cove I traced the path through ghostly gum woods, Port Arthur Bay just discernible through the spooky mist. On that first day I tramped a gentle 2.5 miles (4km) to Surveyors, the first of the three cabin sites, each with different but alluring views. That night I munched dinner on the open deck, gazing across heath grazed by Bennett's wallabies, west to the craggy columns of Cape Raoul, and east to the hump of Arthur's Peak – the next day's main challenge.

The Three Capes Track could generously be described as undulating. There are no huge summits to conquer, but instead

> *"That night I munched dinner in the open, gazing across the craggy columns of Cape Raoul and the hump of Arthur's Peak"*

a rolling trail, sometimes on well-maintained dirt or rocky paths, elsewhere along springy wooden boardwalks. The second day's hike led first through more eucalypt forest, where first a wallaby then a bronze skink darted off the path ahead, to a curious sculpture – the first of some 37 'Encounters on the Edge' studding the trail. Each was created especially for the track, and reflects an aspect of the area's human or natural heritage. 'Punishment to Playground' is a bench filled with snorkel masks, fishing reels and golf clubs, a nod to the changing function of nearby Point Puer; today a golf course, until 1849 it was the site of a boys' prison. A little further on came a pile of large, smooth wooden cubes: 'Who Was Here?', a reminder to look for the square poos of snuffling wombats.

Through scrub and forest scented with eucalypt and tea tree I climbed, to be rewarded with a sweeping new vista to Cape Pillar, the next day's objective. Habitats morphed almost minute by minute: stands of stringybark and mossy forests, cliffs where signs indicated nesting sea eagles, more heath and dense woods where yellow-tailed black cockatoos squawked overhead.

That night at Munro cabin, I peered along the coast to cape number three, Hauy, and listened to surf pounding the cliffs and wind howling through the treetops. The weather was turning fast

THE LONELIEST LIGHTHOUSE

Atop Tasman Island off Cape Pillar perches Australia's loftiest lighthouse. Thanks to sheer dolerite cliffs soaring to 985ft (300m), construction proved an epic challenge: it was nearly 40 years after the initial survey that the prefabricated cast-iron lighthouse first glowed in 1906. Life on this storm-lashed rock was harsh; Jessie Johnston, the first keeper's wife, dubbed it 'Siberia of the south', and communications to the Tasmanian mainland were initially limited to signal flags. The light was automated in 1976.

Clockwise from top: Cape Raoul; a Bennett's wallaby peers from the bracken; the pillars of Cape Hauy. Previous page: approaching the destination at Fortescue Bay

© TassieKarin | Getty

– as it does in Tassie – but it failed to turn back overnight, and next morning I set out through thick cloud and stinging mizzle. The third day is an out-and-back from Munro along the narrow peninsula to Cape Pillar, traversing a path lined with trees bent by fierce winds that scream around the cape. Shapes and sounds were rendered soft and deceptive by the mist: a flash of brown might have been a wallaby hopping off the trail, the calls of birds blending with a chorus of frogs in a nearby billabong.

Nervously I clambered up the sheer-sided ridge named the Blade to reach the cape itself, where the cloud lifted just long enough to reveal a dizzying drop and Tasman Island beyond, the lighthouse-capped, desolate lump of rock dangling off the end of the peninsula. Then the clouds descended once more, and I tramped back to Munro to pick up my pack for the short leg to Retakunna cabin, that last night's stop.

Some creatures, of course, love rain – and on my last morning I had unwelcome encounters with several. In the wet forest below Retakunna battalions of leeches wiggled, latching on to my bare knees till rivulets of blood trickled down my shins. No matter. The mossy, ferny forest is magical enough to counter any parasite loathing. Soon I re-emerged on to the cliffs, soul salved by views back to Cape Pillar and across to Mt Fortescue, the final haul.

Cape Hauy itself, an hour's detour from the main track, was a suitably epic finale: pillars erupted from the spume, tempting rock climbers who tackle the aptly named Totem Pole. For me, though, the end was in sight – figuratively and literally: Fortescue Bay, where I baptised my weary feet in the warm waters lapping the sand. Three capes, two legs: one spectacular introduction to the Tasmanian wilderness. **PB**

© Peter Gudella | Shutterstock, © Kevin Wells | Alamy

ORIENTATION

Start // Denmans Cove
End // Fortescue Bay
Distance // 28.5 miles (46km)
Getting there // The four-day package starts and ends in Port Arthur, and includes a boat to the trailhead and return bus from Fortescue Bay. Port Arthur is 59 miles (95km, 90-minute drive) from Hobart, Tasmania's capital, a little less from Hobart Airport. Daily Tassielink (www.tassielink.com.au), Gray Line (www.grayline.com.au) and Pennicott Journeys (www.pennicottjourneys.com.au/three-capes-track) buses serve Port Arthur from Hobart.
Tours // Currently, the trek is available self-guided only, and places must be booked through the official website (http://threecapestrack.com.au). The fee includes transport to and from the trailhead and end point, as well as accommodation and a guide book. From September 2018, guided, catered tours will be available with Tasmanian Walking Co (www.taswalkingco.com.au/three-capes-lodge-walk).
When to go // The warmer months (Nov–Apr) offer better, though far from guaranteed, weather.

Opposite: on the Overland Track, a boardwalk section winds through Cradle Valley

MORE LIKE THIS
TASMANIAN TREKS

OVERLAND TRACK

The five- to seven-day hike from Cradle Mountain to Lake St Clair is the classic Tassie trek. Traversing a region opened up by Austrian Gustav Weindorfer, who extolled its glories a century ago, its dramatic landscapes are dominated by iconic Cradle Mountain and 5305ft (1617m) Mt Ossa, the island's loftiest peak. Expect boggy trails, strong winds, rapid weather variations and ample wildlife – wombats are ubiquitous around Cradle Valley, and you'll likely spy pademelons and possums, though you'd be fortunate to spot the quolls, echidnas and Tasmanian devils that lurk in the park. Also expect crowds, particularly in peak season (1 October to 31 May), when booking is essential. With limited spaces in basic huts, most hikers camp and all supplies must be carried, though you can join a guided, catered trek staying in comfortable lodges. Either way, you'll experience Tasmanian wilderness at its most elemental.
Start // Ronny Creek, Cradle Valley
End // Narcissus Hut or Cynthia Bay
Distance // 40 miles (65km) or 51 miles (82km)
More info // www.parks.tas.gov.au

FREYCINET PENINSULA CIRCUIT

Against stiff competition, arguably Tasmania's most magical beach fringes the Freycinet Peninsula on the east coast. Wineglass Bay is just one of several glorious strands lining this two-day circuit. Despite the long stretches of surf-lapped sand, don't expect pancake-flat walking – the trail crosses hilly inland areas and the craggy Hazards Mountains, and you must carry your tent and all food. But the rewards are luminous: ample paddling potential at the beaches of Hazards, Cooks and Bryans (a short detour), far-reaching views from Mt Freycinet, bustling birdlife and of course the perfect crescent of sand at Wineglass Bay itself. If time or energy are limited, take a shortcut along the Isthmus Track between Hazards Beach and Wineglass Bay for a delightful five-hour outing.
Start/End // Wineglass Bay car park
Distance // 19 miles (30km)
More info // www.parks.tas.gov.au

SOUTH COAST TRACK

Overland Track not challenging enough? Try tackling this trail snaking along the coast of isolated, untouched Southwest National Park. For experienced bushwalkers only, this six- to eight-day trek is tricksy right from the off – there are no roads to the trailhead at Melaleuca, so you must either fly or hike in. You'll need to bring camping gear, wet-weather and warm clothing, all food and a hardy constitution: weather can be wild, trails muddy, beach and creek crossings unpredictable, leeches persistent and ascents demanding, not least the 2970ft (905m) haul up the Ironbound Ranges. But what a trek. You'll traverse pristine, empty beaches, dense forests and soaring peaks, and watch rare wildlife – including in summer, if you're really lucky, critically endangered orange-bellied parrots, which breed in tiny numbers only at one spot.
Start // Melaleuca
End // Cockle Bay
Distance // 53 miles (85km)
More info // www.parks.tas.gov.au

WAR AND PEACE: THE KOKODA TRACK

Moving from azure beaches, to misty mountains through jungle that's every type of green, this trek in southern Papua New Guinea is an immersive mix of modern history and Papuan culture.

Part-way up the biggest incline on the fourth day, my legs start to feel it. I pause and raise my eyes along the steep muddy jungle track to a misty clearing at the top where some porters have gathered to wait for us. Apes Turia, the 49-year-old head porter, pulls his acoustic guitar from the side of his pack; this is his 104th Kokoda trek. As he strums a few chords and sings in his local dialect, the other porters join in. Their perfect harmonies melt down the mountainside and through the canopy, scooping us all up, somehow delivering us to the peak, beaming and momentarily ache-free. There is no better way to reach this mountaintop here; somehow the music captures the trek and the landscape perfectly, and adds poignancy to the moment we emerge. We're greeted by a breathtaking view back through the valley, small villages dotting an infinite number of greens that perforate the blue horizon.

Our starting point at the Northern Beaches village of Buna now seems a different world. Just a few days before, I was ticking

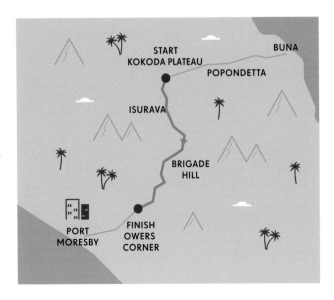

© Ryan Stuart

off tropical clichés as I sat on a crooked palm tree watching local kids play and scream in the crystal-blue water. An old fisherman dragged his nets into his canoe in the distance, and a local woman – Jean – cleaned her pots at the shore with a mixture of sand and leaves. The village sits at the water's edge. Sand stained light grey from distant volcanic eruptions creeps out to sea a few metres before falling off to near white, giving the water its magical blue colouring. Aside from being a startlingly beautiful place to acclimatise to the tropical conditions (and a rare opportunity to spend a few days living amongst locals in a Papua New Guinean village) there are other reasons to start here. Buna and its neighbouring villages were the site of the initial Japanese beach landings at the start of the Kokoda campaign in July 1942, during WWII. Attempting to attack the capital, Port Moresby in the south, Japanese forces chose the Kokoda track as their route. Predominantly Australian Allied forces launched a counter-offensive from Moresby and the two sides each gained and lost significant ground along almost the entire length of the track over six months. The campaign ended with a Japanese withdrawal from these same beaches.

Veterans on both sides recount that battling the terrain was as hard as the fight with their enemies, and it is this reputation that has given the track its mythical status. In Australia, the word Kokoda is synonymous with steep inclines, unforgiving terrain, a tropical climate and both a physical and mental challenge.

> "Australian tank tracks are used to edge garden beds and prop up cooking grills"

It winds up and down for 60 miles (96km) through incredible jungle, wetlands, rainforest, villages, rivers and mountains from the Kokoda Plateau at its northern point to Owers Corner to the south. Initially formed as a network of trails used to connect mountain villages, the track is still in active use and you will meet many locals on your way. In fact, the entire track sits on locally owned private land.

It also sits somewhere between lore and reality in its own world of Kokoda legend, one that fits in a landscape of mythic proportions: other-worldly geographic forms; huge Pandanus trees towering above the canopy; murky swamps; lush rain forest glens; and, of course, the serrated mountains we traversed each day. There are many stories, but one about an Australian soldier on the track during the Kokoda campaign gives a clue to how steep this country is. During a skirmish he stood up and was shot through the ear and the foot – with the same bullet.

Passing through a mountain village I met local David, who hunts birds. Standing next to the track, with a slingshot and fistful of stones, his catch was a good addition to the regular diet of corn,

FLY-BYS ON PARADE

The birds-of-paradise are stunningly beautiful and 40 of the family's 42 colourful species live in PNG. While their tiny size means they can be hard to spot, porters and locals will be able to help. If you are very lucky you may also spot a much larger bird, the cassowary. Much easier to see are the thousands of different-coloured butterflies, 735 species of which call PNG home.

Clockwise from left: cloud threatens to envelop Nauro village; the rickety bridge to Eora Creek; a traditional greeting at Buna village; many hands make light work of landing at Buna. Previous page: the trek leader looks back over the Kokoda Plateau

potatoes and other vegetables grown in the village, some of which we would buy to supplement the food we carried. Taking a more relaxed pace on the track allowed for these moments, and gave more time to take in the surroundings, experience local culture and gain genuine insight into day-to-day living. One evening after a swim in the stream next to the campsite, I watched a porter, Silver, as he fished. After a quick dig for worms he used a small branch for a rod and a bullet for a sinker. Moments later he pulled out a trout.

Living within communities, and walking on local land, the culture is ever present. So too is the history of the Kokoda campaign; from Buna onwards there are signs of it everywhere – out in the open air and part of everyday life, from fox holes, to plane wrecks and supply dumps. Australian tank tracks are used to edge garden beds and prop up cooking grills, every village has its own makeshift war museum attached to someone's private home, and several times during our trek live ammunition rounds were dislodged from the muddy track when trampled underfoot.

After our final ascent, we walk under the commemorative arch at Owers Corner, and the emotion of finishing takes many by surprise. On the bumpy bus back to Moresby, we all say we'll come back and walk it again – me with much less camera gear. As others nod off I watch the jungle fade into the distance, power lines slowly creeping into view, as we wind down the mountains and closer to Port Moresby, and our real lives. **RS**

ORIENTATION

Start/End // Kokoda Plateau/Owers Corner. Walk in either direction.
Distance // 60 miles (96km)
Getting there // Fly into Port Moresby.
Tours // Without the local knowledge of a tour operator travel in PNG is very difficult and potentially unsafe. Try World Expeditions or Escape Trekking Adventures.
When to go // April to November.
What to take // Good boots and poles are essential.
What to wear // Shorts, T-shirts and a light polar fleece for cold mountain evenings. Modest swimwear is important due to local religious beliefs.
More info // www.papuanewguinea.travel; www.dokokoda.com.
Things to know // Allow time for visa processing and hire a porter: it will change your trek experience and supports locals.

MORE LIKE THIS
BATTLEGROUND HIKES

FUGITIVES TRAIL, SOUTH AFRICA

The lonely hill of Isandlwana stands sentinel over the grassy, sun-baked KwaZulu-Natal plains. But it also marks the spot of one of the bloodiest battles in British colonial history. On 22 January 1879, during the Anglo-Zulu War, a British garrison was attacked here by a spear-wielding *impi* (regiment) of Zulu warriors. Outnumbered and unprepared, they were forced to run for their lives across the rugged savannah, through a stream, up a rocky, scrub-cloaked hill and over a raging river, in an attempt to reach safety. It was a gruesome skirmish. Most did not make it; many Zulu were killed too. And now the route of this infamous retreat is scattered with whitewashed cairns marking the spots where soldiers fell. It's a chilling but fascinating hike, best done with an expert guide to bring the grim history to life.

Start // Isandlwana
End // Buffalo River
Distance // 5 miles (8km)

ALTA VIA 1, ITALY

During WWI, the spiky grey peaks of the Dolomites became the most beautiful – if hostile – of battlefields. Between 1915 and 1918, Italian and Austro-Hungarian/ German forces faced off in these magnificent mountains, enduring the freezing cold, precipitous terrain and lung-testing altitudes while also fighting for their countries and their lives. In order to be able to wage war here, they constructed tunnels, trenches and encampments, as well as via ferrata (iron roads), a network of metal ladders, rungs and fixed lines that enabled them to move across the mountainsides. Thankfully the long-distance Alta Via 1 hike is a much more serene way to roam amid these peaks. The route combines the Dolomites' spectacular lakes, wildflower meadows, high passes and welcoming *rifugios* with fascinating relics of the mountains' tragic past.

Start // Lago di Bráies
End // Belluno
Distance // 75 miles (120km)

1066 WALK, ENGLAND

Follow in the footsteps of William the Conqueror across the high weald of East Sussex. In September 1066, William (then Duke of Normandy) landed at Pevensey Bay on the south coast of England and, one month later, defeated King Harold at the Battle of Hastings. The 1066 Walk explores this history-changing swathe of countryside via an array of little villages, ancient towns, woods, windmills and key sites. It begins at Pevensey Castle, which was a Roman fort in 1066 but was converted into a Norman stronghold by William's brother. It also passes through the small town of Battle, where the two sides clashed; Battle Abbey was founded here in 1095 to commemorate the conflict. The battlefield became the abbey's great park, while the abbey church's high altar supposedly stands on the spot where Harold died.

Start // Pevensey
End // Rye
Distance // 30 miles (50km)

Clockwise from top: British war graves on Isandlwana Hill, South Africa; following WWI bootsteps in the Dolomites; Pevensey Castle in Eastbourne, southern England

THE ABEL TASMAN COAST TRACK

One of New Zealand's Great Walks, this world-class beachcombing caper tiptoes around tides and bounds between the bays and golden coves of the South Island.

I f the huge piece of driftwood hadn't suddenly sprouted a head and let out an indignant snort, I'd have sat on it to eat lunch. Apparently, this log isn't wood at all. It's a heaving, breathing, belching lump of grumpy New Zealand fur seal, which had been enjoying a morning snooze under shimmering sun until I ruined its reverie by gatecrashing the secluded beach.

Evidently, my new friend isn't as excited about our encounter as I am – something he makes cacophonously clear when I begin bagging silly sealy selfies. I keep a respectful distance, not wanting to end up in a fist/flipper fight with 330lb (150kg) of rudely awoken sea mammal, especially not quarterway through a 37-mile (60km) walk, beyond limping range of human habitation or help.

So I leave him to snore and seek an alternative snack spot. Fortunately, picnic possies with epic ocean views are plentiful along the Abel Tasman Coast Track, and before long I stumble into another beautiful bay, gilded by golden sand and gently stroked by the waters of Tasman Bay, a glassy puddle becalmed between the protective arms of Farewell Spit and D'Urville Island.

Once lunch is munched, an internal debate begins: should I have a quick swim, or keep walking towards the hut? And therein lies the problem with this trail, a rambling route through rata forests fringing the coastline of Abel Tasman National Park, linking a series of idyllic coves at the top of New Zealand's South Island.

The hike isn't physically tough – not compared with most multiday Kiwi capers – and covering 9 miles (15km) a day allows walkers to enjoy the experience at a comfortable clip. No, here the challenge is different. For round every corner is a beach so fine it would be unforgivable not to stop, strip and plunge into the blue. And then you continue, only to find another sublime bay. And so it goes on.

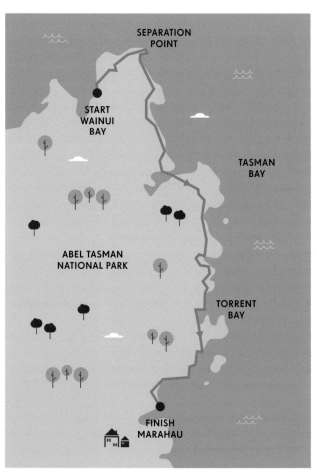

SEPARATION POINT

START WAINUI BAY

TASMAN BAY

ABEL TASMAN NATIONAL PARK

TORRENT BAY

FINISH MARAHAU

© Anna Gorin | Getty

Small wonder the Coast Track is an original member of New Zealand's much-feted group of Great Walks, a list that features the nation's top trails. In a country well-endowed with epic hiking routes, it takes something special to feature in this premier league of paths. Tongariro has dramatic volcanoes and multi-coloured mineral-stained lakes; the Routeburn, Kepler and Milford Tracks make the grade through the magnificence of Fiordland; and the Abel Tasman Coast Track gets the nod because it's one of the world's best beachcombing adventures.

The walk can be done in either direction, but most people start at Marahau and spend several days strolling north, returning via water taxi from Totaranui. A decade earlier I'd walked the route this way. Then, tramping around New Zealand on a backpacker's budget and unable to afford the boat transfers, I had continued to Whariwharangi Hut and spent three days trekking back to Marahau via the Abel Tasman Inland Track (a 25-mile/41km path along Evans Ridge and through the beech forests of Moa Park), a more challenging and less trafficked trail than its coastal cousin.

This experience taught me that the top part of the Coast Track offers quieter paths, better vistas and more wildlife encounters than the rest of the route. Armed with this insight and angling for new views, I've returned to walk north-to-south, after being dropped off at Wainui Bay. Trekking in this direction involves an extra layer of logistics, but it launches you straight into the wildest sections of the trail, and soon after rounding scenic Separation Point, the decision pays off, as I meet the seal in Mutton Cove.

> *"Round every corner is a beach so fine it would be unforgivable not to stop, strip and plunge into the blue"*

KAYAKING THE COAST TRACK

The Coast Track is a cracking walk, but Abel Tasman National Park's shores can also be explored from the cockpit of a sea kayak. Several operators offer combined hiking and paddling adventures, where it's possible to kayak across translucent lagoons and between bays, before swapping blade for boots and walking back. Marahau to Anchorage Bay is a popular paddling section, with walkers wandering onward usually to Bark Bay or Onetahuti before catching a water taxi back.

Clockwise from top: kayaks at Watering Cove; walking the beaches of Abel Tasman; another glorious bay. Previous page: footsteps in the golden sands of Marahau

My dilemma – to take a dip or dawdle on – begins just around the corner, in Anapai Bay, one of the most beautiful bitemarks found along this whole sensationally serrated shoreline. I don't hesitate long. Once past Totaranui, I'll be sharing the huts and the trail with trampers and paddlers aplenty, and the water will be busy with boats, so I embrace the empty beach and dive into the translucent brine that's all mine for a few magical moments.

Sometimes you simply have to get wet. The Coast Track isn't a technical trail, but the tidal range here is large, and there are several estuary crossings to negotiate. At Bark Bay and Torrent Bay, high-tide inland walk-around options exist, but Awaroa Inlet can only be crossed two hours either side of low tide. Campsites and huts have tide tables, and sometimes it's necessary to set off before dawn to avoid delays, but even when you nail the timing, socks and shoes must be removed while you wade across.

The delightful distractions continue as the track tramps over the 853ft (260m) Tonga Saddle and drops to a sensational stretch of sand at Onetahuti Beach, before ambling past Arch Point – an extraordinary exhibition of rock art sculpted by the elements.

I enviously eye kayakers departing from the beach at Bark Bay, and make a mental note to return and paddle the park, for a new view of this epic coastline. Now, though, I have a bigger boat to catch, to the North Island. I wobble over the famous Falls River swingbridge to Torrent Bay, where another tidal crossing lies in wait en route to Anchorage and the trailhead at Marahau. **PK**

ORIENTATION

Start // Wainui Car Park
End // Marahau
Distance // 37 miles (60km)
Getting there // Marahau is easily accessed from Picton, where the Interislander ferry arrives from Wellington.
When to go // The Abel Tasman can be done any time of year, but the trails and campsites heave with hikers (and kayakers) during summer (Dec–Feb). October to November and March to April offer better conditions.
Where to stay // The Department of Conservation (DoC) operates huts and campsites along the route; book ahead.
What to take // A relatively gentle multiday hike, the Abel Tasman can easily be done in running shoes. The route rarely rears above 650ft (200m) and the weather is temperate, but take waterproofs and warm layers for evenings. Pack swimming gear, and a mask and snorkel.

© Janet Teasche | Getty; © Guaxinim | Shutterstock

Opposite from top: Carrick-a-Rede on Northern Ireland's Causeway Coast; crossing the bridge at the climax of New Zealand's Heaphy Track

MORE LIKE THIS
MULTI-SPORTS TRAILS

THE HEAPHY TRACK, NEW ZEALAND

Another Great Walk, the Heaphy Track can also be enjoyed in two distinct ways. As adventurers can explore the Abel Tasman by boot or boat, so the Heaphy can be hiked or biked (mountain bikes are permitted 1 May–30 November). You can tackle the track in both directions, either starting at Kohaihai and tracing the Tasman Sea along the South Island's wild west coast, before crossing the Heaphy River, ascending Gouland Downs and traversing Kahurangi National Park via Perry Saddle, or beginning at Brown Hut and doing the same in reverse. Whichever way you approach it, the Heaphy is an epic challenge. Allow two nights/three days to pedal the route, or four days to walk it, and look out for powelliphanta (a giant carnivorous snail!) and roa (great spotted kiwi) en route.
Start // Kohaihai (near Karamea)
End // Brown Hut (Golden Bay, via Collingwood)
Distance // 49 miles (78.4km) one way
More info // www.doc.govt.nz/heaphytrack

JATBULA TRAIL, AUSTRALIA

A hiking experience punctuated by plunge pools, the Jatbula Trail in the Northern Territory is an epic Australian adventure. Beginning with a boat trip across the Katherine River at 17 Mile Creek, the rugged route can be hiked independently or with guided groups, but the track is only marked in one direction, with blue triangles pointing the way from Katherine Gorge to Leliyn. It typically takes five days to trek the trail, which traverses Nitmiluk National Park, tracing an ancient indigenous songline and passing Jawoyn rock art and spectacular waterfalls tumbling from the towering Arnhem Land escarpment. Campsites at Biddlecombe Cascades, Crystal Creek, 17 Mile Falls, Sandy Camp and Sweetwater Pool are all situated beside swimming spots. This tropical trail is best walked during 'the Dry' (May–August). Some operators combine walks with gorge-exploring canoeing adventures.
Start // Nitmiluk Gorge
End // Leliyn (Edith Falls)
Distance // 38.5 miles (62km) one way
More info // www.northernterritory.com

CAUSEWAY COAST WAY, NORTHERN IRELAND

Stepping out along a super storied section of Ulster's jagged shores, the Causeway Coast Way draws a dramatic line between the historic towns of Ballycastle and Portstewart, taking in a series of iconic sights along the way. These include the nerve-knackering Carrick-a-Rede Rope Bridge, medieval Dunluce Castle and, of course, the enigmatic Giant's Causeway – a semi-submerged geological wonder comprised of 40,000 hexagonal basalt columns created either by a huge volcanic eruption, or a Celtic warrior called Fionn mac Cumhaill, depending on who you listen to. The walk can be done in either direction, over two or three relatively easy days, but if you want to up the ante, try running the route during the Causeway Coast ultramarathon, or paddle it while exploring the North Coast Sea Kayak Trail between Magilligan Point and the Glens of Antrim.
Start // Ballycastle
End // Portstewart
Distance // 32 miles (51km)
More info // www.causewaycoastway.com

FEATHERTOP TO BOGONG TRAVERSE

Grab some altitude on this stunning multiday hike across the roof of Australia, crossing the state of Victoria's fabled Bogong High Plains, home of the wild brumbies.

I n the crisp, still dawn, golden sunbeams creep slowly across the High Plains, falling spindrift-like into my open tent. I take another sip of coffee. Nearby, a copse of gnarled snow gums turn molten orange, while somewhere above, a lonely currawong warbles the new morn. On Feathertop's South Face, remnants of winter snow are burning bright crimson. The temperature is just above freezing.

Content in my sleeping bag, I review my plan to link Victoria's three highest peaks in a leisurely five-day high-country amble. Yesterday afternoon, I'd left the car at 5577ft (1700m) on the Great Alpine Rd and walked north along the Razorback, a spectacular high ridge leading to Mt Feathertop, at 6306ft (1922m), Victoria's second-highest peak. The views were incredible, but nothing surpassed dusk from the summit – a searing, snow gum-framed sun, sinking into scarlet oblivion beyond the 'horns' of distant Mt Buffalo.

Ahead was the Bogong High Plains, a high, desolate plateau sprinkled with historic huts and herds of brumbies (wild bush horses). Soon I'm packed and walking, but not before another quick summit dash to gaze on the aloof, table-topped Mt Bogong – aka Big Man, Victoria's highest peak at 6516ft (1986m) and my final destination. I head for Diamantina Spur, a steep, relentless two-hour knee-breaking descent down to the Kiewa River, through scarred snow gums and blackened mountain ash. Bushfires are a regular occurrence in alpine Victoria, as entire ridges of grey skeletons testify.

Surviving Diamantina, I refill my water bottle from the clear Kiewa, before stopping for lunch at historic Blair Hut, idyllically located in a grassy, stream-side clearing. Echoes of long-gone

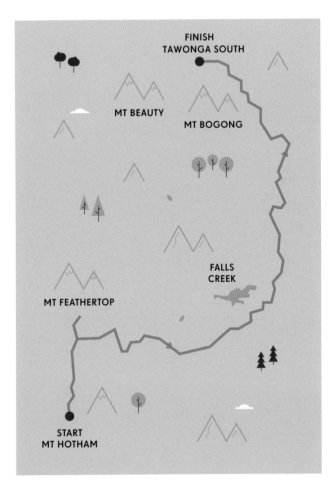

© FiledIMAGE | Shutterstock

mountain cattlemen and their horses resonate from the now-dilapidated structure, until I look up from my cheese and crackers to find I'm surrounded by horse-trekking tourists. I quickly seek solitude in the steep climb to Weston Hut.

Flanking the High Plains, just inside the treeline, the original Weston Hut was constructed by cattlemen in the 1930s, and nearby, horse yards are still visible. It escaped the awful 2003 fires, but was reduced to cinders in 2006. Volunteers erected the present structure in 2011. The grassy surrounds make a pleasant campsite, and the hut offers refuge from the notorious High Plains weather.

The snow gums give way to tussock, brumby dung and alpine grasses as I ascend a snow-pole line on to the plateau. There's a stark, desolate beauty about this barren high country that stretches for miles in all directions. I push on to a track junction, pole 333. A set of numbered snow poles spike in from the south like abandoned telegraph poles – from Mt Hotham, they cross the Cobungra Gap and count the way to Bogong. Another set disappear northwest over my left shoulder, on to the Fainters, but I focus on the string beckoning forwards. In the melancholy late-afternoon sun, all is still, empty, not another soul to be seen.

A few kilometres further I pause to observe a herd of brumbies eyeing me warily. The stallion stands his ground, snorting. I keep moving, eventually setting up camp beside a group of snow gums above Cope Saddle, as the temperature plummets with the sun.

"The last day's trip is short but it's the most magical. The sky is deep blue, the earth blindingly white and the air frigid"

Early the next day, I'm crunching through thin puddle-hiding-ice and the odd snowdrift. The pimply summit of Mt Cope (6027ft, 1837m) sits tantalisingly close to my right, but I've got a more pressing goal – the long-drop dunny at Cope Hut.

Mission accomplished, I rush through this ski area on the eastern edge of the plateau. Missing the moody High Plains solitude, I push on cross-country and bag Mt Nelse North, Victoria's number three at 6181ft (1884m), and only marginally higher than the fire-trail beside it. Massive Bogong is looming ahead as I stroll downhill to Roper Hut.

The original Roper hut, dating from 1939, burnt in the 2003 fires, but arose phoenix-like in 2008 as an emergency shelter. I give myself the rest of the afternoon off, lounging in the sunshine and collecting water from a nearby cascade.

The following fog-shrouded morning is spent laboriously descending and ascending steep spurs covered in wet regrowth and fallen trees as I depart the High Plains, cross Big River and finally climb on to Bogong. From my welcome lunch spot on top

HIGH HORSES

In Australia, 'brumby' refers to any wild bush horse, and though herds are scattered across wilderness areas, they are commonly linked with the High Country, thanks to Australia's favourite bard, AB 'Banjo' Patterson, who immortalised them in his poem *The Man From Snowy River*. Their presence in alpine areas is contentious and while scientists call for culls, many others call for their protection.

From left: Cape Hut; a Bogong High Plains creek; the Kosciuszko Main Range is visible on the walk; here be wild brumbies. Previous page: Mt Feathertop

of T-Spur, it's only a short walk through lush snow meadows to the Cleve Cole Memorial Hut, although I take a detour via the picturesque Howman Falls.

Nestled in a beautiful, sheltered bowl on the mountain's southeastern flank, the hut commemorates a local skier caught in a blizzard. Made from stone, with bunks, indoor plumbing and solar panels, it's one that's popular with walkers, and I exchange pleasantries, though still opt to sleep in my cosy bomber tent – orientated, as always, to catch the sunrise.

Early morning sunlight sparkles off the surrounding snow and draws long shadows from the ubiquitous snow gums as I crunch above the tree line one last time. While this last day's walk is short, it's the most magical of the whole trip. The sky is deep blue, the earth blindingly white and the air frigid as I follow the pole line on to Bogong's wide summit plateau.

The whole of the High Plains lie stretched out along my left, ending in the distinctive cap of Feathertop, while over to my right, a distant long white wall heralds the Kosciuszko Main Range, which is across the border in New South Wales. Clouds fill the valleys. I am absolutely alone, at altitude, and immensely happy. I take the mandatory selfie at Bogong's summit cairn, then drop down the atmospheric, and at times decidedly airy Staircase, until the trees swallow me up and my thoughts stray to how I'm going to recover my car. **SW**

ORIENTATION

Start // Diamantina Hut, Mt Hotham
End // Mountain Creek, Tawonga South
Distance // 48 miles (77km)
Getting there // It's a 4-hour-drive from Melbourne followed by the need for a car at both ends. Try taxis via www.mtbeauty.com or www.ptv.vic.gov.au.
When to go // September to May.
What to take // A good tent, sleeping bag, fuel stove, warm clothes, thermals and wet weather gear. Food for five days. Huts (except Cleve Cole) are for emergency use only.
Things to know // Shorter three-day circuits are possible: Mountain Creek, Eskdale Spur, Cleve Cole, Roper Hut, Timms Fire Trail, Bogong Ck Saddle, Quartz Ridge, Staircase, Mountain Ck; or Razorback, Feathertop, Diamantina, Weston Hut, Cobungra Gap, Dibbin Hut, Swindlers Spur, Razorback.

© Bjorn Svensson | Alamy

Opposite: Nepalese villagers cross
a footbridge spanning dramatic
Himalayan terrain

MORE LIKE THIS
HIGH-COUNTRY WALKING

UPPER MUSTANG, NEPAL

Mysterious and sparsely populated, the magnificently remote Kingdom of Upper Mustang sits on a high, eroded plateau surrounded by snow-capped Himalayan peaks, nestled between Nepal's Annapurna Range and the Tibetan border. The deep gorge of the Kali Gandaki cuts a dark swath through the dry, crumbling badlands and Tibetan culture reverberates across the scattered villages. With a mandatory guide and good fitness, you can make an adventurous 10-day return teahouse trek from Jomsom to Lo Manthang, the capital of Upper Mustang, following traditional footpaths, ancient trading routes, and the odd modern jeep track. Most of the trek sits between 9842ft (3000m) and 13,123ft (4000m) and the sheer scale of the scenery, not to mention the arcane monasteries, ancient frescoes, prayer-flagged passes and amazingly hospitable locals, will literally take your breath away.
Start/End // Jomsom
Distance / 85 miles (136km)
Duration // 10 days
More info // www.uppermustang nepal.com

HOCHSCHWAB, AUSTRIA

In the north of Austria's Styria lies the Hochschwab, a huge limestone plateau, where it's possible to hike for days, staying at rustic (but civilised!) alpine *hüttes*. From Bodenbauer, climb up through pine-fringed alpine meadows to the sobering Das G'hackte, an almost vertical, chained ascent, before reaching the barren and rocky Hochschwab at 7470ft (2277m). Sink *ein radler* (beer and lemon soda) while you watch the sun set from the deck of the nearby Schiestlhaus and listen to the après-dinner singing. The high route heads west across Hundsboden (dog's floor) past various tempting peaks like ZagelKogel (7398ft, 2255m, number two on the plateau) before dropping down to skirt the Sackwiesensee en route to Sonnschienhütte. Consider nailing omnipotent 6965ft (2123m) Ebenstein or meander over to tiny Androthalm for lunch, before heading back to the bright lights of Tragoss via Jassing and the Grüner See.
Start // Bodenbauer (St Ilgen)
End // Jassing (Tragoss)
Distance // 34km (without side trips)
Duration // Three or four days
More info // www.summitpost.org,
www.osm.org

MT ARTHUR AND TABLELAND, NEW ZEALAND

Kahurangi National Park's excellent network of backcountry huts provide many multiday tramping opportunities, and the Mt Arthur and Tableland area is spectacular. One challenging route climbs above Mt Arthur Hut (4298ft, 1310m) to the summit of Mt Arthur (5889ft, 1795m) then follows a high, exposed traverse to Salisbury Lodge (3707ft, 1130m). With good weather, the views are superb, in bad it's abysmal and the alternate low-level route should be used. Continue on to the Tableland, a high limestone plateau covered in tussock, alpine flowers, snow and sinkholes. Pass Balloon Hut on the way to Lake Peel, a photogenic alpine tarn, before climbing the ridgetop for a sensational view of the Cobb Valley. Return to the car by the low-level route or drop down into the Cobb for further adventures.
Start/End // Flora Car Park, Motueka (alt Cobb Reservoir, Takaka)
Distance // 22 miles (35km)
Duration // Two to four days
More info // www.doc.govt.nz

INDIANA JONES AND THE GOLD COAST

Encounter fascinating wildlife, waterfalls and ancient rainforest on this three-day walk through two national parks in southern Queensland.

A glossy blue-black bird is assiduously arranging the scenery of its performance space. Blue petals and bottle tops are placed centre stage and anything that isn't blue is briskly flicked aside. This remarkable scene, starring a satin bowerbird, is happening metres from where I'm staying at O'Reilly's Rainforest Retreat in Lamington National Park, which is two hours' drive inland from Brisbane in the volcanic and forested region of the Gold Coast hinterland.

The park, a Unesco World Heritage site, sits on a plateau almost a mile above the coast and contains a portion of the world's largest stand of sub-tropical rainforest. More than 900 plant species, 200 bird species and 60 mammal species thrive up here, alongside 100 species of reptiles and amphibians. 'Many specialised plants and animals only live here,' says park ranger Kerri Brannon; 'It's all about the altitude.' Lamington National Park is also the starting point for the 34-mile (54km) Gold Coast Hinterland Great Walk, which descends through

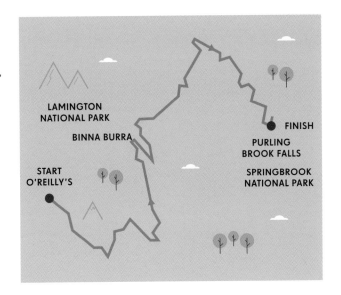

LAMINGTON
NATIONAL PARK

BINNA BURRA

START
O'REILLY'S

FINISH

PURLING
BROOK FALLS

SPRINGBROOK
NATIONAL PARK

dense rainforest, airy eucalyptus woodlands and even grasslands to Springbrook National Park on Queensland's border with New South Wales.

Lamington's altitude has another effect: no matter how steamy it is on the Gold Coast, it will be 50% cooler in the mountains, which makes for comfortable walking conditions in Australia's late summer. Pulling on my boots outside O'Reilly's Rainforest Retreat at the trailhead (you can walk from east to west instead, but you'd be going uphill for most of the way), the sun had yet to warm the chilly mountain air. Filaments of mist filter through the vines and around the buttressed tree roots; if it seems primeval, that's because it is. The forests date back hundreds of millions of years and were part of the ancient continent of Gondwana, before Australia broke apart from Antartica and South America, and ancient species such as cycads (which can be 500 years old), Antarctic beech and hoop pine were once dinosaur food.

On day one we follow the Border Track from the Green Mountains side of Lamington to Binna Burra, where another lodge has cabins and space for camping. This 13-mile (21km) section is the highest stage of the walk, with views to Mt Warning, the first place in Australia to get sunlight every morning.

My first wildlife encounter on leaving O'Reilly's is with a gaggle of unperturbed brush-turkeys. But unless you have sharp eyes or the patience to stand silently, your encounters with birdlife tend to be audio rather than visual. This makes the birds easier to identify. Does it sound like the crack of a whip? That's

"If you hear a car alarm or mobile phone, that'll be an Albert's lyrebird, an elusive but accomplished mimic"

a whipbird. Does it sound like a mewling cat? That's a catbird. A rifleshot? That's a Paradise riflebird. You get the idea. And if you hear a car alarm or mobile phone, that'll be an Albert's lyrebird, an elusive but accomplished mimic.

At the junction of the Border Track with the Coomera Falls circuit I take the Coomera turning, where I meet Rusty and Nev, two park rangers attending to one of the regular rainy season landslips. 'Some parts of the trail date back to the Depression labour of the 1930s and the 1940s, when unemployed men, and war veterans who found it hard to adapt to civilian life, went into the woods to adjust to life,' explains Rusty. 'They'd fill backpacks with rocks from the creek and carry them along the trails. It was hard, dangerous work – there were no safety harnesses in those days.' Snakes were a hazard too, and it's a little later that I encounter Australia's third-most venomous reptile, a young male tiger snake warming himself on the trail.

The natural history lesson continues on the second section of the walk, which connects Lamington National Park with its eastern relative Springbrook. An intense fragrance in the air turns out to be patch of lemon-scented teatrees. A lattice of roots

CATCH SOME NIGHTLIFE

The wildlife-watching doesn't end at nightfall. Wherever you're staying at Lamington National Park, bring a powerful torch and shine it into the trees. Pairs of bright eyes will reflect back at you. They will commonly belong to ringtail or brushtail possums. But you might also spot gliders (sugar or squirrel) in the trees. And more than 20 species of bat flutter around the park.

Clockwise from left: deep in the woods of Lamington National Park; a strangler fig grips its victim; O'Reilly's Rainforest Retreat; an eastern whipbird. Previous page: the forested Gold Coast hinterland of Queensland

around a tree trunk is a strangler fig, imperceptibly killing its host over decades. And then my second Indiana Jones moment occurs: strung across the path, one after another, are spider webs 10ft (3m) wide at head height, each patrolled by a golden orb spider the breadth of my hand.

No sooner do we reach the valley floor than we start on the steep climb up to Springbrook National Park. Michael Hall, who has been a park ranger for 30 years and is the ranger in charge of Springbrook, explains that people have had as much influence on the landscapes of the Great Walk as volcanic power. 'Aboriginal people,' he says, 'burned the woods to create open spaces for hunting, leaving forest for shelter.' Controlled burning is a tool for defending the fragile eucalyptus forests from encroachment by voracious rainforest plants. Once fire has cleared a space, it's a starting gun for new life to race upwards to the light. 'Some forest likes a light burn every 10 years,' says Hall, 'other forest prefers a crowning fire up to the canopy of the trees every 100 years. A crowning fire can produce 100,000 kilowatts of heat per metre.'

Michael is pointing out more plants and trees on the final day's route past Purling Brook Falls, Springbrook's 328ft (100m) waterfall, when his eye is caught by a movement on a branch above us. After three days of prehistoric plants, ancient landscapes and deadly wildlife, he's spied one more little brown bird. 'It's a spotted pardalote,' he whispers. 'I haven't seen one of those for 20 years. Now that is special.' **RB**

ORIENTATION

Start // Lamington National Park
End // Springbrook National Park
Distance // 34 miles (54km)
Getting there // Several tour operators provide transfers from Brisbane airport to O'Reilly's lodge. From the end of the walk at Springbrook National Park there are also transfers to Gold Coast airport (closer than Brisbane).
Where to stay // Accommodation is available along the walk, including at O'Reilly's Rainforest Retreat (www.oreillys.com.au) and Binna Burra Mountain Lodge (www.binnaburralodge.com.au). Camping permits are required for camping in Queensland's National Parks: www.qld.gov.au.
When to go // Winter (Jun–Aug) is best.
What to take // Sturdy boots, a first-aid kit (know what to do with a snake bite), water, hat, sunscreen, warm clothing, waterproof jacket, food and camping equipment if needed.
More info // www.npsr.qld.gov.au.

*Opposite from top: the reason
Kangaroo Island is so named; a pier
leads into the blue on Stewart Island's
Rakiura Track*

MORE LIKE THIS
WILDLIFE WALKS IN OCEANIA

KANGAROO ISLAND WILDERNESS TRAIL, AUSTRALIA

Opened in late 2016, this five-day hike takes in the raw western edges of Australia's second-largest island. It's an area protected as Flinders Chase National Park, and four dedicated campsites have been constructed along the trail, all with tent platforms and cooking shelters. As the island's name suggests, it's a place prolific in wildlife – koalas, seals, platypus and the eponymous kangaroos – but the most striking feature of the trail is the landscape, from the pounding Southern Ocean seen from atop ragged cliffs to the island's emblematic Remarkable Rocks (passed on the third day of the trail), a collection of granite boulders that have been scoured by wind into strange and fragile-looking shapes. A day on you can duck down to the strikingly clear seas of Hanson Bay before finally finishing the hike at the limestone Kelly Hill Caves – how many other hikes can you finish with an underground tour?
Start // Flinders Chase Visitor Centre
End // Kelly Hill Caves
Distance // 38 miles (61km)

RAKIURA TRACK, STEWART ISLAND, NEW ZEALAND

Stewart Island's kiwis – the southern brown kiwi – are extra-large. But that doesn't mean that they're any easier to spot. You'll have to wait until dusk then head for Ocean Beach in the Glory Cove Scenic Reserve, giving the protected Hooker's sea lions a wide berth. Since you'll need a permit to be there after 6pm it's worth joining a guided tour. However, the Rakiura Great Walk on Stewart Island does offer almost-certain sightings of lots of New Zealand birdlife, including kaka parrots, bellbirds, tui, fantails, little blue penguins and an abundance of wading birds. The 20-mile (32km) circuit starts near the Rakiura National Park visitor centre on the east coast of this island, which sits just below the South Island. The walk typically takes three days and you'll need to book huts in advance.
Start // Lee Bay
End // Fern Gully (or the reverse)
Distance // 20 miles (32km)
More info // www.doc.govt.nz

THORSBORNE TRAIL, HINCHINBROOK ISLAND, QUEENSLAND, AUSTRALIA

Lying off the north coast of Queensland, Hinchinbrook Island is part of an important marine nature reserve, encircled by mangroves, dugong, green sea turtles, snubfin dolphins and the occasional estuarine crocodile. The Thorsborne Trail stretches along the east coast and offers challenging, unsanitised but extremely rewarding hiking along empty beaches and through tropical rainforest with some wonderful wildlife viewing opportunities. Hundreds of species of bird live on or visit the island, from kingfishers and cockatoos to honeyeaters and doves. Reptiles range from pythons to monitor lizards. Hinchinbrook's plant life is especially important, with many rare species existing on the island. Hiker numbers are strictly limited so advance booking is essential; April to September are the best months and the walk takes a minimum of four days (three nights) due to the terrain.
Start // Ramsay Bay
End // George Point (or the reverse)
Distance // 20 miles (32km)
More info // www.npsr.qld.gov.au

TO THE LIGHTHOUSE: CAPE BRETT TRACK

Trek along a rugged coastal ridge to a lighthouse-tipped cape peering out to one of the most famous sights of New Zealand's Bay of Islands.

It looks like any other forested pass on any other trail. I've been walking for five hours, and rainforest wraps around me. The trail is climbing towards an obvious notch in the ridge, where I'm expecting to step on to the pass and find an ordinary scene – another slope of forest rolling away ahead of me.

But nothing is ordinary here. I'm hiking on the Cape Brett Track, which runs like an underline beneath New Zealand's famed Bay of Islands, following the high line of the cape's ridge to a lighthouse on its point. I will stay the night in the former lighthouse-keeper's cottage before returning the following day.

As I step on to the pass, the world suddenly plunges away beneath my feet. I'm stopped in my tracks, literally, because to take two steps ahead would mean being toppled into the ocean almost 66oft (20om) below. Ahead of me, across the sea, the cape snakes and contorts to its end, the track looking like a razor cut through its high cliffs.

Nothing has prepared me for the curtains to pull back on a scene quite like this. Until now the hike has been beautiful, but I've just stepped across the line into extraordinary.

I'd begun my hike five hours earlier, setting out from the strung-out settlement of Rawhiti, where steps ascend to a low ridge. Within moments I'm looking down into paradise – unruly bush tumbling down the slopes to empty, cream-coloured sands washed smooth by the tide. I drop my pack and descend to the beach. I've been walking for two minutes after all... I'm due a break.

When I return to my pack, an elderly Maori man is standing beside it. He's come to Rawhiti looking for an ancestor's grave. 'A local guy said the cemetery is over there,' he says, pointing back along the low ridge on which we stand. 'Can you imagine carrying

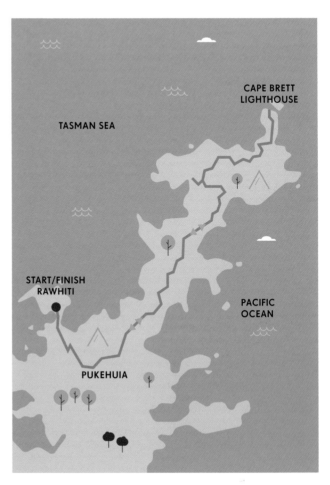

© Evgeny Gorodetsky | Shutterstock

a dead body up here?' I look up to the ridge where I'm heading, close to 1000ft (300m) above us, and the dead weight of the backpack beside me, and just nod.

From here my journey has been simple, if not always easy. The track ascends to the ridgetop that forms the spine of the cape. Like all spines, this one is full of vertebrae, most of which I have to climb, turning the next few hours into a sweaty grind broken by occasional peeps through the forest into the Bay of Islands, which from here look like the scattered pieces of a broken vase.

Atop the ridge, the sound of the ocean rolls up the slopes from both sides – the Pacific Ocean in stereo – and the climbs have the effect of hastening my fantasy of a swim ahead at Deep Water Cove. This narrow slot in the cape is reached on a short side trail just before the Cape Brett Track ascends to the pass that heralds the dramatic final couple of hours to the lighthouse.

At the junction I drop my backpack, and without it it's as though somebody has given me wings. I plunge down the slopes to the cove, where the pebbly beach is covered in driftwood. The track is almost empty today, so I strip down and plunge into the chilly water, washing off more than four hours of effort.

Half an hour later I'm stepping through the pass that's like falling into Alice's Wonderland. The cape spools out ahead of me, attached to New Zealand only by a thin thread of land. Dead trees angle out from the slopes below me, adding yet more drama to an already dramatic scene. Whatever fatigue I've been feeling disappears in an instant as I look ahead to the line of the track etched along the cliff edges. A couple of exciting hours beckon.

At first the track buries itself in bush, but when the views return,

"Nothing has prepared me for the curtains to pull back on a scene quite like this"

SHINING LIGHT

Cape Brett Lighthouse was first illuminated in 1910, and remained a working lighthouse until 1978, with the light from its 40ft-high (12m) station shining almost 32 miles (50km) out to sea. Three men originally staffed it, with a school for the lighthouse-keepers' children on the cape. Conditions were harsh, perhaps best evidenced by a storm in 1951, when a keeper reported waves crashing on to the roof of the cottage (now the hut for hikers), which stands a full 141ft (43m) above the sea.

Clockwise from top: the cliffs of the Cape; the lighthouse at the end of the line. Previous page: Cape Brett Lighthouse seen from afar, standing tall in the Bay of Islands

they *really* return. The cape looms larger with every break in the bush, and the ocean swarms ashore in white fury around the black rock of the cliffs. By the time I return along the track the next morning, after heavy overnight rain, these dry cliffs will be pouring with waterfalls. Is it any wonder there are now helicopters buzzing about, gawking like me at this spectacular tentacle of land?

The trail climbs on and on, a protective handrail briefly testifying to the sudden sense of exposure as the land tumbles away 650ft (200m) either side into the sea. And then, suddenly below me, is the lighthouse and, just offshore, the island that forms the Bay of Islands' most famous attraction, the Hole in the Rock, its cave hidden from view by the angle.

Beside the lighthouse I indulge in a moment of self-congratulatory pride...I have made it. But it's at that moment that I spy a red roof far below – the old lighthouse-keeper's cottage, now converted into a hikers' hut, where I will spend tonight, around 500ft (150m) lower down the slopes. I don't even want to think about the climb back out the next morning, and I'm certainly not the first to be intimidated by this hill.

Before a tramway was built linking the cottage to the lighthouse, a horse was used to haul goods between the two. It's said that the horse quickly learned the sound of the supplies boat arriving, and would run and hide. For me, however, there's nowhere to hide. I have to walk on. I'll worry about dragging my own dead weight back up the hill in the morning. **AB**

ORIENTATION

Start/End // Rawhiti

Distance // 20 miles (32km) round trip

Getting there // The nearest major airport to the Cape Brett Track is Auckland, around four hours' drive from the trailhead. There's no public transport. A couple of homes in Rawhiti offer hiker parking for around NZ$5.

Tours // The walk to Cape Brett Lighthouse takes a full day, requiring an overnight stop at the lighthouse-keeper's cottage before returning along the same track. It's possible to walk just the most dramatic section, from Deep Water Cove to the lighthouse, with two water-taxi companies – Wainot (www.wainot.co.nz) and Bay of Islands Water Taxi (www.boiwatertaxi.co.nz) – ferrying hikers to either point.

Where to stay // Stays in the lighthouse-keeper's cottage must be pre-booked, which can be done through the Department of Conservation website (www.doc.govt.nz).

Cape Brett Track

*Opposite: Phare du Petit Minou
in Plouzané, France, one of 148
lighthouses in Brittany*

MORE LIKE THIS
LIGHTHOUSE WALKS

CAPE TO CAPE TRACK, AUSTRALIA

Tucked into Australia's southwestern
corner, the Cape to Cape Track provides
a unique walking experience, with a pair
of lighthouses serving as its start and
finish posts. In the north, it begins beside
the 1904 Cape Naturaliste Lighthouse,
finishing around a week later at the base of
the 19th-century Cape Leeuwin Lighthouse.
These flashing markers aren't all that
distinguishes this track, which heads along
cliffs and beaches, pressed between the
wineries of Margaret River on one side
and a passing wave of whales for around
half the year on the other side – it's not
uncommon to see breaching humpback
whales as you wander along the clifftops.
Though just three hours' drive from Perth,
and skimming along the edge of the
popular wine region, there's a remarkable
sense of remoteness and isolation as you
hike along the likes of Deepdene Beach
and Quininup Beach.
Start // Cape Naturaliste
End // Cape Leeuwin
Distance // 84 miles (135km)

TE PAKI COASTAL TRACK, NEW ZEALAND

Head even further north than the Cape
Brett Track and you come to Cape Reinga,
near to New Zealand's northern tip and
staked into the earth by a 32ft (10m)
lighthouse. Rounding the cape is the
Te Paki Coastal Track, a three-day hike
through sand dunes, coastal forest and
seven beaches. Cape Reinga is reached
midway through the hike, with its lighthouse
looking out over the line where the Pacific
Ocean and Tasman Sea slam together,
often with dolphins hurtling through,
feeding as they go. It's a highly sacred
spot where Maori traditionally believed
that spirits descended to the underworld,
first sliding down a tree root into the sea
and emerging at the Three Kings Islands
offshore. Beyond the cape, the hike takes
in a beautiful and wild slice of coastline,
including a sweeping dune field at Cape
Maria van Diemen, and the seemingly
endless stripe of 90 Mile Beach.
Start // Te Paki Stream
End // Kapowairua
Distance // 30 miles (48km) one way

GR34, FRANCE

If too many lighthouses aren't enough,
cast your thoughts (and feet) to Brittany
where the GR34 runs along the entirety
of the region's wind- and wave-assaulted
coastline. There are 148 lighthouses
in Brittany alone – one-third of all the
lighthouses in France – and this long-
distance hike is like a game of connect
the dots...or lights, in this case. What
becomes clear as you hike is the reason
for all the lighthouses, as the trail, which
is also known as the Customs Path (it was
first created by the customs service in the
18th century to help in the fight against
smugglers), winds around dramatic rocky
coastlines where the sea charges ashore.
Along the way it passes the likes of Mont
Saint-Michel and the sandy coves of the
Emerald Coast. Walk small sections of the
GR34 between Breton villages, or if you're
really keen come for a couple of months
and hike the entire thing.
Start // Vitre
End // Le Tour-du-Parc
Distance // 1240 miles (2000km)

© pios | Shutterstock

INDEX

Epic Hikes of the World
August 2018
Published by Lonely Planet Global Limited
CRN 554153
www.lonelyplanet.com
10 9 8 7 6

Printed in Malaysia
ISBN 978 1 78701 417 6
© Lonely Planet 2018
© photographers as indicated 2018

Managing Director, Publishing Piers Pickard
Associate Publisher Robin Barton
Commissioning Editor Dora Ball
Art Director Daniel Di Paolo
Designer Ben Brannan
Picture Research Regina Wolek
Editors Bridget Blair, Lucy Doncaster, Nick Mee, Yolanda Zappaterra
Print Production Lisa Ford, Larissa Frost, Nigel Longuet

Although the authors and Lonely Planet have taken all reasonable care in preparing this book, we make no warranty about the accuracy or completeness of its content and, to the maximum extent permitted, disclaim all liability from its use.

Lonely Planet Offices

Australia
The Malt Store, Level 3,
551 Swanston St, Carlton, Victoria 3053
T: 03 8379 8000

USA
124 Linden St, Oakland,
CA 94607
T: 510 250 6400

Ireland
Digital Depot, Roe Lane (off Thomas St),
Digital Hub, Dublin 8,
D08 TCV4

Europe
240 Blackfriars Rd,
London SE1 8NW
T: 020 3771 5100

STAY IN TOUCH lonelyplanet.com/contact

Authors Alex Crevar (**AC**); Andrew Bain (**AB**); Andrew Brannan (**AB**); Brandon Presser (**BP**); Carolyn Heller (**CH**); Carolyn McCarthy (**CMC**); Celeste Brash (**CB**); Christa Larwood (**CL**); Craig McLachlan (**CML**); Daniel McCrohan (**DMC**); Emily Matchar (**EM**); Gregor Clark (**GC**); Isabel Albiston (**IA**); James Bainbridge (**JB**); Kerry Christiani (**KC**); Lucy Corne (**LC**); Mark Elliott (**ME**); Mark Johanson (**MJ**); Matt Swaine (**MS**); Megan Eaves (**ME**); Oliver Berry (**OB**); Oliver Smith (**OS**); Patrick Kinsella (**PK**); Paul Bloomfield (**PB**); Piers Pickard (**PP**); Robin Barton (**RB**); Ryan Stuart (**RS**); Sally Nowlan (**SN**); Sam Haddad (**SH**); Sarah Baxter (**SB**); Steve Waters (**SW**).

Cover and illustrations by Ross Murray (www.rossmurray.com). **Maps** by Callum Lewis (www.callum-lewis.com).

MIX
Paper from
responsible sources
FSC™ C021741

Paper in this book is certified against the Forest Stewardship Council™ standards. FSC™ promotes environmentally responsible, socially beneficial and economically viable management of the world's forests.